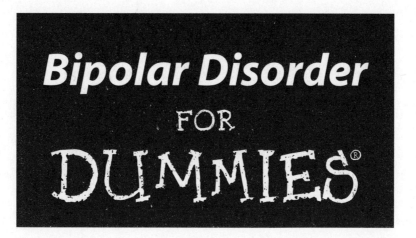

Bipolar Disorder
FOR
DUMMIES®

by Candida Fink, MD and Joseph Kraynak

WILEY

Wiley Publishing, Inc.

Bipolar Disorder For Dummies®

Published by
Wiley Publishing, Inc.
111 River St.
Hoboken, NJ 07030-5774
www.wiley.com

For general information on our other products and services, please contact our Customer Care Department within the U.S. at 877-762-2974, outside the U.S. at 317-572-3993, or fax 317-572-4002.

For technical support, please visit www.wiley.com/techsupport.

Wiley also publishes its books in a variety of electronic formats. Some content that appears in print may not be available in electronic books.

Library of Congress Control Number: 2005924620

ISBN 978-0-7645-8451-0

Manufactured in the United States of America

10 9 8 7

1O/RY/QY/QZ/IN

WILEY

About the Authors

Candida Fink, MD (New Rochelle, New York) is a Board Certified Adult, Child, and Adolescent Psychiatrist in private practice in the New York area. Dr. Fink graduated from Boston University Medical School and did her postgraduate training through Harvard Medical School. She's currently an Assistant Clinical Professor of Psychiatry at Westchester Medical College. She has worked extensively with children and adults with complicated psychiatric illnesses. Mood disorders, especially the diagnostic and treatment questions surrounding bipolar disorder, comprise much of her practice. She also works extensively with schools and other institutions regarding developmental and psychiatric issues. Dr. Fink grew up with mood disorders in her family, so she has seen them from every angle and knows the importance of mobilizing the family as a part of any successful treatment. She has previously co-authored, with Judith Lederman, *The Ups and Downs of Raising a Bipolar Child: A Survival Guide for Parents* (Fireside). She frequently consults and speaks on bipolar disorder in children.

Joe Kraynak, MA (Speedway, Indiana) is a freelance author who has written and co-authored dozens of books on topics ranging from slam poetry to personal computers. Joe received his degree in bipolar disorder from the College of Hard Knocks. On December 10, 1999, Joe's wife, Cecie, a Spanish teacher at the time, was diagnosed with bipolar disorder. Since that day, they have bounced around to a half dozen doctors and even more therapists, broke in a few young marriage counselors, survived several changes in health insurance coverage, attended dozens of support group meetings, and endured the career changes and financial hardships that commonly accompany bipolar disorder. In this book, Joe offers his experience and insight from life in the trenches.

Dedications

From Candida: To my Mom, who loved and taught with compassion and selflessness that profoundly changed all who knew her. She was my rock, and she's deeply missed.

From Joe: To my wife, Cecie, whose zest for life and genuine interest in the lives of others engage and inspire everyone she touches.

Authors' Acknowledgments

Although we wrote the book, dozens of other talented individuals contributed to its conception, development, and perfection. Special thanks goes to Mikal Belicove, who chose us to author this book; Mikal has an uncanny knack for connecting authors who work well together and enjoy the experience. Chrissy Guthrie, project editor, deserves a round of applause for acting as the choreographer — developing chapters, shepherding the text and illustrations through production, making sure any technical issues were properly addressed, and serving as unofficial quality control manager. Thanks also to Josh Dials, our copy editor, who read through everything — forward and backward — to identify and obliterate our many grammatical goofs and typos. We also tip our hats to the folks in Composition Services at Wiley for doing such an outstanding job of transforming a loose collection of text and illustrations into such an attractive volume.

We owe special thanks to our technical editors for ferreting out technical errors in the manuscript and helping guide its content:

Ellen Frank, PhD, professor of psychiatry and psychology at the University of Pittsburgh School of Medicine, Western Psychiatric Institute and Clinic, and Depression and Bipolar Support Alliance scientific advisory board chair.

Paul E. Keck, Jr., MD, professor and vice chairman for Research, Department of Psychiatry, University of Cincinnati College of Medicine, and a Depression and Bipolar Support Alliance scientific advisory board member.

And thanks to Laura Hoofnagle, publications manager, and Susan R. Bergeson, vice president of the Depression and Bipolar Support Alliance, Chicago, Illinois, for their assistance in ensuring the technical accuracy of the material.

And we thank our agent, Faith Hamlin, of Sanford J. Greenburger Associates, Inc., for managing the contract negotiations so we could focus on writing rather than the legal stuff.

We would also like to thank all the people with bipolar disorder and their family members and friends whom we've met along the way. Without these brave souls, along with their stories, their struggles, and their achievements, this book wouldn't be possible. And we acknowledge nonprofit organizations, including the Depression and Bipolar Support Alliance (DBSA), the Child and Adolescent Bipolar Foundation, and the National Alliance for the Mentally Ill (NAMI), for their valuable contributions and continued dedication to educating, supporting, and advocating for all those in the bipolar community.

Publisher's Acknowledgments

We're proud of this book; please send us your comments through our Dummies online registration form located at www.dummies.com/register/.

Some of the people who helped bring this book to market include the following:

*Acquisitions, Editorial, and
Media Development*

Project Editor: Christina Guthrie

Acquisitions Editor: Mikal Belicove

Copy Editor: Josh Dials

Editorial Program Assistant: Courtney Allen

Technical Editors: Ellen Frank, PhD;
Paul E. Keck, Jr., MD; Laura Hoofnagle;
Susan R. Bergeson

Editorial Manager: Christine Meloy Beck

Editorial Assistants: Hanna Scott,
Melissa S. Bennett, Nadine Bell

Cover Photo: © David Evans/Getty Images/
National Geographic

Cartoons: Rich Tennant
(www.the5thwave.com)

Composition Services

Project Coordinator: Nancee Reeves

Layout and Graphics: Carl Byers, Andrea Dahl

Special Art: Medical illustrations by
Kathryn Born

Proofreaders: Leeann Harney, Jessica Kramer,
Robert Springer, Aptara

Indexer: Aptara

Publishing and Editorial for Consumer Dummies

 Diane Graves Steele, Vice President and Publisher, Consumer Dummies

 Joyce Pepple, Acquisitions Director, Consumer Dummies

 Kristin A. Cocks, Product Development Director, Consumer Dummies

 Michael Spring, Vice President and Publisher, Travel

 Kelly Regan, Editorial Director, Travel

Publishing for Technology Dummies

 Andy Cummings, Vice President and Publisher, Dummies Technology/General User

Composition Services

 Gerry Fahey, Vice President of Production Services

 Debbie Stailey, Director of Composition Services

Contents at a Glance

Table of Contents

Introduction

*I*magine yourself cruising down the highway at a comfortable speed of 65 miles per hour when your cruise control goes berserk. The speedometer climbs to 75 and then 85 . . . you hit the button to cancel . . . tap the brakes . . . nothing slows you down . . . 95 . . . your car is shaking and weaving . . . 100 . . . people are honking . . . 105 . . . police are chasing you . . . 110 . . . your spouse is yelling at you to SLOW DOWN . . . 115 . . . 120 . . .

Or imagine the opposite: You're driving through town, 30 mile-per-hour speed limit, nobody in front of you, and your car can only go 3 miles per hour. You're practically pushing the accelerator through the floor, but you can only get it up to 5 miles per hour . . . downhill! Your neighbors are honking, passing you on the right — on bicycles — giving you dirty looks and other gestures of discontent.

When you have bipolar disorder, your brain's accelerator is stuck. At full speed, it launches you into a manic episode. In slow gear, it grinds you down into a deep depression. If this were your heart, somebody would call the ambulance, doctors and nurses would flock to your bedside, loved ones would fly in from other states, and you'd get flowers and fruit baskets. But when your brain is stuck in park or overdrive, people just think you're lazy, you've snapped, or you're too weak to deal with life. Instead of flowers and fruit baskets, you get a pink slip and divorce papers.

The good news is that the mind mechanics — psychiatrists, psychologists, and therapists — have toolboxes packed with medications and therapies that can repair your brain's accelerator. In this book, we reveal those tools, along with strategies and techniques that you can use to achieve and maintain mood stability and to help yourself feel a whole lot better.

About This Book

This book is more than a repair manual for the bipolar brain. Sure, we discuss diagnoses and treatments, available medications and therapies, and the lifestyle changes that can help you cope. But we also go beyond that to reveal some of the causes and consequences of bipolar disorder, let you in on some crisis-survival strategies, and describe ways that friends and family members can support loved ones who have bipolar disorder. Our goal is to help you develop a deeper understanding of bipolar disorder and its symptoms and empower you to take more control of your treatment, eliminate your symptoms, and regain your ability to function.

In the quest to make you or your loved one feel better and maintain stable moods, we focus on the three Cs of bipolar disorder:

- **Continuity of treatment:** In this era of specialization and managed healthcare, patients often get shuttled from one doctor or therapist to another, and each professional may have a unique approach. Any drastic changes to medication or therapy can upset the balance, so this book encourages you to develop a treatment plan that all your caregivers follow and that remains with you when you change doctors or therapists.

- **Comprehensive treatment:** The most effective treatment plan calls for a three-pronged attack of medication, therapy, and lifestyle change. In this book, we explain why your treatment plan should address all three factors, and we reveal the most effective medications, therapies, peer support options, and lifestyle changes currently available.

- **Coordinated treatment:** Communication is the key to coordinated treatment, and communication breakdowns are at the root of most failed attempts. To ensure success, communicate openly and honestly with your doctor, therapist, and loved ones and encourage them to communicate with one another. Throughout the book, we reveal techniques to improve communication among all members of your treatment team.

Of course, this book is no replacement for professional psychiatric care. (We kicked around the idea of bundling the book with a blank prescription pad, but our publisher nixed the idea.) Even so, *Bipolar Disorder For Dummies* can help you gain a better understanding of your treatment choices so you can build a more cooperative and productive relationship with your healthcare providers.

Conventions Used in This Book

We don't like to think of *our* book as *conventional,* but we do have some standard ways of presenting material. For example:

- Whenever we introduce a new, somewhat technical term, such as *expressed emotion,* we display it in italics. We enclose a commonly used term that's not necessarily a technical term "in quotes." If you're reading the book aloud or your lips are moving, make the finger gesture for quotes to get the full effect.

- Web and e-mail addresses appear in `monofont` to help them stand out on the page for easy access.

- In almost every chapter, we include stories about people who have bipolar disorder and their loved ones. These stories aren't necessarily about real people — they represent composites of real people we've met and worked with over the years.

What You're Not to Read

You can skip any text we mark with a Technical Stuff icon because the only people who really care about this stuff are doctors and the lawyers who want to sue the doctors. And sidebars are just what the name implies. They give you somewhere to hang out when you don't have somewhere else to go or something better to do. Most of our sidebars tell stories that are *sort of* based on reality, and they're about the most entertaining parts of the book, so be selective in what you skip. *Note:* However, we don't recommend that you skip the sidebars with Bipolar Bio icons next to them.

Foolish Assumptions

When you (or loved ones) are diagnosed with bipolar disorder, you automatically become a rank beginner. You never needed the information before and probably had little interest in the topic. Now you need to get up to speed in a hurry. With that in mind, the biggest foolish assumption we make in this book is that you know very little about bipolar disorder. If you've been to a doctor or therapist and have already received a diagnosis, however, you know at least a little. And if you got burned by a misdiagnosis or the wrong approach, you know that you don't want it to happen again. But no matter what level you're at, this book can help.

We also assume that you or someone you know has bipolar disorder or that you're at least somewhat curious about it. The more bipolar disorder affects you, your family, or someone you know, the more this book helps.

Finally, we assume that you have a sense of humor. According to Jean de la Bruyère, "Life is a tragedy for those who feel and a comedy for those who think." We're thinking people. We laugh through our tears rather than wallow in our misery, although we, too, have shed our fair share of tears. We have loved ones with bipolar disorder, and we know it's painful for everyone involved, but we've found that most people with bipolar disorder and their loved ones have a healthy sense of humor. Maybe it's because they're smarter than the average Joe, or perhaps they've just had to deal with so much bad stuff in their lives that they need a moment to laugh.

In this book, we wanted to strip away all the politically correct niceties and namby-pamby psychospeak. We chose not to sweeten the bitter facts with butter-cream frosting, and we don't hesitate to laugh at the absurdities of living with bipolar disorder. We certainly hope that you won't find any of this more than mildly offensive and that you'll indulge in a few laughs yourself.

How This Book Is Organized

We wrote this book so you could approach it two ways. You can pick the book up and flip to any chapter for a quick, stand-alone mini-course on a specific bipolar topic, or you can read the book from cover to cover. To help you navigate, we divided the chapters that make up the book into six parts. Here, we provide a quick overview of what we cover in each part.

Part I: Boning Up on Bipolar Disorder

The three chapters in this part comprise a quick overview of bipolar disorder. You begin to discover the characteristics of bipolar disorder and how it affects people who have it and their families. We lift the curtain on the diagnosis to reveal the various ways that bipolar disorder presents itself and the leading theories on what causes it. We introduce some of the most effective treatments, explain why prevention plays such a critical role in treatment, and discuss the positive prognosis that you can expect with the right combination of medication, therapy, and lifestyle adjustments.

Part II: Taming the Bipolar Beast

A half-hour discussion with a doctor or therapist may be enough to raise suspicions of bipolar disorder, but it's certainly insufficient for obtaining an accurate diagnosis. First, you need to see your family physician to rule out other possible causes. Any of several physical ailments can cause symptoms similar to those that come with bipolar disorder, and you need a physical exam and appropriate lab tests to rule them out. In this part, we lay out the process you must go through to obtain an accurate diagnosis. We also show you how to assemble your very own mood-management team, complete with a doctor, therapist, and dedicated friends and family members to help tame the bipolar beast.

Part III: Opening the Treatment Toolbox: A Comprehensive, Integrated Approach

Successfully managing bipolar disorder and maintaining mood stability require a combination of medication and therapy. This part begins by providing an overview of available medications for treating both "poles" of bipolar disorder: mania and depression. Even more valuable than the list of effective medications and their potential side effects is the primer we provide on bipolar psychopharmacology. We tell you which questions to ask your doctor to help you make informed decisions, diminish undesirable side effects, and safely combine medications. We also discuss types of individual and family therapies that have proved useful in preventing relapses. Finally, we provide an overview of alternative treatments to help you distinguish useful supplementary treatments from opportunistic quackery.

Part IV: Helping Yourself

The most valiant efforts of a doctor and therapist to control bipolar symptoms are no match for what patients can do to undermine their own health. Successful treatment requires the person with bipolar disorder to play an active role. In this part, we show you how to take control of your treatment. You discover how to identify common warning signs of an impending mood episode, respond quickly and appropriately, identify stressors and triggers that affect your moods, restructure your life, care for yourself, incorporate peer support into your recovery, and adhere to the recommended regimen of medication and therapy.

Part V: Assisting a Friend or Relative with Bipolar Disorder

If you're reading this book because you have a friend, significant other, or relative with bipolar disorder, this part is for you. We both have family members with bipolar disorder, and we know firsthand just how difficult it is to walk the fine line between over and underinvolvement. The chapters in this part explain what you can and can't do to help, how you can establish an environment of open communication and cooperation with your loved one, and how to prepare for and respond to a crisis. If you have a child diagnosed with bipolar disorder or another psychiatric disorder or if your child is experiencing unexplained behavioral problems at home, school, or with friends, you won't want to miss Chapter 18, which explains the challenges of diagnosing, treating, and parenting children with bipolar disorder.

Part VI: The Part of Tens

Before you head out to see your psychiatrist or therapist, turn to this section for a quick list of 10 questions you should ask. And if you can't pay the bill, this part provides 10 affordable treatment options and sources of financial assistance. When your life calms down and you have time to advocate for the bipolar community, flip to this section to discover 10 ways you can become more involved in the cause.

As if all this other stuff weren't enough, we also include a handy glossary at the end of this book that defines commonly used terms related to bipolar disorder.

Icons Used in This Book

Throughout this book, we sprinkle the following icons in the margins to cue you in to different types of information that call out for your attention:

You can forget the rest of the stuff in this book, but you should remember anything that we mark with one of these icons.

Tips provide insider insight from behind the scenes. When you're looking for a better, faster way to do something, check out these tips.

"Danger, Will Robinson, danger!" This icon appears when you need to be extra vigilant or seek professional help.

Throughout the book, we feature cameo performances of people with bipolar disorder and their families. This icon shows you where to meet them.

When an explanation is more technical than even the technical material we cover in the text, we flag it with one of these icons so you can avoid it (unless you're really into superfluous information).

Where to Go from Here

Think of this book as an all-you-can-eat buffet. You can grab a plate, start at the beginning, and read one chapter right after another, or you can dip into any chapter and pile your plate high with the information it contains.

If you want a quick overview of bipolar disorder, check out the chapters in Part I. Before you visit a psychiatrist for a diagnosis, check out Chapters 4, 5, and 19. If you have a friend or family member with bipolar disorder, skip to Part V. Wherever you choose to go, you find plenty of useful information and advice.

Part I
Boning Up on Bipolar Disorder

The 5th Wave   By Rich Tennant

"Watching game shows all day masked the highs, but when I started weeping through the dog food commercials, I knew I had a problem."

In this part . . .

Take a crash course in bipolar disorder, from the onset and diagnosis to treatment and recovery. The three chapters in this part reveal the many masks of bipolar disorder, including Bipolar I, Bipolar II, Cyclothymic disorder, and Bipolar NOS. You discover the official signs and symptoms of depression, hypomania, and mania and how to distinguish between a bad day at work and a bona fide mood episode. And you find out where bipolar disorder comes from, what triggers it, and how likely or unlikely it is that you have it.

We also unveil the positive prognosis that accompanies the bipolar diagnosis and the conventional treatments currently being developed to successfully treat its most sinister symptoms. And, after you hop on the road to recovery, we provide techniques and tips to steady your course.

Chapter 1

Living La Vida Bipolar

*B*ipolar disorder is a heartless beast that parties with your life and sticks you with the bill. At its best, it inspires brilliant insights and uninhibited joy. At its worst, it drapes the mind in debilitating depression, destroys relationships, empties bank accounts, and fuels suicidal thoughts. Doctors have no test for it and no cure, and one of the main symptoms of the disorder is that the afflicted often deny they have it and resist treatment.

Science knows few more elusive diseases, yet mental health professionals are more skilled than ever at accurately diagnosing bipolar disorder and successfully treating it with the right combination of medicine, therapy, and life changes. Many people with bipolar disorder can now live productive lives and achieve levels of happiness and fulfillment they had never dreamed possible.

In this chapter, we reveal a few of the many manifestations of bipolar disorder and describe its most challenging aspects. We lead you on a brief journey of what a person with bipolar disorder can expect — from diagnosis through prognosis and on to treatment and recovery. And because successful treatment and recovery often require the participation of loved ones, this chapter shows you what you can do to support a friend, relative, or child who has bipolar disorder.

Riding the Bipolar Waves

Some people are so persistently perky that you want to slap them. Most others experience the normal ups and downs of everyday living. You lose your job, and you feel a little dejected. You win the lottery, and you feel ecstatic . . . at least until you blow all the money. Minor fluctuations in mood are normal. Even major fluctuations are normal, as long as they don't last too long or interfere with your ability to function and enjoy pleasurable activities. A temporary bout of unhappiness can even prompt you to make a positive change in your life that leads to greater happiness and self-fulfillment.

If you suffer from bipolar disorder, you also experience the normal ups and downs of everyday living, but sometimes the ups and downs exceed the healthy, socially acceptable limits and persist for inordinate amounts of time.

Finding your comfort level

As Figure 1-1 shows, most people experience mood swings to some acceptable degree, but bipolar mood swings are amplified and extend way past the comfort level, to the point where they impair the person's ability to function and enjoy life.

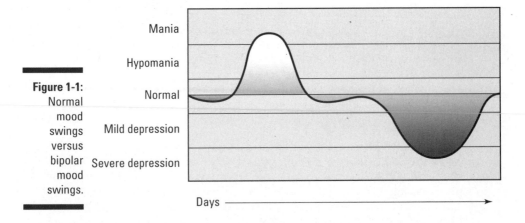

Figure 1-1:
Normal mood swings versus bipolar mood swings.

Of course, intensity of mood alone, especially when it's on the rise, isn't always problematic. In fact, many people who experience *hypomania* — an elevated state of mood and energy that doesn't qualify as full-blown mania — report that their creative drives and clarity of vision are quite exhilarating. Hypomania can often make you more extroverted, entertaining, and engaging. It can increase your sex appeal and make you feel more powerful. It can energize and invigorate, help you focus, and inspire creative vision.

The trick to treating bipolar disorder isn't to flat-line your moods and energies. You want to bring the fluctuations into a range that's acceptable to you and the people who are important to you. You want to ride the waves without being dragged under and without eliminating them entirely.

Crashing on the rocks

When you suffer from bipolar disorder, your mood can occasionally fluctuate *way* beyond normal. One day you're nimbly surfing the sea of life, and the next day a massive wave rises up and smashes you against the rocks. A deep depression can wrap you in despair and sentence you to endless days in bed. A full-blown manic episode can buck you like a raging bull and then toss your exhausted carcass in the trash heap. Whether you fly up or plummet down, an extreme, prolonged mood episode can cause you to crash, which can be devastating to your perceptions, emotions, relationships, career, and other aspects of your life.

Whether you crash via a wave of mania or get swept away by the undercurrents of depression, intervention is usually required in the form of medication, therapy, or a brief stay in the hospital (in extreme cases). However, the preferred method is to avoid the crash altogether by obtaining an accurate diagnosis and receiving preventive treatment and therapy.

Uncontrollable mania

Manic episodes seem to garner all the press, because their stories are often titillating. In episodes of mania, people often rise above the monotony of the moment, pumped up with the following feelings and beliefs:

- I am amazing!
- Everything is wonderful!
- I can do anything and everything!
- I have all the answers! My ideas will change the world!
- No matter what bad things I do, I'm still a great person!
- Sleep is only for people who have nothing better to do!
- I'm always right!
- Everybody loves me!
- I'm the fastest at everything I do!

However, full-blown manic episodes often are accompanied by paranoia and other psychoses that compound the problem. A person may become consumed with thoughts of religious martyrdom or government plots. He or she may believe family members, friends, or even strangers have ill or dangerous intentions. Left to run its course, mania often results in a crash, leaving the victim feeling depressed and physically and mentally exhausted. The episode can also foul up the victim's personal and professional relationships and financial status.

Debilitating depression

Depression is the opposite of thrilling. It can make you feel like you're trudging through the quagmire of life in a lead suit. It dulls your senses and bars you from experiencing any of life's pleasures. You become the resident party pooper, the proverbial wet blanket. If you had the energy to talk, you'd express your feelings as follows:

- I'm terrible.
- Everything is horrible.
- I can't do anything.
- I'm a bad, evil person, even when I don't do anything bad.
- I can't sleep.
- I can't get up.
- Even little things take forever to do.
- Nobody loves me.
- Everything's my fault.
- Nothing feels good.

If you're lucky, the depression eventually burns off like the morning fog. If it deepens, it can lead to a crash, leaving you feeling even more depressed and physically and mentally exhausted.

When most people think of bipolar disorder, they think of the manic side. However, depression is the more common and more damaging of the two poles. In the euphoria of mania, people rarely choose to intentionally harm themselves. In a deep depression, however, self-mutilation and suicidal thoughts and actions are far too common.

Maddening mixed states

A somewhat perplexing cycle in bipolar disorder is the *mixed state,* a condition with characteristics of both mania and depression. During a mixed state, your thoughts may go a mile a minute, but they're all angry or miserable. You may have big ideas but no energy to carry them out or plenty of energy to fuel your irritability. You may even believe that your imminent death is part of some master plan.

Earning Your Bipolar Badge

To begin the process of treating and regulating your bipolar disorder, you need an official diagnosis, and obtaining it can be quite a lengthy process.

Coming to terms with the problem

The first step toward a diagnosis is to realize that something isn't right. Acceptance is usually the most time-consuming step. Most people live with bipolar disorder for an average of 10 years before seeking help. In many cases, people experience multiple major mood episodes — depression or mania — before circumstances or frustrated family members force them to seek professional help.

People with bipolar disorder may avoid seeking treatment for any of several reasons:

- Mania feels great. I've never felt so energized!
- Why bother? Nothing can possibly make me feel any better.
- I'm not ill. I'm just weak. I need to work harder at overcoming this.
- I can deal with this on my own.
- I can't afford any more bills.
- I don't want to be labeled.

Both depression and mania can influence thought patterns that make a person avoid treatment. In a manic episode, you commonly feel all-knowing, all-powerful, full of energy, and at the top of your game. In such a state, few people think they need help. When you feel deeply depressed, you commonly lose hope in the future and begin thinking that nothing can improve your life, so it's understandable not to seek help. In many cases, you need to experience a crash or a loved one has to intervene to provide the motivation to seek professional help.

Obtaining an accurate diagnosis

After you decide that you need professional help, you can begin the process of obtaining an accurate diagnosis. This process typically entails the following steps:

1. **Visit your physician.**

   Other health issues, such as thyroid malfunction, menopause, or nutritional deficiencies, can cause symptoms similar to those of bipolar disorder. Medications and other substances can also generate similar symptoms. Your family physician can help rule out these and other possible causes of your symptoms. (Flip to Chapter 4 for more on this.)

2. **Undergo a psychiatric evaluation.**

   A licensed psychiatrist can review your medical history, family history, and symptoms and offer an initial diagnosis and treatment plan. (See Chapter 5 for more on visiting the psychiatrist.)

Unfortunately, the steps for obtaining an accurate diagnosis and a treatment plan that works aren't always so linear. If you're feeling deeply depressed, manic, or agitated, your physician or psychiatrist may prescribe medication to alleviate the symptoms immediately and work on the diagnosis later.

If you receive a diagnosis of bipolar disorder, your psychiatrist typically narrows the diagnosis by specifying one of the following four flavors:

- **Bipolar I:** Requires at least one full-blown manic episode some time during your life that doctors can't attribute to another cause, such as a medication or substance abuse. You may or may not have experienced a major depressive episode.

- **Bipolar II:** Requires at least one major depressive episode some time during your life that doctors can't attribute to another cause. You must also experience a hypomanic episode.

- **Cyclothymic disorder:** Requires multiple depressive and hypomanic episodes not extreme enough to warrant a diagnosis of Bipolar I or II. In some cases, the depression and mania occur simultaneously, resulting in a state of chronic irritability.

- **Bipolar NOS (Not Otherwise Specified):** Requires manic or depressive episodes that doctors can't categorize as unipolar depression. The episodes also can't fit into any of the other bipolar categories.

Chapter 2 discusses each of these forms of the disorder in detail.

Mixing an Effective Bipolar Cocktail

Your psychiatrist's treatment plan almost always prescribes medications designed to treat your current state (manic, depressed, mixed) and to prevent further cycles. Your job is to provide your doctor with detailed information so she can choose the right medications for you and to stick with the treatment plan. We cover all the bases in this section.

Clarifying the purpose of the bipolar label

If you're like most people, you shun labels — especially labels that carry negative connotations, such as *bipolar.* Used in a sentence, such as "Pat is bipolar," the label seems even more insensitive. It not only stigmatizes Pat, but also reduces her to the illness itself. If Pat had cancer, nobody would say, "Pat is cancer," but people often play fast and loose with the term "bipolar."

Your physician or psychiatrist doesn't use the label "bipolar disorder" to label *you* or minimize your worth as a human being. The label provides a convenient way to refer to your condition that requires treatment. It helps all the people involved in your treatment plan to quickly recognize the disease that afflicts you and to provide the appropriate medications and therapy.

Always remember that you're not bipolar disorder. Bipolar disorder is something you have, and you can manage it with the right medication and therapy.

Getting the right meds for your condition

Chapter 7 introduces you to the medications most commonly used to treat bipolar disorder. The medications fall into the following categories:

- **Antimanics:** Antimanic medications, commonly referred to as *mood stabilizers,* primarily treat the manic side of bipolar disorder. Your psychiatrist may prescribe an antimanic medication to bring you down from the highs of mania, or she may prescribe a maintenance dose as a *prophylaxis* (preventative). Lithium is the gold standard in the antimanic category because it's one of the few antimanic medications that doctors truly consider a mood stabilizer; it can prevent depression as well as mania.

- **Antidepressants:** Antidepressants, such as Prozac, Paxil, and Wellbutrin, treat the depressive side of bipolar disorder and are also used to treat unipolar depression. Your psychiatrist may prescribe an antidepressant to pull you out of an acute depressive episode or to prevent future depressive episodes. Antidepressants can induce mania in some individuals, so psychiatrists typically prescribe them only in combination with an antimanic medication for patients with bipolar disorder.

- **Antipsychotics:** Antipsychotic medications, such as Zyprexa, may be used to treat mania or psychotic symptoms that may accompany a major manic or depressive episode.

- **Sedatives:** Psychiatrists commonly prescribe sedatives to alleviate anxiety and to help patients sleep. As we discuss in Chapter 12, sleeplessness can often trigger a major mood episode, so psychiatrists are highly motivated to help you sleep through the night.

Psychiatrists often prescribe multiple medications to treat all symptoms and to improve the drugs' overall effectiveness. Most people with bipolar disorder take at least one antimanic medication along with an antidepressant. You may take antipsychotics to further dampen the mania or to treat residual psychoses. Your psychiatrist may prescribe an antianxiety medication to alleviate anxiety during the day and sedatives to help you sleep at night.

The prescription medication you take isn't designed to cure bipolar disorder or to solve all your problems. It's designed to treat the physical side of the disorder in your brain so the rest of your being can function without the interference of mania or depression. When your brain begins functioning more normally, you may be able to make some adjustments to your lifestyle and attitudes that can accelerate your recovery, improve your life, and offer additional protection against new episodes.

Sticking to the treatment plan — even when you don't want to

Noncompliance — the tendency to stop taking your prescribed medications — can undermine the most skillfully designed treatment plan. In addition to the normal human proclivity to avoid swallowing pills, people with bipolar disorder often have some seemingly valid objections to taking their medications. The following list discusses some of the most common objections and what you should do if you find yourself thinking them:

- ✔ **I feel fine.** Psychiatrists prescribe many of the medications to prevent recurrences of mood episodes that can worsen the course of the disorder. Of course, when you feel good, you don't see a need to take medication. You have to fight a constant battle against your natural urge to avoid taking your medication in order to remain healthy and prevent the course of the illness from worsening.

- ✔ **I can't tolerate the side effects.** The side effects of some medications for bipolar disorder can be brutal: weight gain, memory loss, anxiety, fatigue, loss of libido, and so on. Psychiatrists often help reduce or eliminate undesirable side effects by adjusting the dosage, recommending a different time to take the medicine, or changing medications.

- ✔ **I forgot.** When you're trying to hold down a job, pay your bills, shore up your relationships, and perform your daily chores, popping pills may not seem like a priority, especially when you feel okay. Chapter 7 discusses some ways to help you stay on top of your medications.

- ✔ **I miss my mania.** Because hypomania can be so exhilarating, an effective mood stabilizer can make life seem dull. The challenge is to establish a baseline level for your moods that enables you to feel vibrant and creative without tumbling over the edge. You and your doctor can work together to establish a baseline that's comfortable for you.

Although you may be tempted to tweak your medications on your own, don't do it. Always consult your psychiatrist before you adjust the dose or times of day that she prescribes. In many cases, your psychiatrist can make a minor adjustment that alleviates a troublesome side effect or improves the effectiveness of the medication. Stopping a medication cold turkey can destabilize your moods and cause other withdrawal symptoms.

Retooling Your Thoughts and Relationships

Some psychiatrists and mental-health activists describe bipolar disorder as a mental illness caused by a chemical imbalance in the brain. Although this is true, it doesn't mean that if you repair the chemical imbalance through medication, you eliminate the illness for good.

Unfortunately, bipolar disorder is much more complicated than that. Yes, balancing brain chemistry is essential, but your brain doesn't live in a petri dish; it lives inside your body. It registers what your eyes, ears, nose, tongue, and fingers perceive. It processes your interactions with others and generates your emotions and thoughts. In short, your experiences influence your brain as much as your brain influences your experiences. And both your brain and your experiences affect your moods.

 Bathing your brain in the right mix of medications helps it maintain normal function, but if you and those around you assault your brain with negative emotions, conflict, and sleep deprivation, no combination of medications can possibly overcome the stress.

In addition to proper medications, you need to receive the right therapy or combination of therapies, such as the following, to reduce the impact of stress on your brain:

- **Psychoeducation:** Finding out more about bipolar disorder often helps patients become comfortable with the diagnosis, hopeful about the prognosis, and more willing and able to adhere to the treatment plan.

- **Cognitive therapy:** Identifies negative thought patterns and teaches your mind to follow a positive train of thought. As we discuss in Chapter 8, cognitive therapy is especially effective in treating depression.

- **Interpersonal and social rhythm therapy:** Living a structured lifestyle and establishing healthy routines can give your life a rhythm that's conducive to mood stability. Studies show that mood episodes commonly erupt when you experience stressful life changes that break down your natural rhythms and often lead to loss of sleep. Interpersonal and social rhythm therapy strives to restore the rhythm to your life.

✔ **Couples therapy:** A rocky relationship with your main squeeze can whip your emotions into a frenzy, especially if your significant other is abusive. Couples therapy addresses areas of conflict and helps couples establish effective communication techniques that reduce stress.

✔ **Family therapy:** If you live in the same house or spend a lot of time with family members, educating them about bipolar disorder and your needs is essential to your mental health. The more your family members know about bipolar disorder and the stressors that can trigger major mood episodes, the more they can do to help alleviate stress and support you in your journey toward recovery.

✔ **Financial counseling:** Money doesn't matter only to people who have plenty of it. For most of us, a lack of sufficient funds can be a prime source of stress and conflict. A good financial adviser may be able to help you manage your finances.

✔ **Career coaching:** If your job is killing you, you may need a change. Being stuck in a dead-end job with a jerk for a boss isn't conducive to mental health. Maybe you can't up and quit right away, but you can start looking around. A career coach or counselor can help you find healthier employment.

✔ **Lifestyle changes:** Streamlining your life can alleviate the stress that comes with owning and maintaining too much. A good therapist can help you avoid overcommitting your time and resources.

 Although medication is an essential component to recovery, it alone can't always overcome the fundamental problems that trigger mood episodes. You may not be able to eliminate all sources of stress, but the more stress you can eliminate or reduce, the better your chances of avoiding a relapse.

Tracking and Managing Your Moods

In business, the pencil-pushers like to plot data on a chart. Raw data is relatively meaningless, but when you chart data, patterns begin to emerge, and the data begins to have meaning. Charting your moods can help reveal similar patterns that highlight seasons of the year or events in your life that often trigger mood fluctuations. You can use this information to draw up plans to head off mood episodes. For example, you may decide to spend a quiet Christmas at home rather than with your dysfunctional relatives, or your psychiatrist may give you something to help you sleep during a stressful period of your life.

In Chapter 12, we describe mood charts in greater detail and provide a sample mood chart that you can begin using right away. If you prefer, you can design your own mood chart. Try to include the following elements:

✔ **Scale:** Rate your mood on a scale from +3 to –3, with 0 as your baseline, feeling-okay level. If you rate a +3, you're crawling-out-of-your-skin manic, and if you're –3, you're barely-can-lift-the-pen depressed. (Use +5 to –5 or +10 to –10 if you have more shades to your mood spectrum.)

✔ **Dates:** Record your mood rating at least once a day. If your moods fluctuate throughout the day, consider adding a little more detail.

✔ **Notes:** If you do anything out of the ordinary on a particular day, note it. Note any changes in medication, diet, or need for sleep as well.

Knowledge is power. The more you know about the way you feel and how you respond to variations in sleep, diet, medication, or activity, the more control you have over bipolar disorder.

Share your mood chart with your psychiatrist, therapist, and anyone else who you count as part of your support network (see Chapter 6). Others may be able to identify patterns that you miss.

Reclaiming Your Life — When You're Ready

Experiencing a major manic or depressive episode is like getting t-boned by an 18-wheeler. If you could turn yourself inside out, you'd see your bruised and battered self and maybe garner a little well-deserved sympathy. Unfortunately, others may perceive you as a person perfectly capable of returning to your home and job. To compound the problem, a major mood episode often leaves behind substantial collateral damage. Your loved ones may feel angry or guilty. Your boss may consider you a liability. And you may still be wrestling with the side effects of the most recent medication adjustment.

At this point, you may feel that you have a responsibility as a loyal employee or family member to patch yourself up and return to service, and if that's what *you* really want to do, it may be best for you. In most cases, however, being selfish pays greater long-term dividends. Taking some time off work to recuperate, enable your moods to stabilize, and pay some attention to your emotional and psychological needs can lead to a full recovery with a much more positive long-term prognosis. To make your convalescence as successful as possible, consider the following tips and techniques:

✔ **Find alternate living arrangements, if necessary.** If you live alone or in a stressful environment, consider moving in with a close friend or relative until your moods and medications stabilize. A strong support person can help you monitor your moods, remind you to take your medications, and offer moral support.

 ✔ **Contact your company's human resources department.** You may be eligible for a leave of absence during your recovery if your doctor prescribes it. You should also check your health benefits. Don't quit your job, even if you think it contributes to your illness. Get the benefits you deserve and then quit when you find something better. Work the system.

 ✔ **Enroll in intensive outpatient therapy.** Many hospitals and clinics offer intensive outpatient therapy that can help you deal with the issues in your life while you recover physically from the trauma. If you take a leave of absence from work, intensive outpatient therapy keeps you busy during the day and provides all-important human contact.

Avoid making any major decisions during your convalescence, such as quitting your job or breaking off a relationship. Focus on becoming healthy. You can deal more effectively with your issues when you feel fully recovered.

Preventing Suicide and Other Self-Damaging Behaviors

Thoughts about death and suicide, plans to commit suicide, and actual attempts to take one's own life accompany all phases of bipolar disorder. Feelings of anxiety, hopelessness, and seemingly unbearable pain during depressions; irritability and thoughts that race faster than you can think them during manias; and paranoia and life-darkening hopelessness during mixed states all contribute to suicidal thoughts. These thoughts may rush into your head all at once and overwhelm you, or they may become obsessions that occupy most of your waking moments.

Other self-damaging behaviors, such as overspending or indulging in risky sexual activity, can complicate or inflame suicidal thoughts.

If thoughts of death or suicide plague you, seek help immediately. If you suspect that a loved one may be considering suicide, contact the person's psychiatrist, doctor, or therapist immediately. If you don't know what people to call, drive the person to the nearest emergency room or call 911. Studies show that nearly 30 percent of people suffering from bipolar depression attempt suicide, so you need to act immediately. Although you may be able to talk your loved one out of attempting suicide, he or she may lie to you just to get you out of the way. Chapter 17 offers some suggestions for how to respond in a crisis.

When experiencing a manic episode or hypomania, you may behave in ways that you never imagined you would. Mania can drive you to make imprudent decisions that you live to regret. To make a serious mistake, you need motive, method, and opportunity. In a state of mania, your motive is out of your control, so you need to work on eliminating the method and opportunity. Try the following techniques:

✔ **Destroy your credit cards.** They make it too easy to spend money you don't have.

✔ **Limit access to your bank account.** If you can't withdraw your money, you can't spend it. Place a loved one in charge of your finances.

✔ **Hand over your car keys.** You may speed and drive erratically during manic episodes, or you may decide to drive to the airport and hop on a plane to Burma.

✔ **Buddy up with a conscience.** Being alone during a manic episode is dangerous in itself. Find a loyal, level-headed friend to accompany you on any outings.

✔ **Avoid alcohol and other mind-altering substances.** Alcohol, marijuana, ecstasy, cocaine, and other drugs tend to make you less inhibited. Less inhibition plus mania equals trouble.

✔ **Stay off the Internet.** Chat rooms, investment sites, online casinos, and a host of temptations line the streets of the information superhighway. Even people with stable moods have trouble fending off the temptations.

For these tactics to work, you need to plan ahead and work with a close friend or relative who can intervene before the risky behavior commences. See Chapter 17 for instructions on how to draw up a contract for intervention.

Planning Ahead for a Possible Relapse

The last thing you want to think about when you're recovering is having to relive the hell of a major depressive, manic, or mixed episode. However, when your moods and medications are stabilized, you have the perfect opportunity to plan ahead. By planning in advance, you can often reduce the intensity and duration of the next mood episode and accelerate your recovery. You may even be able to short-circuit the episode and avoid it altogether.

Select one or more close friends or relatives to act as your support network (see Chapter 6), and set aside a time to discuss your emergency plan. Be prepared to provide them with the following information:

✔ Your psychiatrist's phone number

✔ Your therapist's phone number

✔ Your health insurance company's phone number and your member ID

✔ The name of the hospital you prefer to go to, if hospitalization is necessary

✔ A list of warning signs that indicate you may need help

✔ A heartfelt promise that even though you may resist their help during the mood episode, you won't hold it against them later

The more you educate the members of your support network about bipolar disorder, the better. They need to know up front that you may vehemently protest against their involvement when you need their help the most. Encourage them to read this book or obtain information from other resources or bipolar support groups. (Chapter 21 helps you get involved in the bipolar community.)

Supporting a Friend or Relative with Bipolar Disorder

Bipolar disorder can make or break a relationship. Although bipolar is a disorder that causes suffering, it can also have benefits. People with bipolar disorder can often be the most creative, engaging, intelligent, life-affirming people on the planet. They have fun, and their zest for life is contagious. You can easily fall in love with them.

When someone you care about is in a deep depression, however, you may feel as though the disorder is swallowing you both up into a bottomless pit of despair. During a full-blown manic episode, the arrogance, anger, self-righteousness, or emotional abuse your loved one displays may repel you. It's important to keep the disorder in perspective and maintain a healthy state of mind.

Establishing the right frame of mind

To support a friend or relative with bipolar disorder, the first step is to establish empathy and understand the control that the illness has over your friend or relative. Following are a few important points to keep in mind:

- ✔ Your friend or relative probably wants this illness even less than you want him to have it.

- ✔ When your friend or relative spews abusive or cutting remarks, the disorder is talking. Don't take it personally.

- ✔ Taking it personally is normal, so don't feel guilty if you slip. Being a solid support person isn't easy.

- ✔ The situation isn't hopeless. With the right medication and therapy and your support, you can get your friend or relative back, and he may return even better than before!

- ✔ The more you know about bipolar disorder, the more you can accept it and provide the proper support. By reading this book, you're already doing your job.

Taking action

Here are some ideas for more practical, hands-on things you can do to help a friend or relative with bipolar disorder:

- ✔ Attend a support group or class for friends or relatives of people with bipolar disorder.

- ✔ Ask your friend or relative how involved he wants you to be.

- ✔ Be helpful without being intrusive.

- ✔ During times of crisis, offer to cook, clean, or take care of other necessities.

- ✔ Keep in touch.

- ✔ Offer to drive your friend or relative to appointments.

- ✔ Listen.

- ✔ Treat your friend or relative as you used to, before you knew about the diagnosis.

Diagnosing and Treating a Child or Adolescent with Bipolar Disorder

Bipolar disorder puts on a different mask when it afflicts a child or adolescent. Children and teenagers have immature mood systems to start with; kids are, by definition, less emotionally regulated than adults, so determining bipolar patterns is very challenging. Children and adolescents may experience more mixed episodes with co-occurring depression and mania, or they may have more background noise consisting of irritability and explosiveness in addition to the cycles of mood episodes. A child's mood episodes are often briefer than an adult's. (For more about how bipolar disorder affects children, turn to Chapter 18.)

Because bipolar disorder often manifests itself differently in children and adolescents than it does in adults, the diagnosis can be much more difficult to make. Some symptoms can be similar to symptoms of other mental illnesses, such as unipolar depression, ADD (Attention Deficit Disorder), or ODD (Oppositional Defiant Disorder). Furthermore, the child or adolescent may have two or more *comorbid* (co-existing) conditions — for example, bipolar disorder and ADD. Bipolar disorder in children and adolescents commonly presents itself with the following symptoms:

- Extended periods of sadness or irritability
- Extended periods of silliness/giddiness or raging anger
- Periods of high activity levels and/or racing thoughts or pressured speech (the need to talk constantly)
- Exaggerated emotional sensitivity — huge emotional responses to little things
- Significant changes in sleep patterns and energy levels
- A cyclic quality to the mood and behavior changes classically seen over a period of days to weeks rather than moment to moment
- Noticeable increase in risk taking and pleasure seeking
- Noticeable increase in withdrawal, isolation, or dropping activities
- History of difficult temperament in infancy/toddler periods
- Grandiose thinking: "I am great at everything!" or "I am better than everyone!"
- Night terrors/sleep problems during early childhood
- Suicidal thoughts or self-injury
- Violence or threats to harm others
- Decline in function at school, home, or with friends

As we discuss in Chapter 18, obtaining an early, accurate diagnosis is the most critical step in helping a child or adolescent with bipolar disorder. Too often, a child or adolescent with bipolar disorder is misdiagnosed with ADD or depression, and doctors place the children on medications that can worsen the course of the illness.

Chapter 2

Demystifying Bipolar Disorder

*B*ipolar disorder can make you feel blessed or cursed. It can boost your moods to exhilarating new highs or dump you in the dungeon of despair. It can also morph, becoming increasingly severe or going dormant for years at a time.

Perhaps the most vexing aspect of bipolar disorder is that it manifests itself only through thoughts, emotions, perceptions, speech, and behavior. Your doctor can't perform any medical test that proves beyond the shadow of a doubt that you have bipolar disorder. Moreover, other medical conditions, such as thyroid malfunction and substance abuse, can produce similar symptoms. And because bipolar disorder expresses itself internally through thoughts, perceptions, and emotions and externally through speech and behaviors, doctors and patients may be tempted to dismiss the illness as a character flaw or personality defect.

Bipolar disorder, however, is a very real physical illness. It just happens to affect the brain — one of the most complex parts of the human anatomy, one of the most difficult parts to test, and one of the areas most sensitive to emotional trauma and stress.

In this chapter, we explore the four principal bipolar diagnoses and define the terms depression, mania, hypomania, and mixed state. We examine the biology of bipolar disorder, illustrating the genetic vulnerability to the disease and the brain physiology that causes the most severe symptoms. Because external stimuli commonly trigger mood episodes, we look at some of the stressors and triggers that can provoke depression or mania. Finally, we introduce you to the positive prognosis that current medications and therapies can offer.

You're in good company

Bipolar disorder is often considered the Cadillac of brain disorders, because so many famous and creative individuals are thought to have suffered from it, including Vincent Van Gogh, Abraham Lincoln, Winston Churchill, and Virginia Woolf. Although this may be only a small comfort when your symptoms are severe and painful, it can give you a sense of kinship with people who made an impact and help you find and focus on the talents that make you stand out in this world.

With advances in treatment, patients no longer have to swap creativity for stability. In fact, most people who are receiving treatment for bipolar disorder find that they're more consistently creative and productive with the right combination of medication and therapy.

Peeking Behind the Many Masks of Bipolar Disorder

Bipolar disorder wears many masks. It can be happy, sad, fearful, confident, sexy, or furious. It can seduce strangers, intimidate bank tellers, throw extravagant parties, and steal your joy late into the night. However, psychiatrists have managed to bring order to the disorder by grouping the many manifestations of bipolar disorder into four main categories: Bipolar I, Bipolar II, Cyclothymic disorder, and Bipolar NOS (Not Otherwise Specified). Don't take the labels personally; they describe the disease, not the person, and doctors use them to ensure that you receive appropriate, consistent treatment. Medical doctors use similar labels all the time to make sure that if you go into surgery to have your tonsils removed, for example, you don't wake up missing a kidney.

Bipolar I

To earn the Bipolar I label, you must experience at least one bout of mania or a mixed-mood episode sometime during your life. The manic episode must last at least one week, or it must be serious enough to require hospitalization. It also must negatively affect some aspect of your life — your marriage, your career, or your life savings — to some degree. Depression isn't required, although many people with Bipolar I have experienced a bout or two of major depression at some point in their lives.

As we discuss later in this chapter, a bona-fide mania diagnosis hinges on several conditions, which apply to any bipolar label you may receive. To be considered a genuine manic episode, the mania must satisfy the following conditions:

✔ **The mania can't be drug-induced.** For example, if you were taking an antidepressant, steroid, or cocaine at the time, the manic symptoms don't equal a diagnosis of bipolar disorder.

✔ **Doctors can't attribute the mania to an identifiable medical condition.** If you have a hormone imbalance that may be responsible for the manic symptoms, for example, your doctor can't make a definitive diagnosis of bipolar disorder until you get that condition under control.

✔ **Doctors can't attribute the mania to schizoaffective disorder.** *Schizoaffective disorder* is a different illness. Its symptoms and treatments can be similar to those of bipolar disorder, but other aspects, such as the type and duration of the psychoses (including delusions or hallucinations), are very different.

Many of the medicines designed to make you feel better can worsen your condition or alter the course of your illness. SSRI (Selective Serotonin Reuptake Inhibitor) antidepressants, for example, have helped thousands of people overcome debilitating depressions, but they've also induced mania in others. If an antidepressant induces mania, it may be a sign that you have bipolar disorder. Your doctor is likely to become much more cautious when prescribing antidepressants, and she may consider adding a mood stabilizer. Chapter 7 helps you work with your doctor to decide what to do when the medications that should help make your situation worse.

Bipolar II

Bipolar II is characterized by one or more episodes of major depression with at least one episode of hypomania during a lifetime. The depressive episodes must last at least two weeks, and the hypomania must last at least four days. *Hypomania* is a milder form of mania, characterized by an increase in energy and a heightened state of mind, which can often feel quite pleasant. This condition can make you feel powerful, omniscient, creative, passionate, and uninhibited, but it can also be *dysphoric* — making you irritable, disorganized, enraged, or terrified.

Hypomania doesn't typically result in serious relationship problems or extremely risky behavior, but your behavior can make people around you more than a little uncomfortable.

Cyclothymic disorder

Cyclothymic disorder is a less extreme form of bipolar, sometimes referred to as "bipolar lite," that nevertheless chronically interferes with your life. It involves multiple episodes of hypomania and depressive symptoms, which don't meet criteria for mania or major depression in intensity or duration.

Your symptoms must last for at least two years without more than two months of stable, or *euthymic,* mood during that time.

Some people with Cyclothymic disorder go on to develop a full-blown manic, mixed, or depressive episode, leading to an additional diagnosis of Bipolar I or II. Preventive measures like therapy, lifestyle changes, and medication can make a difference in the course of Cyclothymic disorder.

Bipolar NOS

The three bipolar classifications we cover up to this point are loosely paraphrased from the DSM-IV — the *Diagnostic and Statistical Manual of Mental Disorders,* 4th Edition, published by the American Psychiatric Association. DSM-IV defines a fourth class, Bipolar NOS (Not Otherwise Specified), which covers all other forms of bipolar disorder that don't fall into any of the first three categories.

The Bipolar NOS label often applies to the following cases:

- ✔ Rapid fluctuations in mood that may be intense enough to qualify as manic, hypomanic, or depressive but that don't fulfill the duration requirements for a Bipolar I, Bipolar II, or Cyclothymic disorder diagnosis

- ✔ Hypomania without depression

- ✔ Mania or Cyclothymic disorder occurring simultaneously with schizophrenia, Psychotic disorder NOS, or Delusional disorder (a disorder that typically results in psychoses, hallucinations, and delusional thinking)

- ✔ Chronic depression and/or *dysthymia* (long-term, low-level depression) accompanied by hypomanic episodes

Rapid cycling

Rapid cycling isn't a separate type of bipolar disorder, but your doctor may use the label to describe a particular subtype of Bipolar I or II. To qualify as a rapid-cycling sufferer, you must experience the following:

- ✔ You must experience four or more mood episodes (depression, mania, hypomania, or mixed state) in a year.

- ✔ Your episodes must be full-blown versions — including typical duration (see the following section).

- ✔ Your mania or mixed state must last at least one week or result in hospitalization; your depression must last at least two weeks; and your hypomania must last at least four days. In other words, rapid cycling doesn't describe mood changes from minute to minute or hour to hour.

Rapid cycling is the only manifestation of bipolar disorder to have a distinctly higher rate in women than men. All other bipolar disorders are equal-opportunity mental illnesses.

Not Your Average Moodiness: Characteristics of Bipolar Disorder

Everyone experiences ups and downs, and some people are a little more moody than others. That's human nature, but it's not what bipolar disorder is all about. If you drag yourself into a psychiatrist's office singing the blues, she won't hand you a prescription for an antidepressant. Likewise, if you stay up all night playing poker and howling at the moon with your buddies, don't expect to receive a free sample of a mood stabilizer. Major depression, mania, hypomania, and mixed mania are much more serious and more strictly defined.

Major depressive episode

Major depression makes you feel like you're swimming in a sea of molasses. Everything is slow, dark, and heavy. Along with criteria for the various categories of bipolar disorder, the DSM-IV (see the previous section) lays out the criteria for a major depressive episode. Specifically, you must have five or more of the following symptoms that last for at least two weeks straight:

- ✔ Depressed mood
- ✔ Markedly diminished interest in activities previously considered pleasurable, including sex
- ✔ Five percent or more weight loss or weight gain in one month or less when you're not dieting, or a decrease or increase in appetite that lasts for two weeks
- ✔ Sleeping too much or too little
- ✔ Moving uncharacteristically slow, both in mind and body
- ✔ Fatigue
- ✔ Feelings of worthlessness, excessive guilt, or inappropriate guilt (if you're a Catholic, this may be normal; otherwise, it's a symptom)
- ✔ Uncharacteristic indecisiveness or diminished ability to think clearly or concentrate on a given task (if you're a little spacey all the time, this doesn't count as a symptom)
- ✔ Recurrent thoughts of death or suicide (assuming you aren't a French philosopher)

If you tally your score and find that you have five or more of these symptoms, don't jump to conclusions. You still may not be experiencing a major depressive episode. Any of the following can disqualify the episode from achieving major-depression status:

- ✔ Something terrible happened before you became depressed, such as the death of a loved one, a divorce, or a job loss. In other words, you have good reason to feel depressed.
- ✔ You're dealing with substance abuse, such as heavy drinking.
- ✔ The depression is a component of a mixed episode.

Avoid the temptation to self-diagnose. However, if you're experiencing the symptoms of a major depressive or manic episode, or you feel abnormally energetic and enlightened, we encourage you to consult a psychiatrist for a more in-depth evaluation.

Manic episode

Mania is the flip side of depression — the wired side of tired. Imagine a pinball machine on speed to get a pretty good idea of what mania is all about. However, you don't officially experience a manic episode unless the mania lasts for at least one week or requires hospitalization. The episode also must be characterized by an "abnormally and persistently elevated, expansive, or irritable mood." Three of the following symptoms must also be present during the week; four if your mood is irritable rather than elevated or expansive:

- ✔ Inflated self-esteem or grandiosity
- ✔ Decreased need for sleep (feeling well-rested after three hours or less)
- ✔ Excessive talking or the need to continuously talk
- ✔ Racing thoughts with plenty of ideas
- ✔ Inability to concentrate and easily distracted by insignificant external stimuli
- ✔ Significant increase in goal-directed activity or significant speeding up of thoughts and physical movement (If you plan on remodeling the kitchen, making a killing in the stock market, and buying a private island in the Pacific, all by week's end, you qualify.)
- ✔ Excessive involvement in risky, potentially self-destructive activities, including sexual indiscretions, unrestrained shopping sprees, and investments in pyramid schemes

To qualify as a bona-fide manic episode, the mania must be severe enough to mess up some aspect of your life, such as your interpersonal relationships, your job, or your physical functioning. The mania also must not be substance-induced to qualify for diagnosis, because drugs like speed and ecstasy keep most people up all night. However, if you're still flying high long after your friends' weekend highs have subsided, the substances may have triggered an episode that needs medical attention.

Hypomanic episode

Hypomania is a less-intense mania that doesn't last as long as a full-blown mania and that doesn't cause significant problems with your interpersonal relationships or job. Your mood must be elevated above your normal state and display characteristics that others around you believe are slightly out of character. The episode must last at least four days.

Mixed manic episode

To qualify as mixed mania, an episode must simultaneously meet the requirements stipulated for a major depressive episode *and* a manic episode. Your symptoms must occur nearly every day for a week straight. When experiencing a mixed manic episode, you commonly exhibit uncharacteristic emotional storms. You may yell in the morning and cry in the evening or be boastful one minute and self-deprecating the next. Or you may just experience a constant feeling of agitation or irritability throughout the day.

Psychosis . . . sometimes

Perhaps the most frightening accompaniment to depression or mania is psychosis — delusional thinking, paranoia, and visual or auditory hallucinations. Although psychosis isn't a necessary part of the bipolar diagnosis, it can accompany a mood episode. The extremes of depression and, more often, mania can traumatize the mind to such an extent that it begins to latch on to self-destructive or grandiose beliefs, become obsessed with fears that have no basis in reality, or perceive sights and sounds that are not present. During a psychotic episode, you may

- Feel as though you have special powers
- Hear voices that other people can't hear and believe they're talking about you or sometimes instructing you to perform certain acts
- Believe that people can read your mind or put thoughts into your head
- Think that the television or radio is sending you special messages
- Think that people are following you or trying to harm you when they're not
- Believe that you can accomplish goals that are well beyond your abilities and means

Although psychosis sounds dramatic and easily identifiable, it can be quite subtle and shrouded by enough reality to make "psychosis" seem more like "unusually perceptive." Is your boss trying to fire you, or are you just paranoid? Can you really portend future events, or are your accurate predictions of critical world events just a coincidence?

Digging Up the Genetic Roots

Entire businesses are dedicated to mapping human chromosomes to identify the genes that cause afflictions from Alzheimer's to zits. Although scientists can't point the finger at a single gene that's responsible for bipolar disorder, indisputable evidence proves that the disorder is rooted deep in the gene pool. Check out the following statistics:

- ✔ One percent of the general population has Bipolar I.

- ✔ Two to three percent of the general population likely has Bipolar II, and an even larger percentage is thought to have Cyclothymic disorder.

- ✔ In families in which a member gets diagnosed with Bipolar I, immediate family members (mom, dad, brother, or sister) have a 7 to 10 percent higher risk of developing bipolar disorder than someone in the general population.

- ✔ An identical twin has a 60 to 70 percent chance of having Bipolar I if the other twin has it.

- ✔ A fraternal twin has a 10 to 15 percent chance of having Bipolar I if the other twin has it. (This percentage is slightly higher than the risk for other immediate family members.)

No single gene is the sole culprit that causes bipolar disorder. Intensive and varied research studies have yielded unclear and mixed results, due to several factors:

- ✔ Multiple genes appear to be involved in causing bipolar disorder, and they overlap with genes suspected of causing other psychiatric disorders, including unipolar depression and schizophrenia.

- ✔ If bipolar disorder were 100 percent genetic, 100 percent of identical twins with bipolar disorder would have the disorder, which isn't the case. Studies must look for factors that "turn on" the bipolar genes.

- ✔ Multiple disorders (from different problems in different parts of the brain) are likely to contribute to the symptoms doctors collectively refer to as bipolar disorder. This means the genetic search is actually exploring several disorders rather than just one. The people under the microscope may have a range of bipolar subtypes, making the results confusing and inconsistent.

What are the odds?

Scientists used to believe that about 1 percent of the population suffered from bipolar disorder. Now, this figure applies to the narrow definition of Bipolar I. When you roll in the numbers for Bipolar II, Cyclothymic disorder, and Bipolar NOS, the percentage soars to 5 percent or higher. And that's just for the general population. If your family is genetically loaded with bipolar disorder, your odds of developing it or another psychiatric disorder climb even higher:

- ✔ You have 10 percent odds if you have one parent with bipolar disorder.

- ✔ You have 20 percent odds or higher if both your parents have bipolar disorder. (Some studies show that 50 percent of children with bipolar parents may experience some form of cycling mood disorder.)

- ✔ You have increased risk for bipolar disorder, recurrent unipolar depression, or schizoaffective disorder if you have a first-degree relative, such as an uncle or aunt, with bipolar disorder.

Studies consistently show that genetics makes up about 75 percent of the cause of Bipolar I disorder. Environmental variation may play a larger role in other bipolar subtypes, but this isn't clear yet.

Shaking the family tree

An accurate diagnosis of your condition can benefit greatly from an examination of your family history, but you never know what's going to fall when you start shaking your family tree. If you ask your relatives whether anyone in the family has ever been diagnosed with bipolar disorder, you may receive plenty of blank stares and all too little useful information. Try asking this series of more probing questions:

- ✔ **Has anyone in the family had alcohol or substance abuse problems?** Many people with bipolar disorder self-medicate with alcohol and drugs.

- ✔ **Have any family members been diagnosed with schizophrenia?** In the not-so-distant past, doctors commonly misdiagnosed bipolar disorder as schizophrenia.

- ✔ **Has any family member been treated for any mental illness?** If a family member has received treatment for depression, psychosis, or other mental illnesses, he may not have received the correct diagnosis.

- ✔ **Has anyone in the family had to "go away for a while" to an institution, sanatorium, or rehab center?** Families often like to cover up memories of relatives who had to be hospitalized for mental illnesses by saying that they had to "go away for a while."

> ✔ **Have any family members been known to be particularly energetic or eccentric?** In the past, people politely described relatives with various degrees of mental illness as "eccentric."
>
> ✔ **Has anyone in the family suffered from physical symptoms such as chronic exhaustion, pain, or digestive problems?** These can be physical manifestations of the illness.

If you were adopted, consider tracking down your birth records and contacting members of your biological family for medical information. This can help with diagnosing any genetically related illnesses, including bipolar disorder, heart disease, and cancer.

Families can be particularly secretive, especially when it comes to protecting the reputation of the dead. They can become even more defensive if you confront them while you're in the throes of mania. Explain how important an accurate and detailed family history is for your diagnosis.

Predisposed, not predetermined

Being genetically predisposed to bipolar disorder doesn't guarantee that you'll experience symptoms. Genetic predisposition only makes you *susceptible* to developing bipolar disorder. Think of it as a susceptibility to skin cancer: If you're born with pale skin, you may be susceptible to extreme sunburn and skin cancer, but if you prudently avoid overexposure to the sun, you can prevent the cancer.

The same is true of bipolar disorder. You may have the susceptibility, but if you live a stress-free existence and take care of yourself physically, you may be able to live symptom free. You may also be one of the lucky few who have the susceptibility but don't experience the symptoms.

Scientists don't know all the factors that can activate bipolar disorder. Stress is well documented as a trigger, but other biological events, such as viruses, may be involved. The severity of the underlying susceptibility is also important. Some forms are more sensitive to stress than others.

Examining the Biochemistry of Bipolar Disorder

Many mental health professionals refer to bipolar disorder as a "chemical imbalance," which oversimplifies what's actually going on. It implies that if you could inject the proper mix of chemicals into your brain, you could somehow cure bipolar disorder. Moreover, it creates the false impression that medications are solely designed to replace chemicals that your brain lacks.

Brain chemistry definitely has something to do with bipolar disorder. Your body produces and uses countless chemicals, many of which affect the way your mind and body function. However, your brain's physiology — the way it uses and processes the chemicals — has as much influence on bipolar disorder as the chemicals themselves.

Where in the brain does bipolar disorder form?

Pinpointing the location of bipolar disorder in your brain is almost as difficult as finding affordable health insurance. Your brain consists of about 100 billion cells of two different types: neurons and glial cells. Neurons form the telecommunications network in the brain, enabling the cells to communicate with one another and carry signals back and forth between your brain and the rest of your body. Glial cells act as the brain's caretakers — ensuring that the neurons have the chemicals and nutrients they need to function, repairing damaged brain cells, and keeping infection at bay.

As shown in Figure 2-1, the brain is divided into the following four sections:

- **Cerebrum:** The part of the brain that most people consider to be *the brain,* the part that you see in the science fiction movies. The cerebrum is the uniquely human component in charge of gathering and processing information, making connections, generating thought, and controlling emotions and behavior. Problems in certain areas of the cerebrum, such as the *prefrontal cortex,* are thought to play a role in the emotional over-reactivity observed in bipolar disorder.

- **Middle brain:** A relay station for messages traveling from the cerebrum to other parts of the brain. It includes the *thalamus* and *hypothalamus.* This brain region attends to the day-to-day maintenance of the body as well — sleeping, eating, temperature regulation, and reproduction — earning it the nickname "feed and breed." Many symptoms of bipolar disorder stem from this system, including sleep variations, energy level fluctuations, sexuality issues, and appetite loss/gain.

- **Brain stem:** A less developed part of the brain that regulates life-giving functions, such as breathing. The brain stem is also responsible for the "fight or flight" response, or the kick in the pants that your brain gives you when it perceives a threat. Mania may be the result of too much arousal, whereas depression is the result of too little. This brain region plays at least a small role in bipolar disorder.

- **Cerebellum:** A little ball of neurons at the back of the brain that most experts believe is involved in fine-tuning complex movements, along with performing a host of other functions that remain undiscovered. No one knows yet whether or not the cerebellum plays a role in bipolar disorder.

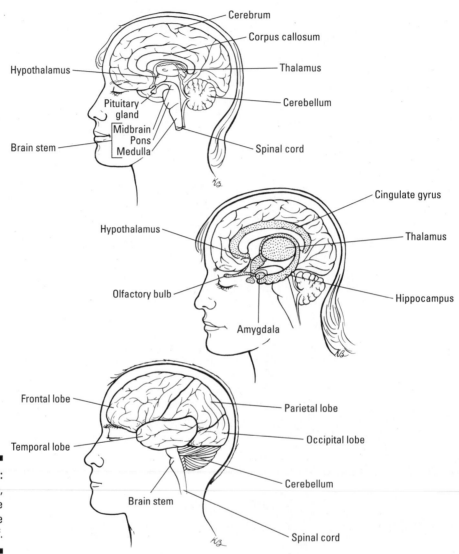

Figure 2-1:
Your brain,
or a close
facsimile
thereof.

Within the cerebrum, the brain is further divided. The *cerebral cortex* is the outermost layer of the brain, commonly referred to as the *gray matter*. Below that layer are bundles of long nerve fibers called *white matter* that carry information between parts of the brain. Deep in the brain are *subcortical* areas, consisting of collections of neurons that regulate different functions. One such area is the *limbic system,* including the *amygdala, hippocampus,* and *cingulate gyrus.* These areas are involved in emotional control, drive and motivation, fear responses, and memory. Many brain function studies reveal that these areas of the brain function differently in people with bipolar disorder or depression compared to those without these illnesses.

The brain science behind bipolar disorder is just beginning to mature. The concept of a simple chemical imbalance, although appealing, isn't quite accurate. Bipolar disorder more likely is the result of various blips in the brain circuitry that foul up the operations of various departments and scramble communications between departments.

Although various areas of the brain are suspected conspirators in producing bipolar symptoms, doctors can't restructure the brain to repair the abnormalities. Instead, they choose the less intrusive option of adjusting the way the brain transfers signals via its neurotransmitters.

What are neurotransmitters, anyway?

Neurons are elongated cells, shown in Figure 2-2, that carry signals throughout your brain and body. The communication system within each neuron is primarily electrical, enabling it to carry a signal at a high speed from start to finish. A very small space, called the *synapse,* separates neighboring neurons and prevents them from communicating directly via the electronic messaging system. Instead, neurons communicate with one another by sending chemicals, called *neurotransmitters,* across the synapse. One neuron sends the signal by releasing neurotransmitters, which the other neuron receives via its receptor sites.

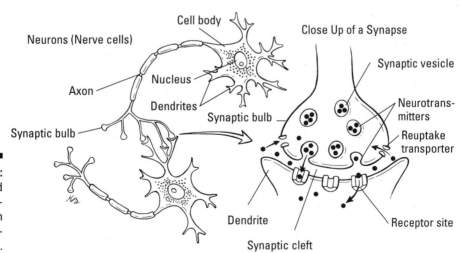

Figure 2-2:
Brain and body communication via neurotransmitters.

The five neurotransmitters considered most responsible for maintaining mood are the following:

- ✓ **Serotonin:** An essential amino acid that has a calming effect on humans, serotonin helps regulate mood, anxiety, fear, sleep, body temperature, the rate at which your body releases certain hormones, and many other body and brain processes.

- ✓ **Dopamine:** Generally considered the feel-good neurotransmitter, dopamine is linked to feelings of pleasure. It modulates attention and focus, as well as muscle movements, and is also related to psychosis.

- ✓ **Norepinephrine:** Best known for its role in your fight or flight response, norepinephrine also functions to regulate mood, anxiety, and memory.

- ✓ **Glutamate:** The primary neurotransmitter in charge of revving up the central nervous system, glutamate may play a significant role in causing mania.

- ✓ **GABA:** Short for gaba-amino butyric acid, GABA is an amino acid transmitter that can cool down or excite brain cells, depending on other chemicals surrounding it.

When the neuron receptor "reads" the neurotransmitter, it releases a cascade of chemicals from inside it referred to as *second messengers,* including various *G-proteins* and *protein kinases.* These second messengers are mediators that help translate the chemical signals from the neurotransmitters into electrical signals that travel through the neuron. Researchers believe these chemicals are showing a lot of promise as possible keys for understanding bipolar disorder and ultimately developing more effective treatments.

Can you achieve better living through chemicals?

The medications doctors prescribe for bipolar disorder primarily alter the way your brain's neurons process the mood-regulating neurotransmitters in your brain. Each medication has a different way of working, and each way is called its *mechanism of action.* Mood medications generally function in one of the following ways:

- ✓ Increase or decrease the actual amount of a particular neurotransmitter in your system

- ✓ Restrict the neuron's ability to receive a neurotransmitter

- ✓ Adjust the second-messenger system to slow inappropriate chemical activity in the neuron

- ✓ Prevent electrical misfiring in the neurons

Psychiatrists and physicians commonly prescribe the following medications to treat mania or depression:

- ✔ **Lithium:** Little is known about lithium's mechanism of action, but it appears to regulate the second-messenger system, helping suppress both mania and depression. Lithium may also reduce the effect of elevated glutamate levels, potentially preventing mania.

- ✔ **SSRI antidepressants:** Selective Serotonin Reuptake Inhibitors are designed to prevent serotonin from being vacuumed back into the first neuron of a synapse, effectively increasing serotonin levels in the synapse.

  Other antidepressants, such as SSNRIs (Selective Serotonin and Norepinephrine Reuptake Inhibitors), work on various combinations of neurotransmitters to bring them to levels that help stabilize moods.

- ✔ **Anticonvulsants:** Valproate (Depakote), carbamazepine (Tegretol), and other anticonvulsants appear to function on the second-messenger system, particularly in systems involving glutamate and GABA. Developed primarily to help treat epileptic seizures, these medications have also proved effective as antimanic medications.

- ✔ **Antipsychotics:** Olanzapine (Zyprexa), clozapine (Clozaril), and other antipsychotic (neuroleptic) agents are typically used to treat symptoms of schizophrenia. They've also proved effective in treating acute manic episodes. Antipsychotics appear to work by blocking receptors for dopamine, although they can affect serotonin receptors as well.

Skip to Chapter 7 for details on the various medications used to treat bipolar disorder.

Trudging Through Stressors, Triggers, and Other Nasty Stuff

Biochemistry tells only half the story of bipolar disorder. Environmental factors play a large role, particularly in the timing of the onset of the disorder. Many people with bipolar disorder experience their first major mood episodes during exceptionally stressful periods of their lives (during a major relationship conflict, job loss, or the loss of a friend or relative, for example). A susceptibility to the illness coupled with an inordinate amount of stress often triggers the symptoms and worsens the course of the disorder.

The brains of people with bipolar disorder are often less effective at managing stress, even between mood episodes. Developing strategies for handling strong emotions and stress is central to the prevention and acute management of mood episodes. Throughout this book, we describe various techniques for reigning in mood episodes.

What really ticks you off?

Many psychologists and self-help gurus try to force-feed people the notion that "Nobody can make you angry." Sure, if you're a groveling sycophant, that may be true, but even Jesus got a little ticked off at times. Anger, in modulated amounts, can be a healthy response to a disturbing situation. If you have control over your moods, it can spark you to take action in the following ways:

- ✔ Determine if your anger stems from a misunderstanding.
- ✔ Identify the reason you feel angry.
- ✔ Resolve any conflicts that may be causing the anger.
- ✔ Deal with internal conflicts that may be causing frustration.
- ✔ Choose to ignore any issues you can't control.

Anger produces an adrenaline rush that can place enormous amounts of stress on your psyche and emotions. The faster you can shed the anger, the faster you eliminate a stressor that can trigger a mood episode.

A brain that angers too easily and calms too slowly commonly carries bipolar disorder. If you can't control your anger, make sure to let your doctor know, because medication adjustments may allow you to have a more normal anger experience.

Can something be too exciting?

Have you ever been involved in a relationship or a project that completely engulfs your mind, body, and soul? You feel like you're walking 3 feet above the pavement. You stop watching the clock. Movement and thought are effortless.

These moments in life can be most exhilarating, but if you have a susceptibility to bipolar disorder, they can also be dangerous. During these periods of blissful obsession, you may believe you need less sleep. Perhaps you decide to skip a meal or two and chug a little more caffeine to stay awake. Your heightened sense can eventually become too high, last too long, and drive you into a full-blown manic state, which leads to an inevitable crash.

Chapter 12 shows you how to map your moods and develop an early warning system for identifying mood swings before they spin out of control. By acting immediately, you can often short-circuit an episode of mania or depression.

Sleep deprivation commonly triggers mania. Fight back by establishing a regular sleep routine and making sure that you obtain a sufficient amount of sleep no matter what's going on in your life. Copy the sleep log you find in Chapter 12 to get started.

Some real downers

Sometimes the tree of life looks more like a lemon tree. You lose your job, your kids revolt, your spouse runs off with the neighbor, and your basement floods. To top it all off, your pastor, mom, or mentor gives you a sermon telling you that if life gives you lemons, you should make lemonade.

If you can make lemonade, that's great. Bad events often act as the kick in the pants you need to solve a problem that's dogging you. Maybe you need a new job. Perhaps relationship issues need some attention. You may need to crack down on the kids to do their chores. If you can trace your sadness back to an identifiable problem, solving the problem can make the blues dissipate. Sometimes, such as when you're grieving the loss of a loved one, you have to work through a period of sadness. These down periods are expected and normal.

When your life is going along pretty well, however, and you really don't have anything to be unhappy about, but you still feel despondent, the sadness may be depression, and it may deepen beyond your control. You may be experiencing a clinical depression that requires medication, therapy, or both.

Seasons change, and so do you

If left to our devices, few of us would remain stable. Humans need structure, routine, and ceremony to order the chaos, make life meaningful, and give us something to celebrate.

The most basic environmental factors that structure routines are the rising and setting of the sun and the change in seasons. All human beings and most animals tune into these environmental cues by using internal clocks. Each individual establishes a unique *circadian rhythm*. In nature, people would generally rise and set with the sun. In modern society, however, you have more control over your environment, and you can set your own internal clock.

Setting your own clock is swell. You can party all night, go to work in the morning, and still have time for dinner with your family. However, if you suffer from bipolar disorder, you may be more sensitive to changes in your daily routine and to any blips in your sleep pattern.

Any major changes in routine, such as the following, can throw you off kilter:

- ✔ Vacation
- ✔ Holidays
- ✔ Return to work
- ✔ Return to school
- ✔ All-nighter
- ✔ Job change
- ✔ Jet lag

Interpersonal and social rhythm therapy, which we discuss in Chapter 8, trains you to establish a healthy circadian rhythm and avoid veering from it. Many people with bipolar disorder have found that this therapy, along with medication, is a powerful combination in stabilizing their moods.

Unharmonic hormones

Although neurotransmitters garner all the attention in most discussions concerning the biochemistry of bipolar disorder, hormones can have a dramatic effect on moods as well. Women wrestle with hormones their entire lives. A few lucky women seem immune to the mood-altering effects of hormones, but the least lucky are bandied about like a bobber on the high seas. Men, too, can suffer from hormonal imbalances; just watch the guys in the stands at any major sporting event.

Women have the circadian rhythm from hell — hormone fluctuations that follow a regular pattern through each and every month and over the course of their lives. The ebb and flow of hormones seem to trigger the vacillations of mood, especially when estrogen levels undergo a dramatic change, such as a girl's first period, after a woman gives birth, or during *perimenopause* — the transition between reproductive years and menopause.

However, you can't pin all the blame on raging hormones. Changes in hormone levels may coincide with other events that have a greater impact on moods:

- ✔ During the teen years, girls' lives explode with new social, emotional, and behavioral demands.
- ✔ The birth of a child may increase the new mother's workload and decrease the amount of sleep she gets.
- ✔ During perimenopause, hot flashes and night sweats can disturb a woman's normal sleep pattern.

✔ A woman's role or perceived role in the family may change.

✔ A woman's self-concept may change.

✔ Relationship issues can compound stress.

Although hormone replacement therapy (HRT) has shown some effectiveness in treating mood symptoms, some studies show that the risks, including a potential increase in risk for breast cancer, outweigh the benefits. Using HRT is highly controversial. Before undertaking the therapy, discuss potential benefits and risks with your doctor.

Overcoming the Power of Negative Thinking

Your mind can be its own worst enemy. Latching on to negative views and allowing them free reign inside your mind can often worsen depression and despair. You can talk yourself into being miserable. You can convince yourself that you're unwanted, that someone wants to harm you, or that certain events will happen if you will them to. You can even think yourself into having a real, physical illness.

Medication can help break the cycle of negative thinking, but therapy, especially cognitive therapy, has proven very effective in breaking the cycle and relieving or preventing depression.

In cognitive therapy, your therapist helps you identify negative thoughts and patterns, such as

✔ **Unrealistic expectations:** If you think that everything and everyone needs to be perfect, that you're entitled to everything you want, or that everyone should be nice to you all the time, you may get depressed when reality smacks you in the face. Cognitive therapy can help you come to terms with reality and adjust your expectations to avoid disappointments.

✔ **Automatic thoughts:** If you assume that another person is thinking negative thoughts about you, that you're a total failure, that everyone hates you, or that nothing you do can improve your life, you may be setting up some self-fulfilling prophecies. Cognitive therapy increases your sensitivity to automatic thoughts and teaches you how to shut them down.

✔ **Maladaptive assumptions:** Forming negative theories about life or what you should do can often lead to depression. Thinking that you need everyone's approval to feel loved, that you can't succeed without the help of another person, or that you're stuck in a dead-end job are all maladaptive assumptions. When you begin to recognize them and come to realize that they're true only insofar as you believe them, you can shed them.

✔ **Low self-esteem:** Beating yourself up over your perceived shortcomings can drive your self-esteem into the ground. Focusing on your unique talents and abilities raises your self-esteem and your mood.

Chapter 8 provides some exercises designed to help you harness the power of positive thinking through cognitive therapy.

Recognizing All-Important Social Factors

Humans are social animals. When you don't socialize to some degree, you lose perspective, your mind turns in on itself, and life loses some of its color. In the midst of a major depressive episode, however, the last thing you want to do is party down with your homies. You may not even have the energy or desire to drag yourself out of bed. But waiting for your mood to improve often makes it worse. Fighting the urge to stay home, although tough, can be just what you need to break the downward cycle of depression and turn your eyes toward the light.

Establishing social contact delivers several benefits:

✔ **Sunlight:** Getting out increases your exposure to sunlight and fresh air, which can have a positive effect on your mood.

✔ **Perspective:** You can see life and your reality through the eyes of others and develop more objective views of reality.

✔ **Rhythm:** Having activities and something to look forward to can provide you with healthy structure and a routine.

✔ **Acceptance:** Interacting with supportive friends and contacts can help you feel more comfortable about your role in a community. You can also find ways to help them, which helps you feel more useful and worthwhile.

In Chapter 8, we discuss interpersonal and social rhythm therapy, designed to teach people how to become more socially involved and how to develop healthy routines. Interpersonal and social rhythm therapy can also help you shut down negative thinking and turn your focus to external stimulation.

Chapter 3

A Positive Prognosis with a Proactive Plan

. . . .

In This Chapter

▶ Gaining hope through a positive prognosis

▶ Attacking bipolar disorder before it attacks you

▶ Implementing effective prevention techniques

▶ Surviving an unavoidable hospital stay

▶ Identifying the warning signs of an impending mood episode

. . . .

*Y*ou can't fight an affliction you can't identify, so an accurate diagnosis is the first step down the path to wellness. If you know your enemy, you can draw up a proactive battle plan to defeat it or to at least keep it from invading your personal space.

In this chapter, we reveal the positive prognosis that accompanies the bipolar diagnosis. We show not only how you can conquer bouts of depression and mania when they afflict you, but also how you can trip them up before they establish their footing. We encourage you to remain as vigilant and unrelenting in stabilizing your moods as the disorder is in affecting your thoughts and emotions. We hope to keep you ever mindful of your right to enjoy a full and fulfilling life.

So, Doc, What's the Prognosis?

The choice between a negative or positive prognosis is up to you, your doctor, and your family and friends. If you accept the diagnosis, if you and your doctor can discover an effective medicine or combination of medicines, and if your family and friends pitch in to support you, the prognosis is very positive indeed. On the other hand, if you try to ignore the problem, it will likely get worse.

It's true that a few lucky souls have only one major mood episode throughout their lives. They experience deep depression or full-blown mania that eventually lifts, with or without treatment, and then they proceed to live out the remainder of their lives symptom free. How often this happens, no one really knows, but it does occasionally happen. In an overwhelming majority of cases, however, when left untreated, when self-treated, or when treated with the wrong medications, people with bipolar disorder can expect the following:

✔ Increase in frequency and severity of mood episodes

✔ Increased stress from the fallout of mood episodes

✔ Damaged relationships

✔ Loss of job or career status

✔ Increased financial problems

That's the bad news.

The good news is that effective medicines and therapies are available, and researchers are constantly developing newer and better treatments to add to the arsenal. Through medication, therapy, and support, you can look forward to achieving the following goals:

✔ Reduce or eliminate symptoms of mania and depression.

✔ Prevent the course of the illness from worsening.

✔ Reduce or eliminate stressors that trigger mania or depression.

✔ Find fulfilling and rewarding work.

✔ Repair damaged relationships and build new, healthy relationships.

✔ Restore your social and financial security.

Responding Proactively and Reactively to Bipolar Disorder

Major mood episodes can sneak up on you with the silence of a brooding sadness or the furtive stirrings of enthusiasm. Maybe you feel a little less tired one day, a little more energetic. That's normal. You have nothing to worry about. After all, you have every right to enjoy your life, and you're looking forward to the weekend — TGIF! After work, you'll head to Wilma's Watering Hole for an evening of rowdiness with your old college pals.

You get home a little late — actually, early Saturday morning — and you're not even tired. You lie in bed for two hours replaying the excitement of the evening on the insides of your eyelids. You finally manage to doze off, expecting to sleep until noon, but you wake up bright and early and raring to go. Why sleep when life's smorgasbord summons you to its feast?

Requiring less sleep and more stimulation, you race through each day of the week. By week's end, pedal to the metal, you're highballing down the hypomanic highway, and you don't even know how you got there.

Now what?

Reacting: Extinguishing the flames

Enveloped by a full-blown mania or depression, you face limited choices. If you pose no threat to yourself or others, you can choose to wait out the storm and hope the raging currents subside. But if your behavior becomes unbearable or dangerous — if you have suicidal thoughts or become increasingly belligerent, for example — you or someone else on your behalf can seek medical intervention in one or more of the following forms:

- ✔ **Hospitalization:** When you pose a threat to yourself or others or need the safety and retreat that hospitalization provides
- ✔ **Intensive outpatient therapy:** Allows you to focus on getting well by day and return home in the evening
- ✔ **Medication:** To lift the depression or quell the mania
- ✔ **Therapy:** To immediately address destructive thoughts or behaviors

Reacting can extinguish the flames, but it can also leave you and those around you burned out. In your weakened state, you're more susceptible to flare-ups. And if your behavior during the episode hurt your loved ones, their frustration or bitterness can compound the stress you already bear.

Proacting: Preventing flare-ups

If you tell the average person he has terminal cancer, he's likely to curl up in the fetal position and weep. Tell Lance Armstrong he has terminal cancer, and he pedals to five consecutive victories in the Tour de France. How you respond to your diagnosis and how ambitiously you pursue treatment and therapy have a huge effect on the outcome. If you deny that you have a problem, lose hope, or try to self-medicate with alcohol and other substances, the disorder wins. If you discover the right medication, confront your hidden demons through therapy, and remain vigilant, you prevail.

Shedding light on the kindling effect

Managing bipolar disorder proactively is important not only in helping prevent mood episodes, but also in thwarting what some doctors refer to as the *kindling effect*—the worsening of the disorder over time. The kindling effect is a process that's known to occur in the brains of people with seizures. *Seizures* are electrical storms in the brain, triggered by chemical changes or other physical stresses on the brain cells. With every storm, the brain can become more and more sensitized. Eventually, the brain can seize over and over again without any type of trigger. The cells seem to "memorize" the electrical storms and repeat them. Neurologists aggressively focus on treating seizures to prevent kindling, which progressively increases the frequency and severity of seizures.

Seizures and mood disorders — particularly bipolar disorder — are thought to have many similarities, chemically and electrically. Some experts suggest that the kindling effect can occur in bipolar disorder — that each mood episode is like a storm and that with each episode the brain becomes more sensitized, eventually having more frequent mood episodes that require fewer emotional triggers. According to the theory, early in the course of the illness, a major stressor is required to trigger a mood episode, but as more and more episodes occur, the brain can develop mood episodes spontaneously instead of waiting for a trigger.

Doctors haven't clearly identified the kindling effect in bipolar disorder, and if it occurs, it's likely much more complex than what happens with seizures. Perhaps some brains are more vulnerable to kindling than others. Whether or not the kindling model accurately pertains to bipolar disorder, reducing the frequency of mood episodes is beneficial for your health and quality of life in many ways.

Practicing an Ounce of Prevention

Maintaining your car's health with regular oil changes and the occasional tune-up helps keep it running trouble free for thousands of miles. Maintaining your physical health reduces the risk of cancer, heart disease, and other major illnesses. Maintaining your mental health delivers similar benefits; yet, even after being diagnosed with bipolar disorder, people often ignore medical orders and continue to roll the dice in a game they're almost certain to lose.

Don't gamble with your mental health. After you've been diagnosed with bipolar disorder, establish a preventive maintenance plan to ward off relapse and minimize the damage of unavoidable mood episodes. Take the following actions:

- ✔ Accept your diagnosis.
- ✔ Take your medicine as prescribed.
- ✔ Monitor your moods for early warning signs, and consult your doctor at the first sign of trouble.
- ✔ Identify and eliminate your stressors.
- ✔ Build a strong support network.

Accepting your bipolar badge

You don't need a Harvard-educated psychiatrist to convince you that you're clinically depressed. For two weeks, you've been sad, tired, and achy, and you've lost your mojo. Mania sometimes takes a little more convincing. You feel better than ever, so what's the problem? When you're symptom free, you also may be a little reluctant to admit that you have an illness. With bipolar disorder, however, accepting the diagnosis is the first step toward recovery.

The path leading from denial to acceptance is a rocky road, but you can stick to the following steps to take the bumps in stride:

1. **Ask your psychiatrist to explain the reasons she arrived at your diagnosis and treatment plan.**

   Knowing the symptoms, background information, and other facts that helped your psychiatrist arrive at your diagnosis is more likely to convince you of its veracity. You deserve an explanation.

2. **Get a second opinion, but don't tell your second doctor what your first doctor thinks.**

   Two concurring opinions weigh more than one. And if the two doctors don't concur, you may need to dig a little deeper by consulting another doctor or doing a little research on your own. Accept your diagnosis only after carefully and honestly assessing all the information from professionals and feedback from loved ones.

3. **Look back at what your life was like before the diagnosis.**

   Did low-level symptoms negatively affect your relationships, your plans, and your happiness? Looking to the past may help you realize that your life wasn't a bowl of cherries before the diagnosis and that your life can be much better with the proper treatment.

4. **Ask your friends and family to provide honest feedback about your moods and behaviors in the past.**

   When experiencing hypomania or mania, you may not objectively perceive your behaviors, which can lead to denial.

5. **Read stories of people who have bipolar disorder, especially those who are on the road to recovery.**

   Patty Duke's *A Brilliant Madness: Living with Manic-Depressive Illness* (Bantam) and Kaye Jamison's *An Unquiet Mind: A Memoir of Moods and Madness* (Vintage) are excellent reads. Jane Pauley has also written a biography that includes a description of her personal experience with bipolar disorder called *Skywriting: A Life Out of the Blue* (Random House). Reading about other people's experiences with bipolar disorder can often help you recognize parallels in your life.

The diagnostic dilemma

Bipolar disorder is actually a number of different disorders — Bipolar I being the most clear-cut and straightforward diagnosis. Bipolar II, Cyclothymic disorder, and Bipolar NOS can be trickier to sort out because the symptoms on the manic end of the spectrum can be harder to specify or notice. On the depressive side of the coin, a whopping major depression can be fairly easy to spot, but variations of it can be less visible. Furthermore, when the first episode of major depression presents itself, you don't know if manic symptoms will develop down the road; although family or personal history may hold some clues, the information isn't 100 percent reliable.

Additionally, bipolar disorder is likely to occur with other symptoms that can be misleading or at least distracting in the diagnostic process.

Anxiety symptoms, psychosis, and substance abuse are the most common overlapping disorders in adults, with ADHD being a common related disorder in kids.

You're more likely to receive varying diagnostic opinions if your diagnosis isn't Bipolar I. When you seek a second opinion, you should pay as much attention to how the doctor arrived at the diagnosis as you do to the diagnosis itself. What symptoms has she considered? How has she put them together with other information, such as family history? What additional diagnoses does she think are present? The answers you receive paint a diagnostic portrait that helps you understand what's going on with your brain; this picture provides you with something much more valuable than a label and a prescription.

6. **Attend a bipolar disorder support group.**

   Having a forum where you can connect with others who face similar struggles can help you bear your burdens and discover useful coping strategies.

7. **Realize the upside of bipolar disorder.**

   Many people go through their entire lives without experiencing the extremes of mood and emotion that you're capable of experiencing. Kaye Jamison's *Touched with Fire: Manic Depression and the Artistic Temperament* (Free Press) can help you appreciate the positive aspects of bipolar disorder.

Of course, working on acceptance assumes that you're in a receptive and rational state of mind. If you're experiencing a mood episode that requires immediate treatment, your doctor may treat your symptoms whether or not you accept the diagnosis, for your own health and safety.

Utilizing your preventive medication

When you're mired in the midst of a major mood episode, your doctor's primary goal is to end the episode as quickly as possible, usually by prescribing psychiatric medication. This process treats the *acute phase* of the illness. If you're having manic symptoms, your doctor likely prescribes lithium or another antimanic medication or increases the dose of the antimanic medication you're taking. If you're having a bout of depression, your doctor may prescribe one or more antidepressants or increase the dose of the antidepressant you're currently taking. In either case, your doctor may prescribe a sedative to help you sleep.

For times when you're symptom free, your doctor likely prescribes a *maintenance dose* of medication to function as a *prophylaxis* — a fancy word for "preventive." You may be tempted to forgo the prophylaxis when you feel fine or when you feel hypomanic (better than fine). However, continuing to take your medication is critical for the following reasons:

✔ Medication decreases your susceptibility to future mood episodes.

✔ Preventing mood fluctuations minimizes the risk of new episodes (see the sidebar "Shedding light on the kindling effect" earlier in this chapter).

✔ Many medications require several days or weeks to build up to a therapeutic level in your system — the level at which they can effectively maintain your mood. By taking your medications as prescribed, you keep them at their therapeutic levels.

✔ Keeping medication levels stable prevents withdrawal symptoms, which can trigger mood episodes.

✔ Retaining mood stability increases the effectiveness of therapy and helps reduce interpersonal conflicts that may lead to stress.

Straying from your meds

Most people have trouble accepting any diagnosis that requires them to change the way they live or increase the energy they must invest to remain healthy. If you tell a guy who eats four Mega Burgers a week that he needs to start consuming more broccoli and spinach and taking pills to control his high cholesterol, you're sure to meet some resistance. Even if he accepts the diagnosis, orders leaner cuts of meat, and increases his dietary intake of fruits and vegetables, he's likely to slip occasionally and gorge on the full-fat menu items . . . with extra mayo.

People, especially those who enjoy life, measure the quality of life not only in how they feel and how long they live, but also in how much they enjoy what life has to offer. The manic side of bipolar disorder not only makes you feel great, but also can make everything you experience more vivid and exciting. When treated successfully, many people with bipolar disorder stop taking their medications because they miss their highs, and who can really blame them? But you should recognize that this is a recipe for disaster and a surefire way to make future episodes harder to control.

Tracking and tweaking mood fluctuations

Human beings are animals programmed by nature to react instantly in response to threats and changes in our environment. You flinch when something flies at your head. You blush when you feel embarrassed. Over the course of any given day, your moods wax and wane. You can feel sad in the morning, elated in the afternoon, and relieved by dinnertime.

Few people make conscious attempts to record their mood fluctuations, but when you have bipolar disorder, tracking your moods can serve some important functions:

- ✔ Reveal patterns to your mood fluctuations
- ✔ Uncover hidden causes, such as changes in medication or sleep regularity, that may trigger mood episodes
- ✔ Provide early warning signs of impending mood episodes
- ✔ Give you something to do while you listen to another lecture on how important it is to take your medications

With a completed mood chart in hand, you can begin to identify the possible causes of your vacillating moods. Perhaps your depression always follows a period of inactivity. Maybe you become hyper when you miss a meal. By identifying the patterns to your mood swings, you can take action to tweak your moods and add a little stability.

Chapter 12 provides a basic mood chart you can copy and use to track your ever-changing moods.

Pinpointing and removing stressors

Stress rarely occurs in a vacuum. Someone or something, commonly referred to as a *stressor,* triggers it. You, the *stressee,* feel stress to the degree at which genetics and your upbringing hard-wired you to feel it. So the obvious and easiest way to avoid stress is to identify and avoid excessive or unnecessary stressors. In Chapter 12, you find out how to avoid or minimize the most common stressors, including the following:

- ✔ Conflicts at work
- ✔ Excessive work
- ✔ Lover quarrels

✔ Parent–child conflicts

✔ Overcommitment

✔ Conflicts at home

✔ Holiday tension

✔ Uncomfortable situations

The demands of everyday life always include stressful events and interactions. How you react and deal with the stress is the most important factor in how it affects your mood disorder. People are wired differently for how they process and manage the strong emotions that come with stress. Some have an easy-going style that allows them to let things roll off their backs; other people are easily inflamed by minor frustrations or irritations. People with bipolar disorder often struggle with "short fuses," even between episodes. The people around you also have a unique stress-response fingerprint, and sometimes the differences in styles can magnify the emotional toll for everyone.

Your therapist can help you identify your unique temperament and develop more effective emotional skills for managing stress. He can also help you and those around you watch out for predictable conflicts that can stem from your different response styles.

Stress has a bad rep, but it isn't always harmful. Negative stress may fill you with overwhelming anxiety and anger; spending too many hours at a job you hate, for example, can make you angry and bitter. Positive events, such as getting a new home or a better job, stir up your emotions and nervous system just as much as negative ones, and your brain and body perceive them as stressful, even if you're happy. Anything that gets your adrenaline going — good or bad — is a potential trigger for a mood episode.

Constructing a safety net

You may be the only person in your circle of family and friends with a bipolar diagnosis, but the disorder affects everyone around you. The people you care about have a stake in your recovery and can contribute significantly to the success of your treatment. Your support group plays several important roles in helping you achieve and maintain mood stability:

✔ Provide objective feedback concerning your moods and behavior

✔ Encourage you to follow your treatment plan

✔ Implement new, low-stress communication techniques

> ✔ Resolve conflicts to remove stressors
>
> ✔ Appreciate your unique abilities and contributions
>
> ✔ Obtain treatment for you when you can't do so on your own

If you've ever witnessed a tightrope walker teetering high above a safety net, you may not even notice the net. That's how unobtrusive you want your safety net to be. You should be confident that you have a solid safety net to catch you if you tumble, but you should be able to live your life without constantly being reminded of your disorder.

Enduring a Pound of Cure: Hospitalization

Before the proliferation of effective psychiatric medications, a major mood episode was likely to land you in the hospital for some voluntary or involuntary R & R. Nowadays, psychiatrists recommend shorter stays in the hospital or in intensive outpatient treatment because hospital bills can be steep, and your home or the home of a loving friend or family member may provide the most conducive environment for recovery.

If you do need to be hospitalized for treatment, keep in mind that you've been hospitalized for your own good and that you'll be released as soon as possible.

The following survival tips can make your stay in the hospital a little more pleasant and productive:

> ✔ Bring any medications you're currently taking or a list of the medications and prescribed doses.
>
> ✔ Bring your doctor's and therapist's phone numbers and other contact information.
>
> ✔ Leave any valuables at home.
>
> ✔ Leave your belt, pocketknife, and any other potentially harmful accessories at home. The hospital won't let you have anything that you or another patient can use to harm yourself or others.
>
> ✔ Bring slippers or loafers. The hospital probably won't let you have shoelaces.
>
> ✔ Bring comfortable but modest clothing — you won't usually wear hospital pajamas.

✔ If you can, bring your own pillow and a comfortable blanket. Hospital linens are distinctly unsoothing.

✔ Contact your regular psychiatrist and therapist before or immediately after you enter the hospital, and make sure that your inpatient team has been in direct contact with your outpatient team to coordinate your care. Your personal team members (family and friends) can help you with this advocacy task if you aren't up to it.

✔ Bring a journal without spirals or wires for your thoughts and feelings and for any useful information you pick up from staff, groups, or other patients.

✔ Cooperate with the staff, as much as your mental state allows.

✔ Get to know your fellow patients. Psychiatric hospitals are populated with interesting and intelligent individuals who understand your experience better than people on the outside.

✔ If you smoke, bring an ample supply of cigarettes (if your hospital is non-smoking, you may receive a nicotine patch).

✔ If you don't smoke, bring a gas mask, because nearly everyone else in the psych ward smokes.

✔ Bring books or magazines for quiet times and a deck of cards if you play (you can usually get a game going).

✔ Pack one or two pictures of family, friends, or pets without glass frames. Photos can warm up your space.

✔ Contact your regular psychiatrist and therapist before being released. The hospital may not discharge you until you have follow-up appointments with your doctor and therapist in place.

Find out your visiting and phone privileges as soon as you can process the information. You can then plan a schedule with your family and other support team members. Continued contact and support from the outside world can be very beneficial, but avoid potentially dangerous or toxic interactions as much as possible. Use phone and visiting time to build an outside support network of healthy relationships and a firm foundation on which to build your recovery.

A brief stay in the hospital may be just what you need to get back into balance. Avoiding conflicts with loved ones, the immediate alleviation of work and chores, and the camaraderie of fellow psychiatric patients can provide a much-needed change of scenery for some people.

Eventually, you must return to your "real" life. To smooth the transition from the hospital back to your home, work with your doctor and support network closely, especially if this is your first hospitalization. You and your family can benefit greatly by knowing what to expect. Recovery can take several weeks. If you, your family members, or your co-workers expect a quick return to your normal level of functioning, the disappointment can lead to further conflict and stress.

Remaining Vigilant for Signs of Trouble

Bipolar disorder is like carry-on luggage: It disrupts your otherwise carefree flight. You need to tote around your medications wherever you go, remember to take them at the prescribed times, and refill your prescriptions *before* you run out. You have more appointments to schedule and keep. And you must constantly be on the lookout for any changes in the way you feel. You have to avoid doing anything that can worsen your illness while remaining vigilant not to be consumed by it.

Self-surveillance is no easy task, but the following tips can help you manage:

- ✔ Identify the symptoms that typically act as warning signs of an impending mood episode. For many people, the symptom may be a change in the amount of sleep needed or desired. Others may notice changes in their appetites, energy levels, thought or speech processes, external appearance, or personal hygiene.

- ✔ Inform your support network of your typical early warning signs so they can keep watch. You may not be able to notice them yourself.

- ✔ Keep a journal, and read it regularly. This can keep you in tune with the ebb and flow of your moods and emotions.

- ✔ Chart your moods, as we discuss in Chapter 12.

During a major mood episode, especially a manic episode, people with bipolar disorder frequently lose *insight,* or the ability to recognize their symptoms. This can actually be a brain-wiring problem — something very difficult to change until the episode calms down. Gradually, as your episode settles down, you can regain your perspective with the help of your personal and medical support teams.

Part II
Taming the Bipolar Beast

The 5th Wave   By Rich Tennant

"Let's see if we can identify some of the stress triggers in your life. You mentioned something about a large wolf that periodically shows up and attempts to blow your house down..."

In this part . . .

Time to tether the bipolar beast that's been ravaging your life. In order to achieve this feat, you must identify the disorder's most serious symptoms, rule out any medical issues that may be causing those symptoms, obtain a thorough psychological evaluation and diagnosis, and then build a mood-management team that's qualified to whip depression and mania into submission . . . or at least remission.

In this part, we recommend that you see your primary care physician first, and we describe the most useful tests and procedures for uncovering medical illnesses that most commonly affect moods. We also help you find a qualified psychiatrist and therapist, lead you through your psychological evaluation, and guide you in building an effective team for treating and managing the ups and downs of bipolar disorder.

Chapter 4

Let's Get Physical: Ruling Out Other Health Issues

*W*hen it comes to bipolar disorder, some doctors take an ill-advised shortcut from symptom to prescription, skipping over the most essential steps: examination and evaluation. You complain about feeling depressed, and instead of searching for the root cause, the doctor hands you a prescription for an antidepressant. When your depression is deep and accompanied by thoughts of death or suicide, immediate treatment is often the only safe option. In other cases, however, forgoing the necessary physical examination and medical tests is both imprudent and irresponsible. The shortcut prevents you from receiving a proper diagnosis and subjects you to potentially useless and unnecessary medication.

Whether you see a physician or a psychiatrist about your problems with depression or mania, the first step is to rule out any other medical conditions that can possibly produce the same or similar symptoms.

In this chapter, we take you back to your physician for a proper physical examination and a battery of medical tests. We introduce you to some of the ailments that can commonly trigger or mimic mood imbalances. We help you through the process of looking for possible causes of your mood and behavioral symptoms. And we show you what to do next, assuming that you and your physician rule out other medical issues.

Can It Be Something Else?

From the time of Aristotle to now, Western thought has endeavored to divide and conquer, label and dissect. Western medicine is no different, holding firm to the distinction between "physical ailments" and "brain disorders," as if people push their brains around in grocery carts.

The fact is that your brain is an integral part of your body, not only acting as the puppet master, but also being subjected to imbalances and illnesses in other organs and physiological systems. Your brain affects your body, and your body affects your brain.

This chapter describes a systematic approach to ruling out other health issues that may contribute to imbalances. Sometimes, however, bipolar disorder is the obvious diagnosis. If you're experiencing a full-blown manic episode and have a strong family history of psychiatric illness, your doctor probably won't waste time ruling out other possibilities.

Singing the body blues

Many physical ailments and conditions can cause changes in your brain function — changes that produce symptoms very similar to those of bipolar disorder. Here's a list of illnesses with symptoms that mimic those of mood disorders or magnify symptoms of co-occurring mood disorders:

- ✔ **Thyroid malfunction:** Located at the base of your neck, your thyroid gland produces hormones that regulate metabolism, growth, development, and reproductive function. A malfunction can cause the thyroid gland to overproduce hormones *(hyperthyroidism),* potentially causing symptoms similar to mania, or underproduce hormones *(hypothyroidism),* generating symptoms of depression.

- ✔ **Hormone imbalances:** Neurotransmitters are often at the mercy of hormones, so when hormones fluctuate, moods commonly follow. During puberty, during a woman's menstrual cycle, and over the course of life, hormone production rises and falls. Staying in tune with these changes and seeking medical attention when necessary can help stabilize moods.

- ✔ **Diabetes:** The inability to process sugars and carbohydrates can result in mood swings very similar to those characteristic of bipolar disorder. Fortunately, most doctors screen regularly for diabetes.

- ✔ **Mononucleosis:** A viral infection that often afflicts high schoolers and college students, mononucleosis, commonly called *mono,* can make you feel extremely lethargic and depressed. A simple blood test can identify the virus.

✔ **Chronic fatigue syndrome:** Also known as *chronic fatigue immune deficiency syndrome* (CFIS), this condition can make you feel persistently tired, achy, and irritable — very much like depression. Research suggests that depression and chronic fatigue have overlapping changes in brain chemistry, so even if he gives a chronic fatigue diagnosis, your doctor may prescribe antidepressants.

✔ **Lupus:** An autoimmune disorder, lupus causes painful swelling of the connective tissue and can inflame numerous organs, including the brain. It's typically accompanied by extreme fatigue and irritability. Your doctor can perform a blood test to rule out lupus if he suspects you may have it. Treatment typically calls for the use of corticosteroids, which can induce mood swings.

✔ **Cancer:** A diagnosis of cancer can obviously trigger depression. Moreover, some cancers and cancer treatments can produce mood instability.

✔ **Cushing's syndrome:** Sometimes referred to as *hypercortisolism,* Cushing's syndrome results in a host of growth and development abnormalities and often mood instability. People with Cushing's syndrome commonly exhibit obesity in the torso, increased fat around the neck, a rounded face, and thinning arms and legs.

✔ **Hepatitis:** Hepatitis is an inflammation of the liver, typically caused by a virus or a buildup of toxins. In addition to the characteristic yellowing of the eyes, hepatitis can make you feel weak, tired, and nauseous and may produce symptoms similar to those of depression. It can even cause hallucinations if toxic levels of certain waste products accumulate in your system. Manic symptoms are uncommon but possible.

✔ **HIV/AIDS:** Human Immunodeficiency Virus and Acquired Immune Deficiency Syndrome compromise the entire immune system, leaving you vulnerable to many kinds of infections — some bothersome and some deadly — that can affect mood. The HIV virus can also directly attack the brain cells, creating problems with thinking and causing mood changes. In addition, the daily stress of living with AIDS can burden you with tremendous anxiety.

✔ **Rheumatoid arthritis:** Causing inflammation and degeneration of joint tissue, rheumatoid arthritis can make you feel chronically weak, tired, and achy, leading to persistent battles with depression. This and other autoimmune disorders (such as lupus) can co-exist with depression and may share underlying disease processes.

Any physical ailment that makes you feel miserable or interferes with your ability to function properly can make you depressed. This is especially true of chronic illnesses. You need to realize that feeling chronically miserable isn't normal. Ask your doctor for help.

Identifying a medical condition that can cause mood instability doesn't rule out the diagnosis of a mood disorder. You may have a medical condition *and* a mood disorder, and both require treatment.

Checking your medicine cabinet for culprits

Because bipolar disorder has so much to do with brain chemistry and physiology, everything you consume, from cocaine to candy bars, can influence your moods. As soon as you start chewing and swallowing any consumable, your body begins breaking it down into chemical compounds and distributing the compounds to your heart, brain, muscles, organs, and appendages.

The list of medications and other substances that can affect your moods is too long to mention, but here are a few of the big names that can cause serious problems:

- Alcohol
- Cocaine
- Amphetamines, which may be used to treat ADD or ADHD or other conditions
- Stimulants, such as those used in diet medications or to stay awake (Vivarin or NoDoz, for example)
- Sleeping aids, including those containing valerian and melatonin
- Antihistamines in cold or allergy medications containing pseudoephedrine, ephedra, or ephedrine
- Corticosteroids, used to treat many illnesses, including lupus, asthma, and allergies
- Dextromethorphan, used in many cough suppressants
- Accutane, used to treat severe acne

If you're taking any of these medications or substances, let your doctor know. Stopping cold turkey isn't always the best option. Your doctor can suggest safe ways to wean you off the substances if he thinks they may be causing the symptoms you're experiencing.

Socially acceptable substances, including caffeine, nicotine, and alcohol, that stimulate or depress brain activity can affect your moods. Avoid or reduce your intake of these substances as much as possible.

Seeking Your Doctor's Advice

Self-diagnosis can be fun or even addictive. You notice something about yourself that seems out of the ordinary, fire up your Web browser, plug a few descriptive words into a search engine, and proceed to convince yourself that you have every ailment known to humanity:

"My torso's pretty large, and I have these weird stretch marks . . . maybe I have Cushing's syndrome."

"Auntie Mildred had to take something for her thyroid . . . maybe that's what I have."

"Cancer! That's it! I must have a brain tumor. I had a premonition that I'm going to die."

Like nature, the human mind abhors a vacuum, so it fills the space with any idea or quack diagnosis that seems remotely possible. To set your mind at ease and avoid making any mistakes that could possibly worsen your condition, visit your doctor.

Your doctor asks you a series of questions and gathers additional information to form a *history* — the story of your condition — that guides her during the physical examination and helps her decide which tests and further studies to order.

What are your symptoms?

The search for the cause of most illnesses begins with a careful examination of the symptoms (how the illness presents itself) and the onset of the symptoms (where, when, and with whom the disease presents itself). During a medical examination, you essentially enlist the aid of your doctor to solve a mystery.

To ensure that your collaboration can successfully unravel the mystery, provide your doctor with a detailed list of your symptoms. You should be able to supply your doctor with answers to the following questions:

- Do you feel depressed? Sad? Blue? Down? Empty? Numb?
- Do you feel inordinately energized or anxious?
- Do you feel angry or irritable more often than usual?
- Can you have fun or enjoy things?
- Have you had any problems getting to sleep or staying asleep?
- Have you been sleeping more than usual?
- Have you been eating significantly more or less than usual?
- Have you noticed behavior changes — doing significantly more or less than usual?
- Have you had any serious conflicts at home or work?
- Have you been drinking or wanting to drink and party more than usual?

Of course, the questions your doctor asks may not be as pointed as the questions we list here. When dealing with mood disorders, doctors often ask more open-ended questions to find out how your life is going in general and to observe how you react to various questions and issues that arise during the interview.

Your doctor also asks you about your other medical symptoms, focusing on particular areas such as the nervous system. Through these questions, she looks for clues that point to other possible conditions that could cause your *presenting symptoms*. Her inquiry is called a *review of systems*. Here are some possible questions:

- Have you experienced headaches, muscle aches, or weakness?
- Have you experienced any nausea, vomiting, or changes in your bowel habits?
- Do you have joint pain or swelling?
- Have you noticed rashes or skin changes?
- Have you noticed any changes in appetite or weight?
- Are you thirsty all the time? Do you have to urinate frequently?
- Has your sex drive or ability to function sexually changed at all?
- Plenty of other questions!

At this point, you may have a question of your own: "What do all these questions have to do with my moods?" Although these questions may seem unrelated to your chief complaint, the answers and information you provide help guide the doctor while she performs a targeted physical examination and chooses the lab tests or other studies she may want to order.

When did your problem start?

When you're looking for your car keys, the last question you want someone to ask you is "When did you have them last?" If you knew that, you wouldn't have asked the person for help. But that's basically what your doctor asks you, and it may come across sounding like some sick joke:

> **Patient:** "Doc, I think I've lost my mind!"
>
> **Doctor:** "When did you have it last?"

Of course, your doctor would never say such a thing, but that's pretty much what she will attempt to do: trace your symptoms back to an identifiable starting point and evaluate what set your mood episode(s) in motion.

Because your doctor doesn't sit on your shoulder observing your daily activity, you need to come up with one or two answers or at least provide her with some likely possibilities. Do your homework, and try to pinpoint events or times of change in your life that correspond to the onset of your symptoms. Here are some events or changes that may help jar your memory:

- ✔ Medication change
- ✔ Illness
- ✔ Accident, such as an auto accident or a fall
- ✔ Loss of a loved one
- ✔ Job loss or conflict
- ✔ Final exams
- ✔ Broken relationship
- ✔ Change in family structure, such as a child leaving or returning home
- ✔ Change in menstrual cycle

Mood disorders can build up over many years, so you may not be able to point your finger at one particular incident or variation in your life that started the ball rolling, but it's worth a try.

The event or change that triggers an illness or begins to make it significantly worse is rarely the entire cause of the illness. Maybe you took a medication that torpedoed your libido, which eventually wore away at your relationship, leaving you more depressed, which led to substance abuse and insomnia, which led to a manic episode. If you catch the initial cause early enough to stop the avalanche, great. If not, you may have a long chain of causes and effects you need to treat.

What makes your symptoms better or worse?

Your symptoms have crept up on you, and you and your doctor can't pinpoint the cause. Frustrating? Yes. Hopeless? No. Time to undertake a new approach. Instead of trying to identify causes, examine and test the most troublesome and annoying symptoms to see if anything improves them or makes them worse. To zero in on possible symptom amplifiers and reducers, answer the following questions:

- ✔ Do you feel better or worse at any specific time of day? In the morning? After lunch? After work? Before bed? Maybe you feel great at work but depressed at home.
- ✔ Are you symptom free during any seasons? Spring? Summer? Fall? Winter?

✔ Do your symptoms worsen near certain holidays or anniversaries, particularly anniversaries of losses or other traumatic events?

✔ Do you feel better or worse after eating specific foods or drinking particular beverages?

✔ Do any medications you currently take make you feel better or worse?

✔ Do any activities make you feel better or worse?

✔ Do any substances, such as caffeine, nicotine, alcohol, or sugar, alleviate symptoms or make them worse? (No, we're not recommending that you try these substances to see if they work.)

What else can you tell the doc?

Beyond a list of your symptoms, your recollections of when the symptoms first appeared, and what makes them better or worse, your doctor gathers the following information:

✔ **Your medical history,** to determine if any past conditions are causing your current symptoms.

✔ **A list of medications you're taking,** to determine if any of them are related to your symptoms. (Refer to the section "Checking your medicine cabinet for culprits," earlier in this chapter, for a list of the most common problematic substances.)

✔ **Your family history,** to identify illnesses that may be genetic.

Finally! Your physical exam

After piecing together a history of your condition, your doctor typically performs a brief physical examination to test your reflexes, check for enlarged glands, and observe your overall physical health and your temperament and behavior. And, as always, the nurse takes your temperature (to check for possible infection) and your blood pressure. Depending on the answers and information you provide as part of your history, the doctor may examine certain parts of you (for example, your joints if you report joint pain) more thoroughly than usual.

On the off chance that your family physician immediately spots the condition that's causing your current mood misery, he diagnoses it, recommends one or more treatment options, bills you, and heads out to the golf course. However, if nothing shows up, you can look forward to some additional medical tests, which we describe in the following section.

Digging Deeper with Additional Tests and Procedures

Depending on what your doctor digs up when taking your history and performing the physical exam, she may order additional tests or procedures. Some tests, such as those that examine blood-sugar levels, are fairly routine. Others, such as tests for thyroid hormone levels, are specifically targeted at finding clues to mood abnormalities.

The following sections describe some of the more common lab tests that your doctor may order and what the results of these tests may reveal.

Standard lab tests

Standard lab tests, including tests for your blood-sugar level and MRIs of your brain and other suspect areas of your anatomy, can often uncover hidden illnesses that may be related to your mood maladies. If your doctor hasn't yet discovered the probable cause, she's likely to order one or more of the following tests:

- ✔ **Blood tests** to check your blood counts (red blood cell count for anemia or white blood cell count for infections); glucose and lipid/cholesterol levels; "chemistries," to screen liver, kidney, and other organ function; and sometimes folic acid or other vitamin levels

- ✔ **Urinalysis** to test for possible pregnancy, kidney problems, drug abuse (particularly in adolescents), diabetes, and other conditions

- ✔ **MRI or CAT scan** to check for structural abnormalities in the brain or other areas that could possibly cause the symptoms you're experiencing

- ✔ **EKG (sometimes called an ECG)** to ensure that the old ticker is still pumping well enough

- ✔ **EEG** if your doctor suspects that you may have a seizure disorder

- ✔ **Spinal tap** if you have an accompanying fever and your doctor suspects an infection of the brain, such as spinal meningitis or encephalitis

Absent from the tests we list is any kind of blood test or scan for bipolar disorder. A common misconception is that your doctor can test you for bipolar disorder. It seems reasonable enough: If bipolar disorder is a chemical imbalance, why can't you just measure the chemicals to see if they're normal or abnormal? As we explain in other chapters, including Chapter 3, the chemical imbalance is a complex set of neurological abnormalities that are hard to pin down. Eventually, scientists will establish tests of some kind, but the medical field isn't up to speed yet.

Thyroid tests

The thyroid gland has a tremendous influence on moods and on the effectiveness of medications used to treat mood disorders, including mania and depression. It produces hormones that regulate your body's energy use, and low levels of thyroid hormones (hypothyroidism) lead to sluggishness, weight gain, and depression; excessively high levels (hyperthyroidism) can have you bouncing off the walls.

Early in the diagnostic stage, your physician or psychiatrist should order thyroid tests to check your level of thyroid hormones to determine if your thyroid gland is functioning properly. During the course of your treatment, your doctor may want to run the tests again, especially if you take medication that can affect thyroid function (such as lithium). A thyroid test is a blood test that checks the levels of the following hormones:

- **T4/Free T4** is the prime suspect in hyperthyroidism and hypothyroidism. Your doctor typically looks first at the T4 level to evaluate thyroid function.

- **T3** is a thyroid hormone that may affect mood stability. Most doctors focus on the T4 level, but if your T4 level is normal, your doctor may examine your T3 level to determine if it's causing problems.

- The pituitary gland secretes **TSH** (thyroid stimulating hormone) to stimulate thyroid activity. If TSH levels are too high or low, the pituitary gland may cause the thyroid gland to produce excessive or insufficient amounts of hormones. A TSH test is the most common screening test for thyroid function.

If your thyroid hormones are out of whack, your doctor may also order a *thyroid scan,* which is basically an X-ray of your thyroid gland that indicates how well it's functioning. Before the test, you down a drink or pop a couple pills laced with radioactive iodine. You lie on a scanner that takes a picture of your glowing thyroid, and your doctor examines the picture. Your doctor may refer you to an *endocrinologist* for this type of test and further workup of your thyroid.

Other hormone tests

Surges of reproductive hormones can make you feel pumped full of superhuman strength or rocket your libido to the stratosphere. Just imagine what they can do when they rock and roll to wild highs and lows during puberty and pregnancy.

Stumbling upon a treatment

Patients and doctors often discover cures and effective treatments unexpectedly by observing positive and negative side effects. Recently, doctors discovered that an antiestrogen drug called Tamoxifen, commonly used to treat breast cancer in women, may also be effective in treating acute mania.

In addition to blocking estrogen receptors in breast cancer cells, scientists discovered that Tamoxifen inhibits protein kinase C, which is part of the second messenger system in neurons. As a protein kinase C inhibitor, Tamoxifen buffers the firing of the neurons. As of press time, scientists were planning more formal studies to prove its effectiveness.

By tuning in to your symptoms and observing what alleviates them or worsens them, you may stumble upon the next medical breakthrough!

Even so, doctors don't routinely run tests to check levels of estrogen, progesterone, testosterone, androgens, or other hormones that may be related to moods. These types of hormones modulate brain development and function throughout life, but their effects are indirect. Normal growth and a changing range of hormone levels tell the doctor little about mood disorders. Some tumors and medical conditions can cause huge changes in your hormone levels, but additional medical symptoms would help identify these problems.

If your doctor suspects that wildly fluctuating reproductive hormones are contributing to your mood symptoms, she may recommend further testing or refer you to a specialist. Or she may consider starting you on hormone replacement therapy (HRT).

During the '80s and '90s, hormone replacement therapy (HRT) was all the rage. Now doctors call it *menopausal hormone therapy* (MHT), and they've become a little more hesitant to recommend it. Some studies show that MHT leads to increased risk of breast cancer and other cancers in women. Although the jury is still out on whether the potential benefits outweigh the possible risks, doctors generally play it safe. (For more information on the benefits and risks of MHT, visit www.breastcancer.org.)

Although the word "hormones" usually makes people think "sex," many hormone systems keep the entire body running smoothly. Thyroid hormones are the best known, but many others chip in to help. Insulin, which is related to diabetes, is a hormone. Cortisol, a hormone from the adrenal gland, modulates energy and wakefulness, fat metabolism, and many other body processes. A cortisol surplus causes Cushing's syndrome, which can be related to mood symptoms. Your doctor examines these and other hormonal systems more closely if blood test results or symptoms point the doctor in their direction.

You Have a Clean Bill of Health. Now What?

Your doctor whacked you on the knee with his rubber mallet, extracted a few ounces of blood, and grilled you on your past health and private indiscretions. He poked and prodded you, but you still don't have an explanation for what's wrong with you.

Now what?

You have a few choices:

- ✔ **Get a second opinion from another physician.** Another physician or specialist, such as a neurologist or gynecologist, may be able to find other potential causes.

- ✔ **Let your physician treat your symptoms.** Physicians can prescribe mood stabilizers, antidepressants, and other psychotropic medications.

- ✔ **Consult a psychiatrist.** After your physician rules out medical issues, you can turn your focus toward psychiatric illnesses, which a psychiatrist is usually more qualified to sort out and treat. As we explain in Chapter 5, a psychiatrist can work through a differential diagnosis to identify or eliminate other psychiatric illnesses that contribute to creating your symptom profile.

Even if you don't receive a clean bill of health — say, your physician identifies and treats a medical condition that may be related to the depression or mania — you may still need psychiatric treatment or therapy anyway. The medical condition may play only a partial role in your mood instability, or it may play no role at all.

Chapter 5

Getting a Psychiatric Evaluation and Treatment Plan

In This Chapter

▶ Tracking down a qualified psychiatrist

▶ Preparing for your first meeting

▶ Sailing through your psychiatric evaluation and diagnosis

▶ Obtaining a treatment plan that works for you

*T*he bipolar tempest not only rocks your boat, but also washes the captain overboard. Your rational mind flails in the waves, and nobody on deck has the wherewithal to throw it a lifesaver. You need someone on the outside to intervene. You need a psychiatrist.

A qualified psychiatrist can help you reset your rudder and steer your ship through the surrounding turbulence. She can explain what happened during your most recent mood episode, provide an objective evaluation of your psychiatric condition, offer one or more possible diagnoses, and develop a personalized treatment plan for you. Your evaluation, diagnosis, and treatment plan chart the course for your recovery, and your psychiatrist's continued guidance helps you stay the course for years to come.

Because your psychiatrist plays such a key role in your evaluation, recovery, and continued stability, this chapter offers advice on finding a qualified psychiatrist who makes you feel comfortable and confident. We show you what you can do to help your psychiatrist develop an accurate assessment of your current condition and psychiatric needs. We also provide a list of items you should bring to your first appointment and a few ideas on how to keep your relationship with your psychiatrist in good working order so you don't rock the boat.

Finding Professional Help

Most people are happy to tell you all about their favorite doctors or healers; they eagerly share the names of their bone doctors, lung doctors, or gynecologists. But if you ask someone for the name of a good psychiatrist, you can feel the temperature of the room drop. Unlike plastic surgeons, psychiatrists don't advertise on billboards: "Depression Lift. Mood Augmentation. Payment Plans Available!" You can flip through the phone book, but don't expect it to steer you in the direction of a bipolar specialist; all psychiatrists are pretty much lumped together.

Is finding a qualified psychiatrist a hit-or-miss proposition? Not exactly. You just need to do a little homework, remain persistent, and be willing to test-drive a few models until you find the one that's right for you. In this section, you find suggestions on where to start your search.

After you identify a psychiatrist, your journey is just beginning. The evaluation process takes time, and your treatments may require lengthy adjustment periods. If you're in a crisis, your doctor is likely to treat you more aggressively, possibly admitting you to a hospital. But even in a hospital, the process of being *worked up* (having a doctor piece together your history, his observations, and test results to arrive at a diagnosis) and developing a treatment plan can be achingly slow.

Ask your family doctor

When you stump your doctor with an illness, he has a list of specialists to whom he can refer you. "Weird heart murmur? See Dr. Pulmonic, the cardiologist." "Skin discoloration? Here's a referral to Dr. Rasho, the dermatologist." The same is true of psychiatrists. Your family doctor, or *internist,* probably knows at least one psychiatrist in his circle of colleagues whom he can recommend — a psychiatrist your doctor has worked with in the past who has a successful track record. When you report mood-related symptoms that your doctor can't trace to a medical cause, he may recommend that you see a psychiatrist. When he does, ask for names.

If you're a woman, and your gynecologist fills the role as your primary care physician (a common arrangement), ask her for a psychiatric referral. The two fields often team up on diagnoses such as PMS and postpartum depression. She can give you some names of psychiatrists with whom she likes to work.

Call your insurance company

Insurance companies have contracts with certain doctors whom they refer to as "preferred providers." These doctors have agreed to the insurance company's rates, making you responsible only for your co-pay. If you go to a doctor who's not on this list, you may have to pay the full fee, so finding a psychiatrist "in network" makes sense for financial reasons and because the psychiatrist probably works with other doctors and hospitals in your network.

When looking at a preferred-provider list from your insurance company, you can ask for more information about the doctors. You can ask whether a doctor is board certified; request information about his level of experience; and check on any areas of subspecialty, such as doctors who deal with mood disorders. If you can't find a doctor qualified to care for your type of illness, you can appeal to your insurance company to cover a doctor outside the plan so you can get appropriate care without paying extra.

Pick your therapist's brain

Treatment need not begin with your family doctor or psychiatrist. You may already be working with a therapist, likely a psychologist or social worker, for when your moods hit a critical point. If you're currently seeing a therapist you like, ask her for a referral. She should be familiar with psychiatrists in your area, possibly within the same office, and she should know which people she works with most effectively.

Successful treatment almost always demands a consistent, coordinated combination of medicine and therapy, so you want a treatment duo who work well as a team. If your therapist and psychiatrist graduated from different schools of thought, they may be unwilling and unable to provide the integrated treatment that you deserve. By obtaining a referral from your therapist, you increase your odds of building a treatment team with a unified vision.

If your therapist and psychiatrist work out of the same office, the proximity often enhances communication. They can share notes and records without the extra work; added costs; and delays inherent in phones, shipping, and fax machines.

Go online

The Internet brings power and information, but it can also bring misinformation and fraud. When searching online for names of psychiatrists, use established, professional Web sites provided by a local medical society or a specialty society, including the following:

- American Psychiatric Association (www.psych.org)
- Depression and Bipolar Support Alliance (www.dbsalliance.org)
- National Institute of Mental Health (www.nimh.nih.gov)

The DBSA site, which is consumer driven, provides a list of recommended professionals (by people being treated for bipolar disorder) and is packed with useful information for people suffering from depression and mania.

University, hospital, and medical school sites also have physician search tools, and they usually list each doctor's subspecialty. By checking subspecialties, you may be able to find someone who's studying bipolar disorder in her research.

If you search more broadly and find other sites about mood disorders and doctors, be sure to get additional references about the doctor or clinic before you make an appointment. The Internet has its share of misinformation. If you're unsure whether a doctor who looks good to you is legitimate, double-check the doctor's licensing and complaint history with your local medical society, which you can do for any doctor you consider seeing.

Consult your support group

As your symptoms develop, you may seek help from a support group — a therapy or self-help group, a 12-step program, or an advocacy group. Maybe a loved one, a judge, or a therapist recommends or demands that you attend anger management or parenting groups. These settings are gold mines of information about local doctors. Seasoned veterans freely vent about doctors they adore and those they despise. Ask around and expect an earful!

Don't limit your search to official support groups. Consult your personal support group as well — your brain trust — the people who provide daily guidance and care and who know you most intimately. If they have any connections with psychiatrists, they can make recommendations with your temperament and needs in mind.

What to Look for in a Psychiatrist

When you're shopping for a psychiatrist, you may begin to wonder who's doing the shopping. Everyone is grilling *you* with questions. When do you get to ask questions and obtain the information you need to make an educated choice? The answer to that question is "The sooner, the better."

Chapter 19 provides a list of 10 questions to ask a psychiatrist or therapist. Before your first visit, review those questions, and prepare yourself. If you're not the assertive type, ask a friend or relative who's a little pushier to join you. Bringing along a trusted ally, especially for the first visit, can make all the difference in getting the information you need and walking away with a good sense of how this doctor may work for you. Your support person can also provide valuable information to the doctor — details you may forget or consider too insignificant to mention.

When scouting for a psychiatrist, use the following criteria to guide your selection:

- ✔ **Experience:** Experience in treating mood disorders usually ensures a more accurate diagnosis and the most effective and current treatments. Be sure to ask the psychiatrist how much experience she has had in treating bipolar disorder.

- ✔ **Sensitivity:** Your psychiatrist should be a team player who accepts your input and adjusts your treatments accordingly.

- ✔ **Willingness to communicate:** Your psychiatrist should not only prescribe medications, but also explain their purposes and possible side effects.

- ✔ **Availability:** Your psychiatrist may need to adjust your diagnosis and medications frequently, especially in the early stages of treatment.

- ✔ **Affordability:** Is this doctor included in your insurance plan? Do the charges for office visits fit in your budget? Does the doctor offer a payment plan?

Your doctor should be *board certified* in psychiatry. This means that she has passed a rigorous set of exams, indicating her mastery of the specialty of psychiatry. The American Board of Psychiatry and Neurology is one of many specialty boards that certify doctors as competent within a specialty. Doctors can have licenses to practice medicine, but they may not be board certified in a specialty. Doctors without board certification may have the required skills, but the designation makes it much easier for you to verify their credentials. Dating back to the mid-1990s, psychiatrists must retest for their board certifications every 10 years to ensure that they keep up with all the rapid changes in the field.

What to Bring to Your First Meeting

If you've never been to a psychiatrist, your imagination may cook up a vision, using ingredients from old movies: you lying on a couch and relating stories from your childhood to an old man who sits in a chair beside you and jots down notes while he strokes his beard.

Reality paints a different portrait: you sitting on a comfortable chair or couch, describing your symptoms to a professional man or woman who sits in a chair across from you or behind a desk and peppers you with questions about your current behaviors and feelings while jotting down notes.

During your first meeting, your psychiatrist tries to write your story in medical terms that accurately describe an illness such as bipolar disorder. She needs a great deal of information about you, so she must ask a string of personal questions. She can't get inside your head to see what you think and feel, so she relies on the following information to guide her diagnosis:

- ✔ **Objective information:** Your psychiatrist's observations of your appearance and reactions to the interview, along with your report of recent behaviors.

- ✔ **Subjective information:** The information and details you provide about how you feel and what you're thinking.

Your best shot at receiving an accurate diagnosis depends on your honesty and openness and on your ability to clearly describe your thoughts and feelings. If you withhold important information because you're embarrassed or for any other reason, you can't expect your psychiatrist to paint an accurate diagnostic portrait.

To prepare for your evaluation, you should collect the information we describe in this section, either in your head or on paper, and get ready to share the intimate details.

Can't you just test me?

Unfortunately, the technology to test for bipolar disorder doesn't yet exist, for several reasons: Bipolar disorder is probably a collection of different conditions; the brain changes are at microscopic levels that scans have a hard time detecting; and blood chemistry doesn't accurately depict brain chemistry. The future holds out hope in the form of some new and improved detection tools. Some innovations currently brewing include the following:

- ✔ **A functional MRI scan** looks at changes in brain chemistry — how active certain parts of your brain are. This technology may someday be able to detect consistent differences between brains with bipolar disorder and those without.

- ✔ **Genetic testing** looks for certain genes associated with the brain-chemistry changes present in bipolar disorder. Particular proteins and patterns of proteins and enzymes may form the fingerprint of bipolar disorder, and detecting the genes that regulate these proteins could eventually help in identifying the disorder.

- ✔ **Neuropsychological tests** (paper-and-pencil testing) may help map patterns of attention, memory, and information processing *(executive function)* that appear to be associated with bipolar disorder. These tests may eventually aid in the early identification of bipolar disorder in children with attention and behavioral problems.

Why you (or others) think you need help

The first thing your doctor wants to know is your *chief complaint:* What's going on that prompted you to seek a psychiatric evaluation? This is a story that starts at the end and then goes back to fill in the details. Perhaps you've been bedridden for days, raging for weeks, watching your mood swings chip away at your marriage, spending extravagantly, feeling completely overwhelmed by everything on your to-do list, or getting into arguments with friends and relatives. If someone recommended that you see a psychiatrist or therapist, explain why that person thinks you need help.

More information, please!

Your chief complaint simply states the problem. After you establish the problem, your psychiatrist can start collecting details about your emotional life and your behavior patterns over the years. She may refer to these details as the *history of present illness* or *review of systems* (organ systems and brain systems). Through this systematic information-gathering approach, your psychiatrist attempts to understand the pattern of psychiatric symptoms that play a role in your condition. To gather a list of symptoms, your psychiatrist is likely to ask many of the following questions:

- ✔ **Depression-related questions:** How sad do you get and for how long? Do you feel hopeless or helpless? Do you think about death and dying? Do you think about killing yourself? Have you ever tried to kill yourself? Do you enjoy things anymore? Can you concentrate? Are you tired all the time?

- ✔ **Mania-related questions:** How happy or angry do you get and for how long? Do you have periods of high energy and productivity? Have you gotten into trouble during those times by spending money, having an affair, or "borrowing" money from your employer? Do you have times when you feel like you're the best at everything?

- ✔ **General questions on your thought processes:** How's your thinking? Do your thoughts feel slow or hyperactive? Do you feel as though you can't think clearly? Does your brain play tricks on you — hearing voices, believing you have magical powers, or thinking people want to harm you?

- ✔ **Questions about anxieties and compulsive behaviors:** How much do you worry about things? Have you ever had a panic attack? Do you have unwanted thoughts that don't go away or illogical behaviors you can't stop doing? Do you freeze in social situations or avoid them altogether?

✓ **Mental health history questions:** What's your psychiatric history? Have you ever been hospitalized? Have you ever been on medications? Have you seen a therapist at some time in your life?

✓ **Questions about your life in the past:** What was your childhood like? How did you do in school? How did you relate to other kids? Did you have close friends? Did you experience any depression or manic symptoms as a teenager or child?

✓ **Questions about your life now:** What's your life like now? Do you work? How's work going? How's your marriage/love life? How's sex going for you? How are things with your kids, your parents, or your siblings? Do you have hobbies? Do you exercise?

As you can tell from these questions, the best way to respond is with a significant other who can offer some details that you may not remember or see in yourself. If your significant other or another family member is willing, and you're comfortable with the person's being in the office with you, the two of you can provide more valuable information more quickly and completely than if you go alone.

Medical history

Have you seen your primary care physician about your chief complaint? If you haven't, refer to Chapter 4 for a better understanding of why this is such an important first step. After you explore that avenue, provide your psychiatrist with the test results and recommendation from your doctor.

Although your primary care physician probably conducted a thorough physical exam and interview, you can expect your psychiatrist to ask several questions about your current physical condition as well. Any headaches, weakness, or dizziness? Diabetes or heart disease? History of stroke or cancer? Eye problems (such as glaucoma)? Have you had any surgeries? Allergic reactions to medications? How about your kidneys, liver, and lungs?

Your psychiatrist needs your medical history for two purposes: to help rule out other physical conditions that may be causing or aggravating your symptoms and to determine the safest, most effective medications to prescribe, if you need medication.

Family history

When you start shaking the family tree of a person who exhibits classic bipolar symptoms, skeletons often rain down from the branches. These skeletons can help your psychiatrist do the following:

✔ **Simplify the diagnosis:** If one of the skeletons happens to be a first-degree relative (immediate family member) with a mood disorder, a schizophrenia diagnosis, or a history of suicide, your risk of having a mood disorder is significantly higher (see Chapter 2). Second-degree relatives (uncles, aunts, cousins) count, too, but to a lesser degree.

✔ **Differentiate between unipolar and bipolar depression:** If you're experiencing depression but have a family history of mania or schizophrenia, you may have bipolar disorder without yet experiencing mania or hypomania. Prescribing an antidepressant alone to a person with the potential of bipolar carries a high risk of inducing mania. If bipolar disorder appears in your family history, your psychiatrist is much more likely to start with a mood stabilizer, with or without the addition of an antidepressant, rather than with an antidepressant by itself.

✔ **Determine the most effective medications:** If a particular medication or therapy has effectively treated one of your first-degree relatives, it's more likely to effectively treat your similar symptoms.

Following are a few points to keep in mind regarding your family history:

✔ You may not have a formal diagnosis for people in your family — especially in previous generations. But if someone in the family showed serious behavioral quirks — never left the house, drank or used pills excessively, or kept tinfoil on the windows to keep out the aliens — that's worth mentioning.

✔ Don't limit your family history to diagnoses of bipolar disorder. Report all psychiatric problems: schizophrenia, depression, anxiety disorders, panic attacks, extreme mood swings, and so on. Different disorders often share common genetic factors.

✔ Your doctor will also be curious about any suicides in the family. The risk of suicide seems to run genetically, even separate from bipolar disorder and depression. Substance abuse in a relative can hint at underlying mood or anxiety disorders. Substance abuse and mood disorders commonly occur in family groupings.

List of legal and . . . yes . . . illegal drugs

Your psychiatrist needs to know about all the chemicals, dietary supplements, and herbs that you pop and pour into your body. You already know that you need to hand over a list of prescription medications, but don't overlook the other stuff, including the following:

✔ Over-the-counter medications you take regularly

✔ Vitamins

✔ Herbs

- ✔ Alcohol
- ✔ Caffeine
- ✔ Energizer beverages, powders, or pills
- ✔ Diet medications or herbs
- ✔ Nicotine
- ✔ Amphetamines or other stimulants or controlled substances
- ✔ Marijuana, cocaine, ecstasy, hallucinogens, narcotics, or other illicit drugs

If you're using illicit drugs, tell your doctor. These substances drastically affect your emotions and behavior, and this information is critical in your psychiatric evaluation. Embarrassment and worry about being "caught" or "found out" have no place here. Your psychiatrist won't report your drug use to anyone unless you pose a risk to someone else. Brutal honesty is the only workable policy.

Hiding drug or alcohol use from your doctor can be fatal. Don't do it. Muster up all your courage, ditch your shame, and spill your guts. You aid in your recovery, and you just may save your life.

Sleep log (or sleepless log)

Whether you're sleepless in Seattle or drowsy in Denver, your doctor needs to know about it. Sleep changes and energy patterns are core biological markers in bipolar disorder; they provide important clues that tell you and your doctor when you need help. Report any of the following:

- ✔ Excessive need for sleep
- ✔ Inability to feel rested even after sleeping for a long time
- ✔ Persistent fatigue
- ✔ Little or no need for sleep
- ✔ Significant changes in sleep patterns

Note your sleep cycles *and* energy levels. Being awake all night and dragging around the next day is a different story from having a three-day wakeful jag and still feeling perky.

Remembering how well you sleep from one week to the next can be a challenge for anyone, so write it down. Also, ask your significant other for help; he or she may have an entirely different read on how well or poorly you sleep.

Arriving at a Diagnosis

You spilled your guts, confessed your sins, and admitted to doing things that could have landed you in jail. All you want in return are clear answers to two simple questions: "What do I have?" and "How do I get rid of it?" You, your friends, and your significant other have slogged through months of unexplained self-destructive and unbearable symptoms, and you need an answer. Unfortunately, unraveling the mystery may take some time.

Evaluating your symptoms

To arrive at a diagnosis, your doctor compares your symptoms to criteria specified in the DSM-IV — the *Diagnostic and Statistical Manual of Mental Disorders, 4.* DSM-IV is the bible of psychiatry that describes various syndromes and conditions and the symptoms that must be present to establish a particular diagnosis.

What symptoms are characteristic of bipolar disorder? Here are some highlights your doctor looks for:

- **Evidence of mania:** You experience a week or more of high energy, excessively happy or angry moods, little need for sleep, excessive activity and pleasure seeking, little judgment or impulse control, grandiose thinking and behaviors, and racing thoughts *(to the degree that they create problems in your life).*

- **Evidence of major depression:** You experience two weeks or more of sad mood, low energy, decreased enjoyment of things, poor concentration, low activity and low productivity, thoughts of death and suicide, excessive feelings of guilt or bad feelings about yourself, and slowed thinking *(to the degree that they create problems in your life).*

- **Evidence of hypomania:** Consisting of an elevated mood that lasts four days, hypomania is a "light" version of mania and doesn't create so many problems in function, but it can be difficult to live with.

- **Presence of psychosis:** Psychosis can go along with either "pole": depression or mania. It can include disorganized thinking, paranoia, delusional thinking (significant distortions of reality), or hearing voices.

- **Presence of mixed states:** Mixed states are combination states that meet full criteria for mania (or hypomania) and depression together.

Climbing your family tree

Because much of the risk for bipolar disorder comes from inherited genetic vulnerabilities, family history is an important piece of the diagnostic puzzle.

Although the DSM-IV doesn't list family history as one of the diagnostic criteria, if the bipolar diagnosis seems plausible but a little fuzzy, a strong family history may tip the scales.

Considering other causes

After the picture of your mood symptoms has developed, and your family history is on the table, your psychiatrist must look closely at other symptoms and problems that you're having. This *differential diagnosis* allows her to explore all the possible causes and to determine if she needs to address additional diagnoses. The types of symptoms most important at this point are the following:

- ✔ **Substance abuse** can mimic mood disorders or can occur with and exacerbate mania or depression.

- ✔ **Medical conditions** — such as thyroid disorder or other hormone imbalances, infections, autoimmune disorders, cancers, heart disease, or stroke — can produce similar symptoms.

- ✔ **Anxiety disorders** can sometimes look like mood disorders. Panic attacks may look like brief manic episodes, for example, and they're often *comorbid* (co-occurring) with bipolar disorder.

- ✔ **Psychosis,** which may be a symptom of mania or depression but also of schizophrenia or schizoaffective disorder, must be addressed in order to rule out those disorders.

- ✔ **Attention Deficit Hyperactivity Disorder** seems to overlap with bipolar disorder in many people and should be identified when it does. Alternatively, the high energy of mania can sometimes be confused with ADHD, and the similarity can blur the diagnosis, especially in young people.

Receiving the diagnosis

You've been poked and prodded, examined and cross-examined. Your psychiatrist has even rummaged through your family tree. Now you want to know: What is it? What do you have that's causing you so much discomfort and misery? This section reveals the most common bipolar diagnoses.

Typecasting your illness

If you're "lucky," you step right out of your psychiatrist's office with a clear, textbook diagnosis. You have one of the following types of bipolar disorder:

BIPOLAR BIO

When diagnoses converge

Kevin went to see his doctor after dropping out of college for the third time. Every time he tried to go to class, he would shrink into the back row and spend the whole time worrying that people were thinking about how stupid he was. He stopped going to class and then dropped out. After his latest failure, he stayed in his apartment all day and didn't answer the phone. He felt like a freak and could barely drag himself out of bed. All he did was sleep.

While relating his history to his doctor, he recalled that he had survived high school only by borrowing friends' notes, because he hardly ever went to class. He also confessed that during his senior year, he started drinking a lot, and he got into trouble with his parents for stealing money from them and spending it with his friends. Senior year was the only time in his life that he got into trouble with the law — after he and his friends stole his parents' car and took a midnight road trip to check out a bar two states away. He told the doctor that he slept very little that year — he spent his nights on the Internet and practicing his guitar and then

stayed up the following day. He described it as the "happiest time" of his life, but he had almost failed all his classes. He noted that his mom had a drinking problem and seemed to have some pretty depressed times, but she had never been diagnosed with a mood disorder.

The doctor arrived at a diagnosis of Bipolar I, along with Social Anxiety Disorder (see the next section for more on the different types of bipolar disorder). Over time, as Kevin stabilized with his mood and anxiety disorder, he tried to go back to school and discovered he had terrible trouble paying attention and focusing. Eventually, the doctor added medication for ADHD. Given Kevin's family history, the doctor also counseled him that he was at high risk for alcoholism. Stopping drinking became an ongoing challenge for Kevin, but he remained vigilant. He returned to school — only one class to start — and found success there. Although Kevin continues to struggle, he's gradually leaving the past behind and learning to effectively deal with his dual diagnosis.

- ✔ **Bipolar I** is the classic form of bipolar disorder that includes clear-cut manic episodes, periods of major depression, and *euthymic* (even-mood) times in between. Bipolar I has been recognized for the longest time and has the most predictable course and response to treatment.

- ✔ **Bipolar II** differs from I in that depressive episodes alternate with hypomanic periods rather than manic ones. This variety is often harder to identify, because hypomanic periods can be tricky to spot and may remain unreported. Its course is also more variable, and the response to treatment is less predictable.

- ✔ **Cyclothymic disorder** is a more subdued version of bipolar disorder, characterized by depressive spells and hypomanic times that never have sufficient intensity or duration to meet full diagnostic measure. It

---

Treating unipolar depression with mood stabilizers

Current scientific evidence suggests that people with recurrent, severe depressions are more like people who suffer from bipolar depression than they're like people with single or infrequent episodes of unipolar depression. Some research has revealed a significant overlap between the family histories and treatment-response profiles of all patients with severe, cycling mood episodes, even if they experience only one pole (depression) instead of two poles (bipolar). (Frederick K. Goodwin, MD, former director of the National Institute of Mental Health, is a leader in this field of research.)

If the research proves true, the treatment recommendations for unipolar depression may change significantly. Traditionally, doctors treated most cases of unipolar depression with antidepressants. Now, doctors are becoming more cautious in their use of antidepressants. Psychiatrists will look closely for red flags, such as a family history of bipolar or particular patterns of the patient's depression, to try to determine the risk of triggering agitation or mania in a depressed patient. If the doctor spots red flags, she may consider using a mood stabilizer or a potentially less irritating antidepressant as a first choice.

---

has to be chronic — two years or more — and it must interrupt your life in some way.

✔ **Bipolar NOS** is the "leftover" category, characterized by variations of cycling mood disorders that reflect episodes of mood problems that interfere with your life but don't fulfill the complete diagnostic requirements.

For more information on each of these possible diagnoses, refer to Chapter 2.

If you're not so lucky, and you don't present textbook-variety symptoms, your diagnosis may be murky and tentative. Maybe you have an anxiety disorder with some depression, obsessive compulsive disorder with some characteristics of attention deficit disorder, or a touch of mania with paranoia. In other words, your diagnostic portrait may look more like an abstract painting. Your doctor may provide you with an initial diagnosis and then continue watching your progress over time to confirm, refute, or modify it.

Finding your place on the bipolar spectrum

Having four bipolar categories sure simplifies the diagnosis, but does this model jibe with reality? Not according to some experts in the field. Psychiatrists are beginning to find that the four categories are too limited; they fail to accommodate symptoms and patterns that don't neatly fit into one of the four categories. A growing trend is to diagnose mood disorders on a sliding scale, or *spectrum*. You may hear of the *bipolar spectrum* or the *unipolar depressive spectrum*.

The purpose of the bipolar spectrum is to help identify the disorder in people who don't exhibit classic symptoms — for example, a depressed bipolar sufferer who has never experienced hypomania or mania. Misdiagnosing this person with unipolar depression can be dangerous, because treatment with an antidepressant alone is likely to induce mania. By finding the person a place on the bipolar spectrum, the psychiatrist can begin treatment with a mood stabilizer and probably achieve better results.

Don't be surprised if your diagnosis changes over time; symptoms commonly change over the course of the illness. You may be diagnosed with Bipolar II and then experience a full-blown manic episode that changes your diagnosis to Bipolar I. This doesn't mean that your initial diagnosis was wrong — only that that course of your illness has changed.

Gauging the severity of your illness

The severity of bipolar disorder varies from one person to the next. Some people may go for years without a major mood episode, whereas others cycle four or more times a year. A depressive episode can drag on for months or end in a matter of days. Some individuals have only mild depressions and hypomanic episodes that barely interfere with their ability to function. Determining the severity or predicting the overall course of the disorder is difficult, but the following factors clue you in to what you can expect:

- The presence of psychosis commonly marks more severe mood episodes.

- Early onset of the disorder, in childhood or adolescence in particular, often indicates increased severity and predicts a worsening of the mood episodes over time.

- An increase in the frequency, duration, and intensity of mood swings over time often indicates that the disorder is more severe.

- An early and full response to medication, such as lithium, often indicates a milder form of the disorder with a more positive prognosis over the course of your life.

- Rapid cycling may indicate a type of bipolar disorder that may be more difficult to treat.

You and your doctor can and should discuss these factors. Although some factors may indicate a harsher outcome, no factor locks in your destiny. Stress management, lifestyle changes, and careful and comprehensive medical management over time can significantly diminish the severity of symptoms and improve the course of the disorder.

Pushing the Limits of Psychiatric Labels

Your reaction to your diagnosis depends on many factors, including but not limited to your personal experience with people who have bipolar disorder, your awareness of the science and information about bipolar disorder, the attitudes about mental illness you grew up with, and your recollections of Hollywood characters with "manic depression." In the movies, people with bipolar disorder are wildly out of control; they're either dangerous villains or pitiful victims. Psychiatrists are always weird and creepy, and the "cure" is magical and complete or a sadistic failure.

A host of social reactions to mental illness may influence your responses. How will people see you and judge you? Will your employer fire you? Will your landlord evict you? The questions swirl through your mind and spark panic. So what exactly is the point of the bipolar label? Why do you need this in your life, and what are its benefits and limitations? The following list provides some answers:

- ✓ **A diagnosis guides treatment decisions.** Just like a diagnosis of diabetes tells the doctor to initiate a certain treatment regimen, a diagnosis of bipolar disorder triggers the planning process of medication and therapy choices.

- ✓ **A diagnosis lets you know what to expect over time.** Although the doctor can't see the future outcome of a complicated illness like bipolar disorder, he can anticipate certain risks and patterns you're likely to encounter over the course of the illness and possibly help you avoid them.

- ✓ **A bipolar diagnosis doesn't define you.** You're not bipolar; you *have* bipolar disorder. This is a huge difference, because language conveys powerful meanings. Always refer to your illness as something you're managing, not as a label that identifies you.

- ✓ **You choose whether and with whom you want to share your diagnosis.** Your doctor and therapist can't reveal your condition to anyone unless you give them permission to do so. You can't be fired or evicted based on your diagnosis, even if the word does get out. Your civil rights demand that you not be discriminated against because of the diagnosis.

✔ **Some people may judge you based on your diagnosis.** Judgment is a risk that comes with the label. Your task is to remember that these people are uninformed and afraid. You may choose to advocate, educate, and inform sometimes, but in other situations you may choose to limit your interactions with these people and keep a healthy distance from them.

✔ **Your label places you in a community of people with similar concerns.** You have opportunities for support and networking that will be invaluable over the years. People who are going through the same situation band together in many ways — formal and informal — to take care of one another and advocate for the group. Others have "been there" — you know that from your labels — and they "get it."

Walking Out with a Treatment Plan

When you're ready to leave the doctor's office, you should have more than a diagnosis. You want to have a well-defined treatment plan that covers your immediate needs and future directions. Ask questions about anything in the plan that you don't understand. Don't be afraid to bring a written list of questions to ask your doctor. With all that goes on during your first few appointments, you may easily and understandably forget to express your most pressing concerns and ask your most important questions. Write down the treatment plan as your doctor describes it (if you have someone with you, this can be a job you assign).

Get several of your doctor's business cards so that you can give them to other caregivers, such as your therapist, family doctor, and cardiologist. Nobody expects you to carry around contact information in your head — just keep it in your wallet or purse.

Your treatment plan should include the following:

✔ Medication names, dosing schedules, potential side effects, and time frames for them to begin working (you should have some understanding of why your doctor chose these particular medicines for you at this time)

✔ Any changes in your current medications — decreasing doses or changing times of medications you were taking before this visit, for example

✔ A plan for therapy, including the recommended type of therapy, names and phone numbers of potential therapists, and/or consent forms for your psychiatrist to speak to your current therapist

✔ Forms necessary for any blood tests, other medical consultations, or examinations that your psychiatrist recommends

✔ Instructions on how to reach your doctor if you have a problem or emergency before the next visit

✔ Information about how often you need to meet with the psychiatrist, how long the appointments will be, and how much the follow-up visits cost

✔ (Optional) Names of support groups in your area or online resources or books that your doctor feels can help you

Psychiatrist appointments, particularly at times of the day that work for you, are hard to come by. Before you leave (or right after your visit, if you have to call the office to make the appointment), schedule a series of appointments for four to six months out. This gives you the appointments that you need at times you can get there without turning your life inside out. If you stabilize and need less frequent appointments, you can always cancel, as long as you let the doctor know well in advance.

Chapter 6

Building a Winning Mood-Management Team

*Y*ou can successfully treat many common ailments on your own. You can pop an antacid tablet to relieve indigestion, sip some lemon tea at the first sign of a cold, or down a couple of aspirin to ease headache pain. Bipolar disorder is more sinister. You can be so blinded by the darkness of depression or so bewildered by the maelstrom of mania that you can't recognize your altered state of mind, let alone settle on an effective treatment.

If it takes a village to raise a child, it takes at least a small team to help you prevent your moods from swinging out of control: a psychiatrist, a therapist, and one or more supportive family members or friends. Your psychiatrist typically makes the diagnosis and prescribes the medications that enable your brain to function properly; your therapist helps you solve problems, develop coping skills, and let go of issues beyond your control; and family members and friends provide feedback, support, and encouragement.

In this chapter, you begin to build your mood-management team. You discover the key role that each person on your team plays and the criteria required for each position. You also find out how to track down and select qualified professionals and supportive friends and family members to add to your team roster.

The Head Doctor: Your Psychiatrist's Position on the Team

When your brain functions properly, it reacts appropriately to stimulation. Someone cuts you off in traffic; you angrily honk your horn. You win a spot on *American Idol;* you jump for joy. When your brain malfunctions, it may overreact or react inappropriately. You may feel depressed at parties or excited when your sister-in-law starts showing slides of her new kitchen cabinets.

When your moods are out of sync with reality, your brain's physiology or chemistry may be off balance. A psychiatrist, fondly referred to by many with bipolar disorder as a *p-doc,* helps adjust the biochemistry of your brain to enable it to respond appropriately. This doesn't cure your bipolar disorder, but it helps regulate your moods so you can function and begin to deal with real-life issues that may trigger mood swings.

Your psychiatrist's two main functions are to accurately diagnose your illness and to prescribe the appropriate medications to treat it.

A psychiatrist is a medical doctor who has specialized training in treating mental illnesses. Doctors who've successfully completed this rigorous training may not be the most warm and fuzzy individuals, although many are very amiable. When choosing a psychiatrist, remember that knowledge and experience trump congeniality.

Diagnostician

Before you can begin any sensible treatment, you need a diagnosis, and your psychiatrist is the one who gives it to you. During your first visit, your psychiatrist typically asks a series of questions:

- ✔ What events brought you here?

- ✔ What are your symptoms?

    The psychiatrist may pry out symptoms that you may not think to report but that indicate important diagnostic information for bipolar disorder or another co-existing condition. Psychiatrists often refer to this as a *review of systems* (see Chapter 5 for more on symptoms).

- ✔ How long have you been experiencing these symptoms?

- ✔ Have you consulted your primary care physician concerning these symptoms (see Chapter 4), and what diagnosis, if any, has your physician suggested?

✔ Are you currently receiving treatment for your condition?

✔ Are you currently taking any medications, supplements, drugs, or alcohol?

✔ Have any family members, past or present, been diagnosed with a mental illness?

Your psychiatrist may also have you complete questionnaires or scales, such as the *Hamilton Depression Scale* or the *Young Mania Rating Scale,* to aid in the diagnosis. Your psychiatrist uses all this information to perform a psychiatric evaluation, which he or she uses to determine a likely diagnosis. The diagnosis probably won't become official until the psychiatrist observes how you and your condition progress over time and in response to treatment.

If you're seeking treatment for depression, and you or your relatives have experienced mania or hypomania, make sure that you inform the psychiatrist. Many antidepressants can induce mania and worsen the course of your illness.

Medicine man (or woman)

In the old days, psychiatrists handled all aspects of treatment. The psychiatrist diagnosed the illness, prescribed any necessary medications, and offered therapy and counseling. Managed healthcare has redefined the role of the psychiatrist. Nowadays, some psychiatrists spend more time scribbling on prescription pads than they do counseling their patients. Insurance companies often allocate no more than 15 minutes per visit for "medication management." Caseworkers, social workers, and psychotherapists provide the talk therapy that many psychiatrists performed in the past.

If the time you spend with your psychiatrist is insufficient for successfully communicating your needs, voice your concern. Your insurance company may allow an exception for one or two visits, or you may be able to make special arrangements with your psychiatrist.

The Lifestyle Director: Your Therapist's Roles

Some people mistakenly believe that after a psychiatrist effectively tweaks brain function with the right brew of medications, the problem is solved. However, your body constantly showers your brain with mind-altering substances that it manufactures 24 hours a day in its own chemical factories.

Perceptions and your body's reaction to those perceptions play a significant role in the flow of those chemicals and in how your brain responds to them. You may be taking an effective maintenance dose of a mood stabilizer, but if you live under constant stress, your system's reaction can easily override the mood-moderating effects of the mood stabilizer.

Your therapist's primary role is to help you make positive lifestyle changes that reduce stress and establish healthy thinking patterns, enabling you to cope more effectively with unavoidable stress. A therapist, for example, may teach you techniques for identifying problems and developing solutions rather than allowing your brain to follow a defeatist thought pattern.

A therapist can play many additional roles on your mood-management team, acting as coach, career consultant, mood monitor, and wellness manager. We discuss these roles in the following sections.

The therapist and psychiatrist often function as co-leaders of your team, and their roles may overlap to some degree. Psychiatrists often play some role in therapy, education, and support functions, and therapists, with their patients' permission, may contact psychiatrists to voice concerns when they think medication adjustments are needed.

Coach, trainer, and referee

An effective therapist treats all aspects of your life that may be suffering from bipolar disorder or worsening the illness:

- ✔ **Your thought process,** which can often darken your perceptions and create a vortex that spins you into a deeper depression
- ✔ **Relationship issues** that may act as stressors

  The issues may have arisen from something you said or did as a result of your mood-disorder symptoms.

- ✔ **Family issues,** such as raising children or managing finances
- ✔ **Career changes,** problems on the job, or personality conflicts with co-workers that may cause stress at work
- ✔ **Social situations** that stress you out or that have suffered due to your illness

Scout for a therapist who specializes in the form of therapy you need most. Chapter 8 describes types of therapies proved to effectively treat bipolar disorder.

Mood monitor

You can and should monitor your moods, as we explain in Chapter 12, but when depression weighs on you like a lead blanket or mania thrusts your moods into the dizzying stratosphere, remaining motivated and objective enough to create an accurate mood map may be nearly impossible. And friends and family members may be too busy tending to their own needs to be of much help.

Your therapist can function as a mood thermometer, providing you with objective observations concerning your moods and demeanor. Sometimes mood observations are easier to accept from a third party than from a loved one.

Resident soundboard

Some of the best therapists offer the least advice. They sit and listen attentively as patients rant and rave about a particular issue. They use a little body language to indicate their interest, but they say very little. Often, airing out your issues allows you to calm down and begin to realize that you already know the solution to your problem.

If you can find a therapist who listens well and who inspires you to solve your own problems, you've struck gold. But keep in mind that this is only one role that a therapist plays. When your moods are cycling, a good therapist usually needs to play a much more active role.

Wellness manager

One of the most important factors in the success of long-term management of bipolar disorder is the *continuity of treatment.* If you shuffle from one psychiatrist or therapist to the next, your moods are likely to fluctuate with every shift in treatment. Unfortunately, changes in health insurance and other factors outside of your control often lead to changes in doctors and treatments. To achieve continuity of treatment, you must often rely on yourself or on a caseworker or therapist to establish and maintain your treatment plan.

Referral service

Therapists are people who know people. If your therapist can't solve your problem, she probably has the name and contact information of a specialist

Therapy: It's a family affair

Bipolar experts have found that family therapy (see Chapter 8), including a healthy dose of education about bipolar disorder, is highly effective in helping people with bipolar disorder establish and maintain a stable mood. Family therapy has two primary goals: to build empathy for the person who has the disorder and to improve communication skills among family members. Family members discover how to listen to one another, express themselves without appearing confrontational, avoid unproductive arguments, and set limits that prevent the illness from overtaxing the family. Family members who can empathize and communicate effectively remove one of the primary stressors that can trigger a mood episode.

Family therapy is even more critical to families that have more than one member with bipolar disorder. People with bipolar disorder often gravitate to one another because of their mutual appreciation for the highs and lows, and pairs of sufferers often end up marrying — a phenomenon called *assortative mating*. Marriage pairs two people who have fluctuating moods, which can often make for a very volatile relationship. If the couple has children, the kids have a higher likelihood of developing bipolar disorder.

who can. She'll dig through her desk and hand you a business card or flip through her day planner and rattle off the name, address, and phone number of a specialist you need. Buried in debt? Here's a financial consultant that my other clients rave about! Need a job? Here's the name of a career coach I know. Need a break from the drudgery of daily life? Here's the travel agent I use. Can't pay me? Here's some information on government-subsidized health insurance.

Assembling the Rest of Your Support Staff: Family and Friends

A strong support network of family and friends can function as a valuable ally in the battle against mood swings. However, if your allies have their own agendas and their own emotional baggage to lug around, they can compound your problem and trigger mood swings by being a little too helpful. When you begin recruiting your support staff, you need to decide whom you can trust, establish an understanding of everyone's fears and anxieties, and educate your network about your illness and what they can do to help.

Building a network based on trust

When scouting for family members or friends to add to your support network, look for stable and trustworthy people. Ask yourself the following questions:

- ✔ **Can I confide in this person?** Some parasites buddy up to people who have problems just so they can obtain some juicy gossip to pass along. Your support staff should know how to keep discussions confidential.

- ✔ **Is this person stable enough to help me?** People with bipolar disorder commonly are drawn to others who enjoy roller-coaster moods and emotions. Only someone who's steady can help you steady yourself.

- ✔ **Do I see this person frequently enough?** An ideal support person sees you at least once a week to determine if you've experienced any significant shift in mood. Of course, the more people you have in your support network, the more objective observers you have to monitor your moods.

- ✔ **Does this person judge me for having a mental illness?** If this person thinks that your mental illness is due to a character flaw, he or she can't provide the support you need. You don't need people who make you feel guilty for having the illness.

- ✔ **Is this person reliable?** If you foresee this person bailing out at the first sign of trouble, you know he won't be there when you need him most.

- ✔ **Does this person respect me?** You don't want an intrusive caretaker who constantly nags you about your moods and meds and treats you like a child.

Understanding their fears, anxieties, anger, and other emotions

Family and friends who genuinely care about you and appreciate your unique gifts can often get under your skin, especially when they want to help and especially during a mood episode. They have fears, anxieties, anger, and other emotions, too. As you're battling a lengthy bout of depression, they may be anxious, not knowing how long it will last, or angry that you don't "seem" to be doing enough to help yourself. When you're in the throes of mania, your loved ones may be unable to understand you or tell you to calm down. Something you say or do may trigger strong negative emotions. Although some people have thicker skins than others, nobody's skin is impervious. Chapter 10 reveals how people commonly perceive and respond to manic and depressive episodes.

Educating your supporters

Whenever you throw a party, you usually have several guests who strategically avoid the after-party cleanup. If you're lucky, one or two close friends who know their way around your kitchen will start tidying up. You may see a couple others who linger around, waiting to be told what to do.

You can observe many of these same human behaviors in your support staff. If you're depressed or manic, most people who don't understand what's going on or what you expect of them flee the scene. If they don't bolt, they stick around, become frustrated by not knowing what to do, and lose their tempers or pepper you with sarcasm. What you want is a close friend or relative who knows about mood disorders to intervene and provide a firm, guiding hand to help you stabilize.

You want as many knowledgeable people on your mood-management team as possible, and the only way to achieve that goal is to educate the members who want to learn and are committed to helping you succeed. Knowledge gives people the information they need to help and the confidence to jump in when you need them most. Whenever friends or family members ask what they can do to help, encourage them to discover more about bipolar disorder, drawing from any of the following resources:

- ✔ **You:** You're the most qualified expert in the world on *your* moods and what keeps them stable. If you feel ready to discuss your situation with others, you can be an incredibly valuable source of information.

- ✔ **Depression and Bipolar Support Alliance (DBSA):** An organization focusing on bipolar disorder and depression and run by and for patients, DBSA offers free and confidential support groups for patients, families, and friends living with depression or bipolar disorder. DBSA also offers free educational materials written in a language you can understand. Check out the DBSA Web site at www.dbsalliance.org.

- ✔ **NAMI Family to Family:** The National Alliance for the Mentally Ill (NAMI) offers a 10-week course called *Family to Family* that educates friends and family members about major mental illnesses and the available treatments. The course also functions as a support group, encouraging friends and family members to express their feelings about the illness and how it has affected them. Check out the NAMI Web site at www.nami.org.

- ✔ **Books:** This book and many others on bipolar disorder can help friends and family members empathize and can teach them what they can do to help. Chapter 16 focuses specifically on what you can do to help a loved one who has bipolar disorder.

- ✔ **Audio and videotapes:** Audiotapes, videotapes, and television specials about bipolar disorder typically don't delve into what loved ones can do to help, but they do help build empathy, which is the first step toward loved ones becoming more accepting and understanding.

- ✔ **Movies:** Although Hollywood takes a little poetic license with "true" stories, some movies, including *A Beautiful Mind* and *Frances,* help remove the stigma of mental illness.

- ✔ **Web sites:** Several Web sites offer excellent information about bipolar disorder and provide information specifically for friends and family members of people who suffer from bipolar disorder.

When researching bipolar disorder on the Web, remain skeptical. The Web has plenty of excellent information, but it also attracts its share of quacks and weekend quarterbacks. Before following any home remedies or miracle cures, consult your doctor.

Setting your team's level of involvement

A good supporter remains vigilant, helping you monitor your moods and watch for signs of trouble. The person needs to have the sensitivity to know when to remain silent and when to voice concerns and the strength to step in and help when you need it most, especially when you can't or don't want to ask for or accept assistance. Although such people are rare, you can help your loved ones become a better support staff by educating them about bipolar disorder and by communicating your needs and defining the parameters for assisting you.

You're probably aware that some people, if you let them, will gladly volunteer to live your life for you. They'd be happy to cook your meals, clean your house, raise your kids, and maybe even pay your bills (with your money, of course), all in the name of charity. Such assistance may seem nice in the short term, when you really need help, but when charity becomes chronic and invasive, the lifesaver quickly becomes an anchor. Beware of the following personality types:

- ✔ **The Nagger:** "Did you take your meds today?" Every day, sometimes two or three times a day, you can expect this nagging question. If you want or need to be reminded to take your medications, the Nagger can be useful; otherwise, nagging is just another stressor.

- ✔ **The Clueless:** A Clueless helper watches you, but he never does or says anything that he thinks may offend you. You can be teetering on the edge of the cliff, and Clueless will patiently watch the events unfold.

- ✔ **The Party Animal:** If you're prone to having fun and enduring hypomanic episodes that entail spending sprees, bar-hopping, wild sex, and other frenetic activities, you can find plenty of Party Animals to join you, but they usually don't stick around very long after the hangover. Avoid people who try to inspire you to do things that you wouldn't do in a healthier frame of mind.

✔ **The Heavy:** Unlike the Party Animal, who encourages you to have too much fun, the Heavy doesn't let you have any fun at all. And that's not . . . well, any fun. You should be able to enjoy a full life within the limits you set for yourself.

Encouraging open communication

Announcing that you have bipolar is a foolproof way to silence an audience. Most people don't know what to say, so they instantly go mute. In some cases, that's the desired effect, but when approaching your support staff, you want to encourage open communication.

Communicating openly about bipolar disorder serves two main functions:

✔ It helps your supporters understand you and your condition more intimately.

✔ It helps you become more in tune with how your moods, emotions, and behaviors affect those around you.

Establishing a relationship is like learning to dance together. You and your partner must move in sync, and communication is the key. At first, you step on each other's toes quite frequently, but as you become more accustomed to each other's movements, you begin to instinctively move to the rhythms that surround you. Here are some techniques that can open the channels of communication so you can start working on your rhythm:

✔ Write down what you want to discuss in advance.

✔ Sit down in a quiet, private place whenever you need to discuss confidential topics.

✔ Agree on a physical sign or secret word that you can use to end the discussion, no questions asked, if it becomes too heated.

✔ Encourage your friend or loved one to ask questions about bipolar disorder and how it makes you feel.

✔ Ask your friend or loved one to describe his or her observations and emotions concerning your moods and behaviors. How is bipolar disorder affecting your loved one's life and his or her ability to satisfy personal needs?

You can help a person become more knowledgeable about bipolar disorder and about your needs, but you can't force anyone to accept you or the illness. Some people, due to their own limitations, may not be ready to accept the illness and adapt to a new reality. For your own mental wellness, you may need some distance from these people for a while.

Working as a Team

The key players on your mood-management team should all be able to communicate openly with one another to ensure that you receive comprehensive, integrated treatment. If your therapist notices that your moods are fluctuating or that you seem more anxious and irritable than usual, she should be able to contact your psychiatrist to make a joint decision on how to proceed. You may need a medication adjustment or additional therapy sessions.

An effective strategy is to put one member of your support staff (or yourself, if you feel up to it) in charge of communications. Your communications manager should introduce the members of your mood-management team and ensure that critical information gets passed along. Such communication is especially important in situations when complications or transitions, such as the following, arise:

- **Hospitalization:** Some hospitals have their own doctors in charge of treatment, so when you're hospitalized, the psychiatrist who usually sees you may no longer be in charge of your care. Communication between your psychiatrist and the new doctor at the hospital is essential.

- **Hospital release:** Before the hospital releases you, your regular psychiatrist, therapist, and the person acting as your primary caretaker need to be informed in advance so they can provide a smooth transition to the outside world and make any necessary arrangements.

- **Changing doctors:** When you change doctors or therapists, you should make sure that your records are transferred to the new doctor or therapist.

Because of privacy laws, you may need to sign a release with each doctor and therapist you see so they can openly communicate with one another. You may also need to sign a letter that enables your doctor or therapist to discuss your treatment with specific friends or family members.

Extending Your Family to Local Support Groups

Friends and family have much more invested in your health and well being than any third party, including your psychiatrist or therapist, but others who suffer from bipolar disorder may have much more to offer in terms of empathy, information, and connections. Bipolar support groups commonly offer the following perks:

- ✔ A place where you can vent your frustrations

- ✔ Camaraderie with others who share your experiences and emotions

- ✔ Understanding that a mood disorder doesn't define who you are

- ✔ Motivation to follow your treatment plan

- ✔ The ability to rediscover strengths and humor you thought you lost when you became ill

- ✔ Information on medications, treatments, and therapies

- ✔ Patient perspectives of local doctors and therapists, both positive and negative

- ✔ Information about your legal rights

- ✔ Information about education and IEPs (Individualized Education Plans) for children with bipolar disorder

- ✔ A library of books and videos

- ✔ Featured speakers

You can tap into the resources a support group offers by joining up. Organizations such as the Depression and Bipolar Support Alliance (DBSA) and NAMI (National Alliance of the Mentally Ill) sponsor support groups in most cities and many towns to help people who suffer from mental illnesses find peer support and to encourage advocacy. To find out about support groups in your area, contact the following organizations or resources:

- ✔ **Depression and Bipolar Support Alliance:** Call 1-800-826-3632, or look on the Web at www.dbsalliance.org.

- ✔ **National Alliance for the Mentally Ill:** Call 1-800-950-6264, or look on the Web at www.nami.org. Click the link for State & Local NAMIs to locate contact information for local NAMI groups.

- ✔ **National Mental Health Association:** Call 1-800-969-6642, or look on the Web at www.nmha.org.

- ✔ **Your place of worship:** Many churches provide meeting places for support groups, including those affiliated with DBSA and NAMI.

✔ **Your psychiatrist or therapist:** Ask your psychiatrist or therapist for information about local support groups. Your therapist may run a support group that meets regularly.

✔ **State or county mental health centers:** Most states and large counties have mental health services that can refer you to support groups in your area.

What can you expect when you walk through the doors into your first support-group session? That depends on the makeup of the group and its organization. Some support groups are more structured than others and may include a featured speaker. Others encourage members to vent their emotions or exchange any information they have about medications, treatments, doctors, and therapists. Generally, you can expect members to welcome you with open arms. People in support groups are very open and are more than willing to lend an empathetic ear.

Every support group has its own chemistry and dynamic, so don't give up if you feel out of place at the first support group you visit. Try a few groups until you find one that feels comfortable.

Teaming Up for Crisis Prevention and Management

In the depths of depression and in the irrational throes of mania, you may be much less able to make wise decisions. When overcome by your symptoms, taking your own life may seem like a good idea to you. It never is. This is the time when the people closest to you can do the most to help protect you from yourself.

With so much riding on the outcome, those around you may need to make healthcare choices for you. They may need to contact your psychiatrist or another person on your support team, call an emergency number, or even help you check into the hospital.

Although you may need to pass the decision-making duties to someone else, you can retain some control by making your preferences known in advance, and we explain how in the following sections. For more information about advance directives — legal documents that can help you state your treatment preferences — visit www.DBSAlliance.org/Resources/ AdvanceDirectives.html.

When you're in a healthy frame of mind, the last thing you want to think about is being sick again, but healthy times are the best times to write up your emergency plan.

Providing your team with contact information and emergency numbers

Few people carry around lists of phone numbers to call if they get hit by a car or fall off a cliff. If you're physically harmed to the point where you can't dial a phone, somebody will call an ambulance, and the authorities will manage to get in touch with your family.

But what happens when depression has you bedridden or when mania has you so wired that your thoughts, words, and actions are out of your control? As long as you aren't physically harmed or you're not physically harming someone else, destroying property, or stealing stuff, society pretty much looks the other way. Unfortunately, looking the other way compounds the problem, so make sure that the people on your support team know whom to contact when your mood swings outside of your control:

- ✔ Primary physician's name and phone number
- ✔ Psychiatrist's name and phone number
- ✔ Therapist's name and phone number
- ✔ Health insurance company name, phone number, and your identification number
- ✔ Workplace phone number and supervisor's name

    You should also state how much detail your workplace needs to know. It may be sufficient for your support people to tell your boss you're very ill if you haven't made your bipolar disorder common knowledge at work.

- ✔ Close relatives' names and phone numbers
- ✔ Primary support person's name and phone number (typically, a spouse, parent, sibling, or close friend)

Type the contact information on a small piece of paper, and make copies to place in your wallet or purse and to provide to the members of your support team. See Chapter 17 for more information on planning for a crisis.

Opening and closing your team's lines of communication

Banks, doctors, dentists, insurance companies, and even cable companies that have potentially sensitive information on file about you have privacy policies that specify the limitations of how they can use and share the information you provide. Unless you specifically request otherwise, your doctor, psychiatrist, and therapist are required by law to keep your information confidential — in most cases, anyway. If a doctor believes you're at imminent risk of hurting yourself or someone else, he's legally obligated to break confidentiality to try to prevent harm.

However, if you designate a support person to make decisions for you and to help ensure continuity of treatment while you're incapacitated, that person needs to have access to your doctor and therapist to obtain and provide information critical for proper treatment. When you feel well, make sure you communicate to your psychiatrist and therapist that you want them to share information with this person or people on your support staff. Also, make sure that you sign any necessary releases.

To ensure that you receive comprehensive, integrated care, make sure that your psychiatrist and therapist sign a release so that they can communicate openly with one another and coordinate the various components of your treatment plan.

Expressing your desires regarding inpatient or outpatient treatment

Nowadays, hospitalization is reserved primarily for crisis management and safety intervention. In most cases, you don't check in for the long term. Although you may be scared and unwilling to check in, keep in mind that the ultimate goal is to get stable. Listen to the support people around you. Ask yourself as honestly as possible: Are you functioning? Can you go about your day-to-day life? If not, get the help you need so you can function on the outside.

If you're actively harming yourself or others or pose an imminent risk to yourself or to someone else, hospitalization may be necessary. Voluntary hospitalization is much easier for everyone than involuntary hospitalization. Signing yourself into the hospital may be the best action you can take to liberate your mind and life from the chaos they're in. You have the most control over the course and length of your hospitalization if you sign in voluntarily. Hospitalization is almost always a short-term solution intended to stabilize your moods and emotions. Most hospital personnel are highly motivated to return you to your home and support network so you can begin to manage your recovery with or without the assistance of outpatient care.

You may be scared going in. That's normal. If you're experiencing paranoia as one of the symptoms, you may even believe that someone is hospitalizing you to harm you or get you out of the way.

BIPOLAR BIO

Finding alternative living arrangements

The Christmas holidays always put Debra on edge, but this one was shaping up to be the worst. The stress at work was unbearable, and she became irritable at home when everything wasn't just right. Discussions with her husband, Paul, quickly escalated into yelling matches, and everyone in the family felt as though they needed to walk on eggshells to keep from upsetting Debra.

Debra was seeing her family doctor for depression and anxiety and tried several different anti-depressants, each of which temporarily eased the sadness but made her more anxious and uptight. She wasn't sleeping and began to feel as though her marriage and family were slipping away. She became convinced that Paul was planning to move out and take the kids.

Debra's doctor referred her to a psychiatrist, but by the time she got in, she felt as though she was ready to crawl out of her skin. During her interview with her doctor, her moods shifted visibly. One minute she was ranting about her boss, and the next minute she began crying because her family had turned against her. During the session, she accused Paul of having her followed, which he denied.

The psychiatrist recommended that she check into the hospital, where he could observe her and adjust her medications, but she flatly refused. She glared at Paul and warned, "Don't you dare!" She said she would do anything to stay out of the hospital. Paul had his own reservations about hospitals, so he agreed that hospitalization should remain the last resort, but he was exhausted and angry and didn't want Debra back home in her state. He recommended that she stay with a relative or friend, which Debra was willing to try. She became too stressed at her parents' house, so they ruled out that option. They also ruled out Debra's friend Susan's apartment, because Susan and Debra often partied late into the morning. Debra and Paul decided to contact their church, and the pastor directed them to a couple who had a bedroom available. One of them was always home, and the house was very peaceful and orderly.

Debra stayed at the couple's home for two weeks while she received intensive outpatient therapy. The doctor started her on Depakote. After her stay, she returned home to continue treatment. She and Paul also began seeing a therapist to work on financial issues and other disagreements, and the entire family learned new communication skills that cut down on the emotional noise. Debra and Paul haven't lived apart since, and they'll always be thankful to the generous couple who gave Debra a safe place to stay during their crisis.

If you're not a threat to yourself or others, other options may be more appealing and just as effective:

- ✔ **Home:** Assuming your home isn't full of stressors that exacerbate your mood swings, home is generally the best place to recover.

- ✔ **A friend's home:** If your home environment is too frenzied, try staying at the home of a friend who has a more placid, organized household. You want a quiet place to recover. Moving from one stressful environment to another is futile.

✔ **Halfway house:** If you can't live at home or don't have a place to stay, you may be able to stay in a halfway house until your moods stabilize.

✔ **Intensive outpatient care:** In intensive outpatient care, you generally receive therapy, monitoring, and medication adjustments during the day and return home in the evening.

Stating your preferred hospital

When preparing for a possible crisis, choose the hospital that best meets your needs — assuming, of course, that you have two or more hospitals nearby that provide appropriate care. When comparing hospitals, consider the following:

✔ Does the hospital provide inpatient care for mental illnesses?

✔ Is the hospital covered on your insurance, assuming you have health insurance that covers mental illness?

✔ Does your doctor/therapist think highly of this hospital?

✔ Can your psychiatrist continue to treat you at this hospital?

✔ Does the hospital seem to be clean and orderly? You may want to visit the hospital when you're feeling well; however, due to privacy issues, you may be able to see only the waiting area.

Part III

Opening the Treatment Toolbox: A Comprehensive, Integrated Approach

The 5th Wave — By Rich Tennant

"Fortunately for you, Ms. Dobbins, at this clinic we firmly believe in alternative medicine."

In this part . . .

*I*n order to achieve success in any field of endeavor, you should get to know the tools of the trade. That goes for using your computer, playing golf, and even whipping up a gourmet meal in the kitchen. But it's even more critical when it comes to treating bipolar disorder. The right mix of medication, therapy, and persistence can bring mood swings under control and maintain their stability. But which medications are most effective? What are the risks? And which therapies hold out the most promise?

The chapters in this part answer all these questions and more. Here, we open the medicine cabinet and take a look at what the most promising pharmaceuticals have to offer. We explain the challenges of treating bipolar disorder with medications and reveal some tips and techniques to improve success. We explore therapies that continue to help those with bipolar disorder and additional therapies to assist families and relationships. Finally, we explore optional and complementary treatments, including herbs, vitamins, nutrients, and light therapy.

Chapter 7

Touring the Bipolar Pharmacy

*W*ithout some changes in mood, life would be agonizingly boring, and nobody wants that. What you really want is a regulator that you can affix to your mind's speedometer — something that keeps it traveling between 0 and 65 miles per hour and prevents any sudden changes in speed.

Prescription medications offer great hope, but the magic pill remains elusive. Medications work differently for everyone; a godsend to some may be a disaster for others. Medications that you find effective in normalizing your moods may cause irritating side effects for others. And medications that work today may lose their effects later.

We can't tell you which medications are best for you, but in this chapter, we explore the basics of developing and maintaining a safe and effective medication regimen. We introduce you to currently available medications that have proved useful in treating the most common bipolar symptoms. We explore the benefits and risks of mood stabilizers and survey other antiseizure and antipsychotic medications that are often useful in treating mania. Finally, we examine antidepressants, antianxiety medications, and sedatives.

Grasping the Basics of Bipolar Psychopharmacology

Psychopharmacology is the use of *psychotropic medications* (any prescription drugs that affect mood, emotion, behavior, or perception) to treat mental illness.

In the case of bipolar disorder, psychopharmacology has three primary goals:

- ✓ Alleviate acute manic and depressive symptoms, often at the same time (such as during mixed episodes; see Chapter 2)
- ✓ Maintain mood stability
- ✓ Treat any additional symptoms, such as anxiety

Meeting all the goals is certainly a tall order, but they seem straightforward enough, so why do psychiatrists sometimes seem to have such a tough time prescribing the right medications? Several reasons come to mind:

- ✓ **Symptoms differ among patients.** For one patient, hopelessness and loss of energy are the biggest problems; for another, racing thoughts and sleeplessness; and for a third, irritability and loss of interest.
- ✓ **Patients can have multiple disorders.** A patient may have bipolar disorder coupled with attention deficit disorder, for example.
- ✓ **Each medication treats only specific symptoms.** Some medications treat only mania. Others treat only depression. One or two may help prevent or reduce the chances of experiencing another mood episode in the future.
- ✓ **Effectiveness varies for each patient.** A medication that works for one patient can have no effect or the opposite effect on another.
- ✓ **Side effects differ**. One patient may feel fine taking a particular medication, but another may feel groggy or gain weight.
- ✓ **Medications can worsen symptoms.** Some antidepressants can induce mania or increase anxiety.
- ✓ **Medications can interact with one another.** Treatment often requires the use of two or more medications at the same time, which can affect the efficacy of either or both medications.

In this section, we discuss ways to deal with these complications (with the help of your doctor, of course) and treat your illness the best way possible.

Selecting the best medications for you

Your brain profile is unique, which challenges you and your doctor to discover the most effective potion — the medication or combination of medications that works best for you. Discuss medication choices with your doctor. Just because your boss's son took Lamictal and is showing improvement doesn't mean the medication is right for you; in fact, it may be dangerous for you. Planning and patience are the keys, but when you're feeling the pain, these keys are in short supply. Hang in there, and stay focused and committed. Your persistence will eventually pay off.

Family history may be able to provide you with a shortcut for finding the right medications for you. If a family member has bipolar disorder and is responding well to a particular medication or combination, the same medication(s) may work well for you. This pattern is particularly true for lithium; researchers have found a strong genetic relationship to "lithium responsiveness." In short, if you have an immediate family member who's receiving successful treatment for bipolar disorder, you can often save time by simply saying, "I'll have what he's having," or at least by letting your doctor know what's working for the other family member.

We encourage you to work closely with your doctor whenever you consider your treatment options, including medications. If you think a particular medication may be effective, ask your doctor about it. Also, review your medication choices, and make sure you can answer the following questions *before* you start taking any medication:

- Why am I supposed to take this medication?
- What is the medication likely to do?
- What are the side effects? Which ones (such as drowsiness) are likely to go away after a few weeks?
- What side effects need immediate medical attention, such as a rash, shortness of breath, or suicidal thoughts?

Managing side effects

As a child, you probably learned not to play with fire the first time you got burned. Likewise, the first impulse you have when you experience a negative side effect is to stop taking the medicine you suspect is causing it. In the case of psychiatric medications, however, stopping treatment can harm you, and side effects often decrease with time and may be manageable. Your psychiatrist probably knows some simple tricks, such as the following, for curbing many common side effects:

- **Change the time of day you take the medicine.** If a medication makes you too drowsy, for example, you may be able to take it before bed rather than first thing in the morning.
- **Tweak the dose.** A little more or less can make a big difference.
- **Add a medication to treat the side effect.** If a medication causes trouble, another medication can often help.
- **Change the medication.** Your psychiatrist may be able to switch you to a similar medication with fewer side effects.

Don't play doctor. Stopping a medication cold turkey or adjusting your medications on your own, especially without informing your psychiatrist, can lead to mood instability and a host of other problems (such as seizures or increased anxiety). Always consult your doctor before making any changes. Also contact your doctor right away if you develop a rash or extreme shortness of breath after starting a new medicine — any medication can cause an allergic reaction.

When starting a new medication, ask your psychiatrist if a free sample is available. If the medicine doesn't work or produces undesirable side effects, at least you don't lose any money. Another way to save money on medications that work for you is to order them in bulk; many insurance companies have pharmacy plans that enable you to order a 90-day supply at a discount. (See Chapter 20 for more money-saving tips.)

Getting tested for medication levels and general health issues

Many medications require regular medical tests to ensure that they meet but don't exceed their recommended therapeutic levels (the levels at which they work) and that they're not causing any other medical problems. Common tests include the following:

- **Blood levels** to test the concentration of the medicine in your blood
- **EKGs (electrocardiograms)** to monitor heart rhythms
- **Thyroid function tests** to make sure your thyroid gland is working properly
- **Liver function tests** to ensure that your liver is filtering your blood properly

Throughout this chapter, we don't mention the tests required of a particular medication unless it has a unique side effect that generates significant concern. Ask your doctor if tests are required for any of the medications you're currently taking.

Mixing your pharmaceutical cocktail

The key to finding the right medication or combination of medications is to remain persistent and in regular communication with your doctor. By providing detailed feedback on your feelings and behaviors, you can help your doctor more expertly mix a pharmaceutical "cocktail" that's both safe and effective for you. (Chapter 12 features a mood chart designed specifically for this purpose.)

BIPOLAR BIO

Harmonizing Harry

Harry was diagnosed with bipolar disorder in college when he experienced classic episodes of depression and mania. His response to lithium was dramatic — his moods leveled off, and the cycles disappeared for a while. But Harry was a music major — a pianist — and the tremor from his lithium was unmanageable for him. He couldn't prepare or perform during his final exams, and he began to give up hope of ever performing his final recital — a requirement for graduation.

It was clear that lithium wouldn't work for him — at least at the doses he was on. At lower doses, he again became depressed, so Harry's psychiatrist added a small dose of an antidepressant. A hypomanic cycle erupted quickly, which responded nicely to low doses of an antipsychotic. Harry tried to get off of his lithium entirely, but below a certain dose, even with the other medicines on board, he became irritable and couldn't get out of bed. He worked closely with his psychiatrist to establish a lithium level that was effective but didn't cause a tremor. Along with the other medications, this plan kept him stable. He completed his exams and performed his graduation recital — a semester later than planned but with great success. The time and persistence he invested in his medication trials laid the groundwork for truly successful management of his symptoms.

Practicing safety first

Always make sure that any medication you add is safe to use with any medications you're already taking. This includes over-the-counter remedies and "natural" or herbal supplements.

Most prescription medicines include a list of *contraindications* (medical conditions that preclude the use of a medication) and drug interactions, which your psychiatrist uses to determine one of the following degrees of safety:

- **Dangerous:** Some combinations can be toxic. For example, you should never combine an MAOI (Monoamine Oxidase Inhibitor) with an SSRI (Selective Serotonin Reuptake Inhibitor) or lithium with certain antibiotics or with the weight-control drug Meridia. We discuss MAOIs and SSRIs later in this chapter.

- **Very risky:** Some combinations may be dangerous to some people, but the potential benefits may outweigh the risks. For example, taking lithium with some diuretics or older antipsychotics is risky but may improve symptoms for some individuals.

- **Risky:** A combination with minimal risk may be reasonable in some situations.

- **Safe but with possible changes in medication effectiveness:** Some medications cause others to become less effective, and some can increase the effectiveness of your medications. These combinations can sometimes work to your advantage.

✓ **Safe:** Frequently, two medications have a very low risk of negatively interacting with one another, making them safe to combine.

Consult your doctor if you have any questions concerning the effectiveness or safety of a medication or combination of medications. Common problems when mixing medications include one medication decreasing the effectiveness of another or amplifying its negative side effects, such as increased blood pressure. Inform your doctor of any medications, supplements, herbs, or natural remedies you're currently taking.

Taking a gradual, systematic approach

Few psychotropic medications act as quickly as aspirin. Your doctor may ramp up the dosage over time to reduce the occurrence of some side effects, and the medicine may take several weeks to achieve full effectiveness. Furthermore, whenever you add a medication to your cocktail, you and your doctor need some time to observe the effects, side effects, and interactions. Under psychological distress, your patience, understandably, may be strained, but following a steady course is critical.

Because so much can change with each medication adjustment, we strongly recommend that you make changes in only one medicine at a time. Such patience isn't always possible — particularly in emergencies — but when the time is available, a systematic, scientific approach can reduce variables and make it easier to track down the cause of any side effects. If you introduce two or more new medications to the mix at the same time and experience a negative side effect, you may not be able to tell which medication is causing it.

Staying abreast of the changes

Over the course of your life, your brain physiology and chemistry change, your symptoms change, and your environment and relationships change. To remain in sync with these changes, check in with your doctor regularly, even when you're feeling fine, to determine if you can make any of the following adjustments:

✓ Increase or decrease a medication dosage to reduce side effects

✓ Increase or decrease a medication or change a medication to address a new or nagging symptom

✓ Eliminate or reduce a medication to minimize exposure to long-term risks

A common trap is to start taking a combination of medications during a period of crisis and then continuing on the same medication regimen after you resolve the crisis. As soon as the crisis is no longer an issue, visit your doctor to determine if you can scale back or eliminate some of your medications. Most people with bipolar disorder require some medication throughout their lives, but you and your doctor should seize any opportunity to strip away unnecessary layers of medication.

Juggling medications for co-existing conditions

As you weave your way through the brambles of bipolar disorder, you're likely to pick up a few burrs — diagnoses of additional, comorbid conditions. *Comorbid* is a fancy word for *co-existing*. In bipolar disorder, psychiatrists use the term to describe any psychiatric or medical conditions that accompany your bipolar diagnosis. Of course, the bipolar category already assumes two co-existing conditions: depression and mania or hypomania. Comorbidity doesn't apply to that. It applies to other distinct psychiatric illnesses, such as these:

- **Attention Deficit Hyperactivity Disorder** can co-exist with bipolar disorder, sharing symptoms such as hyperactivity and impulsivity. Amphetamines treat ADHD effectively but can jump-start mania or psychosis in people with bipolar disorder. However, leaping back into a job or school with untreated ADHD may have failure written all over it. Certain antidepressants may be effective in treating ADHD, but both stimulants and antidepressants need to be used with care in treating bipolar disorder. Cautious use of stimulants may be possible in some circumstances, especially in children.

- **Anxiety disorders (panic, obsessive compulsive disorder, generalized anxiety, or social anxiety)** show up in about 25 percent (or more) of people with bipolar disorder. Some medications used for bipolar disorder (such as the atypical antipsychotics) can reduce anxiety, but they may not be adequate, and the anxiety may shut you down and prevent your return to daily life. SSRI antidepressants effectively reduce anxiety symptoms in most cases, but you should use them in conjunction with mood stabilizers, and they require close work with your doctor and support team.

- **Substance abuse,** particularly alcoholism, occurs in one third to one half of people with bipolar disorder. Many medications for bipolar disorder, including lithium, are dangerous with alcohol. Tranquilizers, such as valium, are chemically similar to alcohol and create addiction more easily if you have a tendency toward alcoholism. In combination, alcohol and tranquilizers can kill you.

- **Memory and thinking problems** commonly accompany bipolar disorder. Adding insult to injury, some of the medications used for bipolar can cloud your thinking. Work with your doctors to find a medication combination and dosage level that can stabilize your mood without mucking up your thought processes.

✔ **Personality disorders,** such as borderline, narcissistic, or obsessive compulsive, appear to frequently co-exist with bipolar disorder. This layering of conditions creates a higher likelihood that your function will be impaired in between mood episodes and complicates your recovery. Personality disorders typically respond poorly to medications and can actually work against the medications. Psychotherapy is crucial to managing these issues and must be a part of the treatment package.

Managing your meds during and after pregnancy

Women with bipolar disorder who want to have children face daunting challenges and often express the following concerns:

✔ **How will the medications affect the developing fetus?** Many of the medications used to combat bipolar disorder can be dangerous to the developing fetus. Even if a medicine doesn't pose a well-known risk, little may be known about its safety to the baby's developing brain and body.

✔ **How will the pregnancy affect my moods?** Pregnancy and especially the postpartum period are high-risk periods for mood instability. Hormonal shifts create brain changes that can trigger cycles or other symptoms such as anxiety.

✔ **Can I handle the stress?** Pregnancy, delivery, and raising an infant and child can add to your stress levels, whether you're a mother- or father-to-be. The sleep deprivation that comes with a new baby can make anyone a little cranky, but it can hurl a parent with bipolar disorder right into a manic episode. When planning a pregnancy, be sure to discuss these issues with your family.

If you're a woman with bipolar disorder, and you plan on having a child, work with your doctor to develop a strategy to facilitate the pregnancy, minimize the risk to the fetus, and prevent mood cycling. You should also have backup plans for dealing with any mood episode that occurs during the pregnancy. Plans can include steps like intensifying your psychotherapy, getting help at home from friends or relatives, taking a leave of absence from work, or entering a day treatment program or hospital if necessary. If you unexpectedly become pregnant while on medication, you, your psychiatrist, and your OB/GYN should meet and plan the course of action most appropriate for you and your pregnancy.

You transmit most medications through breast milk, so breastfeeding becomes another concern. Because postpartum is such a high-risk time for a mood episode, many women feel more comfortable returning to their medication and bottle feeding. This is a personal decision you need to make with your physician.

Unlocking the Bipolar Medicine Cabinet

This section introduces you to many of the most common medications that treat bipolar disorder. We base our information on the knowledge available during the writing of this book and on the prescribing practices at the time. And although we mention the primary benefits and the most common potential side effects of each medication, we don't cover all benefits and side effects. If you want to know why, just try slogging through a pharmacy printout for any prescription medication you currently take. You can use the information we provide when consulting with your doctor to determine medications that may be most effective and safe for treating your symptoms.

Lithium (a.k.a. old faithful)

Successfully treating bipolar disorder since the 1960s, lithium is the grand-daddy of bipolar medications. Lithium continues to be the gold standard, treating the range of bipolar symptoms more fully than any other medication in use today. It treats mania. It treats depression. It can reduce the cycling of mania and depression. And perhaps most important, it's the only medication that's proven to reduce the risk of suicide in bipolar disorder. Lithium is truly in a league of its own.

Interestingly, this wonder drug wasn't cooked up in a multimillion-dollar lab. Lithium is a naturally occurring salt that just happens to calm the nerves and, when used under a doctor's supervision, has mild side effects for most people.

Table 7-1 provides a quick rundown of the potential benefits and some of the potential side effects of this rock star of bipolar disorder.

Table 7-1	Lithium's Potential Benefits and Risks
Potential Benefits	*Potential Risks*
Antimanic	Stomach problems, weight gain
Reduces cycle frequency	Frequent urination, kidney damage
Antidepressant	Thyroid damage
Reduces frequency of suicide	Foggy thinking, fatigue, tremor

You must keep lithium blood levels in a very narrow range, so always take the prescribed dose; your doctor tests the levels every few months (more regularly when you first start taking it) and also orders additional blood and urine tests. If your lithium level dips below its therapeutic level, the drug isn't effective. If it rises too high, the drug can become toxic, and severe lithium toxicity can lead to death. Lithium levels can rise as you lose fluid, so be wary of hot weather and vigorous exercise, and limit your consumption of diuretics, including coffee and alcohol. If you experience diarrhea, vomiting, dizziness, lack of coordination, blurred vision, or other signs of lithium toxicity, contact your doctor immediately. If you can't reach your doctor, head to the nearest emergency room.

On the Web or at your local health food store, you may hear of a form of lithium purported to be safer: lithium orotate. The theory behind this claim is that the chemical compound delivers lithium to the brain more efficiently than lithium carbonate, the standard compound, so it requires less lithium in your bloodstream to be effective. However, no studies currently show that lithium orotate is effective in treating mania or depression. Taking the recommended dose of lithium orotate probably won't harm you — but it also won't help.

Effective antiseizure medicines

Your brain and central nervous system form an intricate power grid carrying very low-level electricity. With serious central nervous system malfunctions, such as in epilepsy, neurons misfire to such an extent that they can cause seizures. Antiseizure medications — including valproate, commonly known as divalproex (brand name Depakote) — are designed to regulate neuron firing to prevent seizures. A bonus is that many antiseizure medications also effectively treat the manic or depressive side of bipolar disorder.

Table 7-2 shows the antiseizure class of medications, in which Depakote is the golden child, rivaling lithium as the most effective in treating acute mania. Tegretol (carbemazapine) has also proven effective. Lamictal (lamotrigine) is growing in popularity because of its effectiveness in preventing depression as well as reducing the frequency of cycles.

Table 7-2 Potential Benefits and Risks of Antiseizure Medications

Brand Name	Generic Name	Potential Pros	Potential Cons
Depakote	divalproex sodium	Antimanic; particularly effective in treating acute mania; safer than lithium (greater range between therapeutic and toxic levels)	Pancreas and liver problems; weight gain; sedation; nausea; possible fertility problems in females; hair loss; weak antidepressant properties

Brand Name	Generic Name	Potential Pros	Potential Cons
Lamictal	lamotrigine	Reduces cycle frequency; strong antidepressant properties; not usually associated with weight gain	Rare but dangerous skin reaction (you can usually avoid it by increasing dosage gradually); nausea and vomiting; dizziness; blurred vision; headache; may have weak anti-manic properties
Tegretol	carbemazapine	Antimanic; doesn't cause significant weight gain in most patients	Can reduce effectiveness of birth control pills; blood cell problems; liver problems; blurry vision; dizziness; nausea
Trileptal	oxcarbazepine	Possibly antimanic; similar to but safer than Tegretol (carbemazapine); studies proving mood benefits are still pending	Can reduce effectiveness of oral contraceptives; low sodium level; nausea, vomiting, and diarrhea; dizziness; sedation; clumsiness and poor coordination
Topomax	topiramate	Commonly used to help weight gain from other medicines; studies haven't supported its use in reducing cycling or symptoms of depression or mania	Weight loss (can be a benefit for some); mental dulling or slowed thinking; can reduce effectiveness of oral contraceptives
Neurontin	gabapentin	May help with anxiety symptoms (not proved by studies); not associated with weight gain; very limited side effects; studies haven't supported its use in reducing cycling or symptoms of depression or mania	Fatigue; muscle aches; blurred vision

Never stop taking any medication cold turkey, especially an antiseizure medication. Withdrawing an antiseizure medication too quickly can actually cause seizures. Always consult your doctor before you stop or decrease your medication.

Typical atypical antipsychotics

Atypical antipsychotics, sometimes referred to as *atypical neuroleptics,* are formulated to treat psychosis in schizophrenia, depression, and mania, as well as in other psychiatric illnesses. The "atypical" moniker stems from the fact that this newer breed of antipsychotics works a little differently than the older, *standard* neuroleptics, such as Thorazine and Haldol. Table 7-3 lists the most common atypical antipsychotics used to treat bipolar disorder, along with their primary benefits and potential risks.

Atypical antipsychotics have some typical side effects. Table 7-3 mentions the most prevalent and risky side effects for each medication, but as a group they share many (but not all) of the following potential side effects as well:

✔ Diabetes and problems with sugar metabolism

✔ Weight gain and increases in cholesterol and other fats

✔ Movement problems like Parkinson's disease (tremors and stiffness)

✔ Irreversible uncontrolled movements called *tardive dyskinesia* (facial twitches or uncontrolled movements of the tongue, lips, arms, or other body parts)

✔ *Akathisia,* a feeling of extreme restlessness commonly described as the overwhelming desire to "jump out of your skin"

✔ Changes in cardiac rhythms

✔ Increases in the levels of the hormone prolactin — sometimes causing breast enlargement in men and lactation or menstrual problems in women

Table 7-3	Risks and Rewards of Atypical Antipsychotics		
Brand Name	**Generic Name**	**Potential Pros**	**Potential Cons**
Zyprexa	olanzapine	Antimanic (FDA labeled); may reduce cycling; antipsychotic	Weight gain

Brand Name	Generic Name	Potential Pros	Potential Cons
Risperdal	risperidone	Antimanic; may reduce cycling; antipsychotic	Weight gain; increased prolactin levels
Seroquel	quetiapene	Antimanic; may reduce cycling; antipsychotic	Sedation; heart rhythm changes; possible cataract risk
Geodon	ziprasidone	Antimanic; may reduce cycling; antipsychotic	Heart rhythm changes; sedation
Abilify	aripiprazole	Antimanic; may reduce cycling	Akathisia (severe restlessness); insomnia or sedation
Clozaril	clozapine	Antimanic; may reduce cycling; antipsychotic	Weight gain; *agranulocytosis* (a serious blood disease); elevated cholesterol; possible increased risk of diabetes

Mood-boosting antidepressants

Although mania grabs all the headlines, recurrent and severe depressive episodes can be significantly more devastating and potentially dangerous. Depressive periods are when bipolar sufferers most often seek treatment, which often makes antidepressants the first medication prescribed.

Unfortunately, in bipolar sufferers, an antidepressant taken without the protection of a mood stabilizer can induce mania and worsen the course of the illness. Because of this, if you (or your doctor) have any suspicions that you have bipolar depression, strongly consider taking a mood stabilizer first (preferably one that controls depression as well as mania, such as lithium or Lamictal). If the mood stabilizer controls the depression, you're in luck. If not, you can add an antidepressant with less concern about inducing mania.

The following sections discuss the various types of antidepressants and the specific drugs that fall within these groups.

In addition to their antidepressant qualities, many of these medicines are effective in treating anxiety, which commonly accompanies both mania and depression.

SSRIs

SSRIs are Selective Serotonin Reuptake Inhibitors. Serotonin is a brain chemical that helps regulate mood, anxiety, sleep/wake cycles, sexual behaviors, and many other brain functions. SSRIs increase the level of serotonin in the *synapses* in the brain — the spaces between brain cells *(neurons)* — reducing symptoms of depression and anxiety in many people. Table 7-4 lists the most common SSRIs on the market, as well as their potential pros and cons.

Table 7-4	The Potential Benefits and Risks of SSRIs		
Brand Name	*Generic Name*	*Potential Benefits*	*Potential Risks*
Prozac	fluoxetine	Antidepressant; antianxiety	Insomnia; sedation; agitation or mania; suicidal ideation; change in sexual function; nausea or diarrhea; weight gain
Zoloft	sertraline		
Paxil	paroxetine		
Celexa	citalopram		
Lexapro	escitalopram		
Luvox	fluvoxamine		

SSNRIs

SSNRIs are Selective Serotonin and Norepinephrine Reuptake Inhibitors. They work by increasing the levels of two brain chemicals — serotonin and norepinephrine — in the synapses between brain cells. Like serotonin (described in the previous section), norepinephrine is important in regulating mood and anxiety, along with alertness and concentration. Check out Table 7-5 for a list of the most common SSNRIs available, along with the potential side effects, both good and bad, for these medications.

Table 7-5	The Potential Benefits and Risks of SSNRIs		
Brand Name	*Generic Name*	*Potential Benefits*	*Potential Risks*
Effexor	venlafaxine	Antidepressant; antianxiety; Cymbalta treats some pain syndromes associated with depression	Insomnia; sedation; elevated blood pressure; change in sexual function; nausea or diarrhea; weight gain
Cymbalta	duloxetine		

Wellbutrin (bupropion)

Also marketed as Zyban, the antidepressant Wellbutrin appears to work by increasing the levels of dopamine and norepinephrine in the brain synapses. It has a completely different mechanism of action from antidepressants in other classes, such as SSRIs, SSNRIs, and tricyclics; therefore, it belongs in its own category. Other uses include treating nicotine addiction (as with Zyban) and possibly treating ADHD. Table 7-6 lists the potential pros and cons for this popular drug.

Table 7-6	The Potential Benefits and Risks of Wellbutrin
Potential Benefits	*Potential Risks*
Antidepressant	Jitteriness, insomnia, anxiety
Reduces cravings for nicotine; no sexual side effects	Decreased appetite, weight loss
May be less likely to trigger a manic episode than other antidepressants	Seizure

Tricyclics and MAO inhibitors

Tricyclics and MAO (monoamine oxidase) inhibitors are older classes of drugs that work differently from the antidepressants we list previously and differently from one another. Tricyclics (so called due to a three-ring chemical structure) affect norepinephrine and serotonin levels primarily, but they also touch a number of other brain chemicals, such as histamine. These "extra" chemical events cause many of the side effects of tricyclics. MAO inhibitors work by preventing the action of an enzyme that breaks down norepinephrine, serotonin, and dopamine, along with a number of related brain chemicals, resulting in an increase in the levels of these chemicals in the brain. See Table 7-7 for a comparison of potential risks and benefits.

Table 7-7	The Potential Benefits and Risks of Tricyclics and MAO Inhibitors
Potential Benefits	*Potential Risks*
Antidepressant	Heart rhythm changes
Antianxiety	Increased pulse and blood pressure
	MAO inhibitors require dietary restrictions and have many risky medication interactions
	Dry mouth, constipation, and dizziness

Safely weaning yourself from antidepressants

Doctors used to prescribe antidepressants to treat acute depression and then recommended that you stop taking the antidepressant six months or so after you fully recovered. Some doctors now prefer a much longer-term use of antidepressants because of the devastating toll of depression and its tendency to recur. In any case, if your doctor recommends that you stop taking your antidepressant, do it gradually. Newer studies show that withdrawing the antidepressant, especially if you stop cold turkey, can result in a high risk of relapse. Before you stop taking an antidepressant, consult your doctor. Follow these steps to gradually wean yourself from the medication:

1. **Seek professional assistance during the process.**

2. **Inform your support network of what you plan to do (see Chapter 6).**

3. **Obtain therapy for any ongoing depression triggers.**

4. **Reduce your intake of the medication by no more than 10 percent each week over the course of 10 weeks.**

Be aware that some SSRIs and SSNRIs have a notorious reputation for producing extreme withdrawal symptoms. Stopping cold turkey makes you feel quite ill, almost like having the flu. Don't stop any medication without speaking to your doctor first.

Calming tranquilizers and sleep agents

Sometimes you can get so revved up with your moods and the medications you take to stabilize them that you can't think straight or even fall asleep at a decent hour. To help, your psychiatrist may prescribe one or more antianxiety medications (tranquilizers) or sleep aids, which we discuss in this section.

Antianxiety medications

Antianxiety meds (also known as *tranquilizers*) are central nervous system depressants — they slow down the whole nervous system. This reduces agitation and anxiety levels, both of which can be problems in bipolar disorder. They appear to work at the level of a brain chemical called GABA (gamma-aminobutyric acid), which has a calming effect on neurons. These medications can also be used as sleep aids when given at night. Table 7-8 lists the pros and cons of these meds.

Table 7-8	The Potential Benefits and Risks of Antianxiety Medications		
Brand Name	*Generic Name*	*Potential Benefits*	*Potential Risks*
Valium Ativan Xanax Klonopin	diazepam lorazempam alprazolam clonazepam	Antianxiety; antiseizure	Severe sedation; dependence/ addiction; lethal combination with alcohol; inability to drive or work

Sleep aids

Doctors commonly prescribe sleep aids for the short-term treatment of insomnia, which is often associated with depression and mania. You don't usually use them with the tranquilizers we list above, because they're actually closely related. Table 7-9 lists the pros and cons of sleep aids.

Table 7-9	The Potential Benefits and Risks of Sleep Aids		
Brand Name	*Generic Name*	*Potential Benefits*	*Potential Risks*
Ambien Restoril Sonata	zolpidem temazepam zaleplon	Improved ability to sleep	Dependence

Chapter 8

Retooling Your Mind through Therapy

In This Chapter

▶ Training your mind to think positively

▶ Gaining insight into symptoms and solutions

▶ Tuning in to your circadian rhythms

▶ Allowing your family on board

*T*he right medicines can alleviate bipolar disorder's most serious symptoms, but even during periods when you're symptom free, your functionality — your ability to work, maintain relationships, and enjoy yourself — may be impaired. Lost dreams, broken relationships, a ruined career, and the sullen looks of loved ones can weigh heavy on your emotions. Over time, the pressure can begin to fracture the protective shell of medication, and the vicious cycle begins anew.

Effectively treating bipolar disorder requires not only medication to balance the biological components, but also therapy to repair the psychological aspects (your thoughts and emotions), stressful environmental conditions (relationships, career, finances, and so on), and behaviors (words and actions that can cause more problems). By attending to all the contributing factors, you can work toward slowing and eventually stopping the whirling vortex.

In Chapter 7, we explore commonly used medications for treating the biology of bipolar disorder. In this chapter, we turn the focus to psychology, problem solving, and relationships. We cover the most successful therapies for addressing psychological disturbances. We reveal how relationship and family therapy can remove many of the most tenacious stressors. And finally, we explain ways to hone your problem-solving skills and reduce stress.

Fixing Me: Individual Therapy

The flight attendant on a plane always instructs you before the plane takes off to put on your oxygen mask before worrying about the person sitting next to you. If you pass out, you can't do much to help others. The same is generally true in therapy: Make yourself feel better and then tackle other issues.

Several individual therapies are available and have shown some degree of success in treating bipolar symptoms and improving the course of the illness:

- ✔ **Psychoeducation** helps you develop an objective view of your symptoms and the need for treatment.
- ✔ **Cognitive behavioral therapy** trains your brain to stop negative thought patterns and establish positive patterns.
- ✔ **Interpersonal and social rhythm therapy** resets and maintains healthy circadian rhythms and improves relationships with others.

This section explores each of these therapies and provides exercises and resources that you can use right now to sample each approach.

Psychotherapy is most effective when your brain is capable and receptive to what therapy has to offer. Try to plan your therapy for times when your moods are relatively stable. If you're currently experiencing a major mood episode, seek medical treatment first.

Gaining insight through psychoeducation

Although the diagnosis of any chronic illness is a tough pill to swallow, accepting the bipolar diagnosis is like trying to swallow an egg. You have no blood test to show your friends and family, you have no X-rays, and you rarely even have a brain scan that suggests you have a bona-fide illness. The only symptoms you have are depression, hyperactivity, irritability, and anger — symptoms that every human being experiences at some time to some degree. You may wonder, "If my moods and emotions are the result of the illness, who am I?" and "If I successfully eliminate the symptoms, who will I become?"

Throughout the course of your illness, your ability to accept the fact that you have bipolar disorder may wax and wane. Your ability to objectively observe and evaluate your moods and behaviors may improve or worsen. Your desire to seek treatment may also rise and fall.

Psychoeducation can improve your treatment outcome by educating you about bipolar disorder and making you more aware of symptoms and early warning signs so you can more effectively maintain mood stability. Through psychoeducation, you take the following positive steps:

✔ Gain a clearer understanding of bipolar disorder (its causes and treatments)

✔ Understand why medication is necessary

✔ Find out how therapy can help

✔ Improve your ability to recognize symptoms

✔ Become more vigilant of early warning signs

✔ Gain insight into the stressors and triggers that cause your mood shifts

✔ Obtain confidence that proper treatment can improve your condition

✔ Strengthen your resolve to adhere to the recommended treatment plan

You can receive psychoeducation therapy from a variety of sources, including the following:

✔ Books

✔ Audio recordings

✔ Video recordings

✔ Media broadcasts (news, talk shows, and movies about bipolar disorder)

✔ Doctors, psychiatrists, and therapists

✔ Support groups

✔ Group therapy

✔ Internet sites that provide accurate information (some don't)

During depressive episodes, insight that something is wrong typically rises; you're hypersensitive to the fact that you feel miserable, although insight about the possibility of improvement declines. During hypomanic and manic episodes, lack of insight becomes a bigger problem, because increased energy and self-confidence can conceal the symptoms and convince you that you don't need treatment. One of psychoeducation's prime goals for bipolar disorder is to improve insight as your mood becomes elevated.

Restructuring thoughts and behaviors through cognitive behavioral therapy

According to Socrates, "The unexamined life is not worth living." Well, the overexamined life is no picnic, either. When your brain browbeats your self-esteem, latches onto self-defeating beliefs, or persuades you that the future is bleak, you need to hit the emergency OFF button to get your brain back on the right track.

The trick is in knowing how to find and use the OFF button, because thoughts are often symptoms of the illness and are created by chemical changes. To develop new thought and behavior patterns, you need to train your brain, not just "change your mind." *Cognitive behavioral therapy* (CBT) helps you do just that by training you to do the following:

1. **Identify distorted thoughts and beliefs.**
2. **Quiet your brain, and settle down distorted thoughts and beliefs.**
3. **Develop and practice rational beliefs and logical thought processes.**
4. **Develop and practice positive and effective behaviors based on the new thoughts and beliefs.**

Psychotherapists have used CBT for years to successfully treat both unipolar and bipolar depression. Because antidepressants commonly aggravate mania, CBT serves as an important tool in helping to alleviate depression without the potentially undesirable side effects of medication. Brain scans have shown that CBT actually changes the chemical processes in the brain in patients with unipolar depression — an effect similar to medication. CBT is powerful stuff.

CBT can also help with the manic pole, toning down overly positive, optimistic beliefs to bring them more in line with reality. During mania, for example, you may begin to believe that you can easily make a million in the stock market and completely lose sight of potential risks, such as losing your home.

Treating mania is a more daunting task than treating depression, because in mania, you don't see the problem, and for CBT to work, you have to identify a problem in order to work on it. But you may be able, through CBT, to cool down your brain and take a more rational approach with the following steps:

1. **Identify your overly optimistic thoughts and perceptions.**
2. **Quiet your brain, and slow down your thinking.**
3. **Consider the potential consequences and more realistic possibilities.**
4. **Develop and practice techniques for controlling your impulses and choosing safer alternatives.**

In sports, you practice your skills well before the big game so that they become second nature under pressure. For similar reasons, do your CBT work when your mind is quiet and life is settled — not during a full-blown mood episode — because the brain has a tough time learning anything new when it's out of control. With these new skills firmly in place, when the dust hits the fan, your brain will be poised to keep itself clear and focused. The time and effort you invest in practice now pay huge dividends during the hard times.

Identifying distorted thoughts and thinking

Distorted thoughts commonly cloud perception and spark an irrational internal dialogue that can spiral your mood down into depression or up into mania. Thinking that any endeavor will lead to failure, for example, can produce a self-defeating domino effect that results in hopelessness and despair. On the flip side, thinking that any endeavor will lead to success, no matter what, can inspire reckless abandon.

Through cognitive therapy, you can identify the distorted thoughts and thought patterns that permeate your thinking. Table 8-1 lists the most common distortions, along with examples of how each type can generate depressive or manic thoughts.

Table 8-1	Common Distorted Thoughts and Thought Processes	
Distortion	*In Depression*	*In Mania*
Overgeneralizing	"I'm no good at investing — I lost a pile of money on Enron."	"I won a thousand dollars in Vegas. I can't lose!"
Mind reading	"He thinks I'm stupid, so why should I bother expressing myself?"	"She thinks I'm a genius, so I'll just keep dazzling her with my wit and charm!"
Fortune telling	"I'll never get the job, so why bother submitting a résumé?"	"I can get any job I want and make double what you're paying me. I quit!"
Labeling	"I'm unattractive."	"I'm adorable."
All-or-nothing thinking (also called black-and- white thinking)	"The game of life is rigged; the rich get richer, and the poor get poorer."	"Life is my oyster. Nothing can possibly get between me and what I want."
Filtering	"Sure, I'm debt free, but what do I have to show for it?"	"Yeah, I'm unemployed and have $100,000 in credit-card debt, but the sports car and speedboat are a blast!"
Exaggerating/ minimizing	"We can't agree on finances, child-rearing, or even where to live. This marriage is over."	"Big deal — I had an affair with your best friend. It really didn't mean anything."

(continued)

Table 8-1 *(continued)*

Distortion	In Depression	In Mania
Emotional reasoning	"I feel stupid, so I must be an idiot."	"I feel like I'm plugged in to a higher power, so I know more about what you need than you do."
Entitlement/ disentitlement	"Nobody owes me anything. I don't deserve to be happy."	"I have a right to anything and everything I want. Why should I be denied?"
Should-ing	"I have no right to feel this way. I should feel happy."	"People should accept me for who I am, no matter how I behave."
Blaming (self or others)	"Everything is my fault."	"It's not my fault we're bankrupt; the credit companies charge too much interest."

Maladaptive thoughts and thought patterns become so ingrained that you may not even notice them at work. A cognitive therapist can lead you through a series of exercises that help you identify the way you perceive, evaluate, and respond to actual events and conflicts in your life.

Evaluating how you view yourself

Distorted thinking not only rattles your moods and emotions, but also reinforces your *personal schema* — your long-held, overarching beliefs that lead to negative thought patterns in situations of stress and your total view of your world and your future.

Personal schemas often become more active during mood shifts. Strong moods distort your sense of self, and that in turn influences thinking and further mangles perception, emotion, and logic. Faulty personal schemas cause distorted thinking, and in turn the distorted thoughts reinforce the faulty personal schemas that they generate. If you go to a party feeling as though nobody loves you, and then you start wondering if everyone there thinks you're a loser, the distorted thought reinforces your personal schema that nobody loves you. Furthermore, your personal schema has a direct effect on how other people respond to you, which in turn reinforces your irrational beliefs about yourself.

Through cognitive behavioral therapy, you can break the negative cycle and begin to build a personal schema that's more in line with who you really are.

This creates behavior patterns that are more likely to get you what you need and want and that encourage more positive responses from the world around you.

Restructuring your behavior

Thought precipitates action or inaction. If you don't think you can ever have a fulfilling relationship, you may not have the motivation to try. If you believe you're entitled to have everything you want, despite the cost, you may not hesitate to act, no matter how high the risk. The ultimate goal of CBT is to change your behavioral responses from self-defeating and negative to productive and realistic. This change creates positive experiences that support positive moods.

Cognitive behavioral therapy goes beyond thought to behavior, or action. In the case of debilitating depression, CBT attempts to identify the restrictive thought, question its validity, reveal other possibilities, and encourage you to take action. Table 8-2 provides some examples of how CBT can work to short-circuit depressive behaviors.

Table 8-2	Cognitive Behavioral Therapy Working in Depression		
Distorted Thought	**Negative Action or Inaction**	**Rational Thought**	**Positive Behavior**
"Nobody will hire me."	Won't look for job	"Maybe my friends can help."	Call friends and relatives for possible job leads
"All antimanic medications have terrible side effects."	Avoid medication	"Low doses of lithium seem relatively safe."	Try lithium for one month
"I'm unattractive."	Don't go to party	"I usually have fun at parties."	Go to the party for one hour
"Nobody cares about me."	Won't call friends or family members	"Bill asked how I was doing the other day."	Call Bill

In the case of unchecked mania, cognitive behavioral therapy attempts to identify the grandiose thought, question its validity, introduce potential risks, and encourage safer options. Table 8-3 provides some examples of how CBT can work to sidestep maladaptive behaviors in mania.

Table 8-3	Cognitive Behavioral Therapy Working in Mania		
Distorted Thought	**Negative Action or Inaction**	**Rational Thought**	**Positive Behavior**
"I can't lose."	Gamble everything	"If I lose, I can't pay the bills."	Take only a small amount of money to gamble
"I'm irresistible."	Go to party and flirt with everyone	"I may not be able to control myself."	Party with a friend who can rein me in
"I know what's best for everyone."	Tell everyone what to do	"People may get offended when I offer advice."	Withhold advice unless friends ask for it
"School is a waste of time and money."	Quit school	"If I quit school, I won't get my diploma."	Go to school part time or just long enough to get the diploma

Changing your mindfulness

Quieting irrational thoughts, inserting more logical ones, and developing and acting on new behavioral plans demands more than just recognizing the patterns. Recognition and insight are critical first steps, and you can't go on without them, but the wrinkles of old mental habits rarely fade because of insight alone. Knowing that eating too much makes you gain weight rarely keeps a person on a diet. To change behavior, you must fundamentally change emotions and impulses.

The key technique to invoke these changes involves reducing anxiety. The brain and body resist change. Change is uncomfortable. To help your brain and body tolerate changes to your thoughts and behaviors, you need to practice techniques that calm your brain to keep it from bolting back to the old, comfortable patterns.

CBT includes many forms of anxiety reduction, including breathing exercises, meditation, and progressive relaxation techniques. The common feature of these techniques is *mindfulness* — the process of focusing your brain on the moment and experiencing only the moment. Mindfulness clears your brain, calms your nerves, and allows you to discover new ways of responding emotionally and behaviorally. A subtype of CBT called *dialectical behavioral therapy* (DBT), developed by Marsha Linehan, uses mindfulness as a core technique for quieting overpowering emotions and reengaging the logical part of your brain.

Be sure to include some form of anxiety reduction and mindfulness training in your CBT work. Possibilities include

- ✔ Breathing exercises
- ✔ Visualization techniques
- ✔ Progressive muscle relaxation procedures
- ✔ Yoga
- ✔ Meditation (most any kind)
- ✔ Mindfulness exercises (available in DBT skills training groups or through your therapist or other groups)

A quick mindfulness exercise involves doing an inventory of your five senses. While you perform a chore, such as folding laundry or pulling weeds, bring your mind to what you're experiencing in the world at that moment. What do you see? Smell? Hear? Touch? Taste? You may be surprised at what you hadn't noticed around you, and in the meantime, you've focused your brain and gotten out of your head and its list of worries, demands, and judgments. Take a deep breath, and move forward with some new mental energy.

Practicing cognitive behavioral therapy: An exercise

After you understand the principles of CBT, you can begin to use various techniques to identify distortions and disable them. The following steps lead you through a brief exercise that takes you from avoidance to action:

1. **Describe a positive activity that you refuse or strongly resist doing because of how you feel or feel about doing it.**

   For example, confronting a friend about an issue that needs to be resolved.

2. **Jot down any and all thoughts that may be holding you back, such as the following:**

   - "So-and-so always yells at me when I confront her."
   - "I get nervous about confronting people."
   - "Confronting so-and-so never solves anything."

3. **For each negative thought, jot down anything that challenges or refutes that belief.**

   For example, if you think, "Confronting so-and-so never solves anything," you may come up with the following challenge statements:

   - "Just because confrontation hasn't solved anything in the past doesn't mean it can't solve the issue this time."
   - "So-and-so is a reasonable person who may be convinced this time."

- "By confronting other people in the past, I've been able to resolve some issues."

4. **Jot down possible benefits that may result from taking action, such as the following:**

   - "We can resolve our differences and become closer."

   - "So-and-so may respect me more for standing up for myself."

   - "After the confrontation, I can move beyond the issue one way or another."

5. **In your mind, rehearse various scenarios of how the action will play out.**

   Try to invent a scenario in which you approach the situation in a way that's comfortable for you. Use your relaxation techniques to calm the anxiety that arises when you imagine the scenario. Imagine yourself relaxing and focusing when you perform the action in real life.

6. **Write down a plan for proceeding with the action, including a date and time and what anxiety reduction techniques you can use at that time.**

7. **When the day arrives, perform the action as you planned.**

8. **Don't be frustrated or angry at yourself if it doesn't go as planned. This takes practice.**

The example exercise represents only one way of approaching a problematic thought distortion. Approaches vary, depending on the distortion and how it works in a particular instance. A qualified therapist can recommend several techniques for identifying and ridding your mind of distorted thoughts, including the following:

- **Journaling** to monitor distorted thoughts and identify how they can possibly affect your behavior

- **Envisioning** how an action or event will unfold so you can become comfortable with it

- **Challenging,** in which the therapist acts as a devil's advocate, arguing on the side of your distorted belief, and you voice challenges to refute its truth

- **Role playing** to enable you to act out an uncomfortable scenario with your therapist before you try it out in the real world

- **Experimenting** with different options that you discuss in therapy

- **Desensitizing,** in which you slowly work toward performing an action that you're uncomfortable doing (this is more of a behavior-modification tool)

- **Acting "as if,"** when you perform the role of someone acting out the new behavior, even if it doesn't feel real or genuine yet

BIPOLAR BIO

Building a balanced perspective

JoAnn was a middle-aged piano teacher, diagnosed with bipolar disorder later in life. Her depressive times spilled over into her life even between episodes, and she constantly berated herself for her many perceived failures. She avoided many activities and opportunities because she felt so incompetent. As she worked on identifying her negative thoughts, she was astounded at how often she judged and criticized herself — it seemed like every moment of every day. It didn't help that due to her illness and not receiving a diagnosis for so long, other people had reinforced her negative self-image by judging and criticizing her openly.

As a piano teacher, she often viewed things in terms of her left hand and her right hand — the two parts of any piano composition. She gradually began to think of her negative "laundry list" as weighing down her left hand, and she started to build a new laundry list of achievements and positives on her right hand to balance her thoughts. She tapped on her right hand with each positive thought, reinforcing it with a physical touch along with her visual image of the two hands. She could perform this ritual quietly, even while teaching lessons, to help her stay focused and to prevent herself from getting lost in negative thoughts. Her right-hand list included bringing music into the lives of hundreds of children, achieving a successful marriage in spite of all her difficulties, and expanding her own love of music and sound.

JoAnn's confidence improved, and she took on new challenges in her teaching — including music therapy for children with emotional difficulties. She began to view herself in a more positive light and always kept tapping her right hand.

Resetting your circadian clock through interpersonal and social rhythm therapy

The world has a rhythm to it: the tick-tock of the clock, sunrise/sunset, the phases of the moon, the ebb and flow of tides, the work week, seasonal shifts, paydays, showtimes in *TV Guide*. You subconsciously move to the rhythms around you, and as long as they remain relatively in tune with healthy routines, you do just fine. But when an event throws off your natural rhythm, your moods can shift out of their normal orbit.

Bipolar sufferers commonly find solace in a structured routine. Routine calms. It orders the chaos. It removes unpleasant surprises. It simplifies planning. And it helps you get a good night's sleep, night after night. (Sleep deprivation is a known trigger for mania.) Unfortunately, keeping a routine can be a drag, especially when you're a little manic, which is when you need your routine's calming effects most.

Marching to the beat of your zeitgebers

Your moods, emotions, and behaviors tend to follow a pattern over a 24-hour period (give or take an hour); scientists refer to this pattern as your *circadian rhythm.* To keep your rhythm relatively stable, your body looks for environmental cues, called *zeitgebers* (German for "time givers"). Back in the good old days, and even today in some rural communities, the main zeitgebers were the rising and setting of the sun. In modern, industrial societies, individuals and communities establish their own zeitgebers. Your morning wake-up call, meal times, exercise schedule, and even your daily television shows function as zeitgebers.

Because you largely control where they occur, your zeitgebers are much more prone to fluctuations than the rising and setting of the sun, and they often vary from one day to the next, making it much more difficult to establish a consistent rhythm from one day to the next. IPSRT helps you establish consistent zeitgebers and retain a daily rhythm.

Interpersonal and social rhythm therapy (IPSRT) can superimpose structured routine onto your life, providing you with a stable framework to support your life and anchor your moods. Its goal is to reduce the frequency of mood episodes by balancing the stimulation and rest cycles of your day-to-day life and resolving interpersonal problems. Therapy typically follows a four-stage process: initial, intermediate, maintenance, and termination.

Surveying the IPSRT process

Here's a breakdown of IPSRT's four-stage process:

- ✔ **Initial:** In this phase, you and your therapist develop a detailed history of your disorder, identifying significant mood episodes and their severity, and any life events, medications, or work history that may have coincided with each episode. The therapist helps you develop an interpersonal inventory, highlighting important people and the roles they play in your life, and assists you in identifying interpersonal problem areas that you need to address. During the initial phase, the therapist also provides psychoeducation about the disorder.

- ✔ **Intermediate:** In this phase, the therapist helps you identify your rhythms and create a more structured daily schedule. You also begin to address interpersonal problems that may be affecting your moods.

- ✔ **Maintenance:** Maintaining routines in the midst of discord can be quite a challenge. This phase, which can last for several years, helps you identify events and anticipate and resolve conflicts that threaten your rhythm and routines.

- ✔ **Termination:** When you no longer need your therapist's help to maintain your rhythm and routines, the therapist leads you through a termination phase, essentially weaning you from therapy.

Identifying your natural rhythm

An ideal situation would involve everyone tuning in to the rhythm of the rising and setting sun. Keeping a farmer's schedule would ensure optimum exposure to the mood-brightening sun, sufficient and regular sleep, and very little variation in schedules. But even with such a natural external rhythm, people all have their own biological tendencies and cycles. Morning people (the larks) feel most energized in the early hours and get sleepy in the early evening. Night people (the owls) just get started as the sun goes down. Balancing your rhythms with the world's demands can be tricky.

The first step in moving toward a more predictable and stabilizing schedule is to determine your current schedule and preferences. Figure 8-1 provides a daily grid you can fill out to record your activities for a representative week. For each day, log your activities from the time you wake up until the time you go to bed, including meals, work, social activities, family time, exercises, naps, and any other activities.

Structuring your daily routine

IPSRT doesn't attempt to burden you with a lockstep schedule you must adhere to. Instead, it helps you identify your most out-of-sync patterns and work toward changing your schedule so that it follows a regular pattern from one day to the next. For example, if you go to bed at 10:30 every night except Friday, when you stay out until 3 a.m., IPSRT attempts to bring your Friday bedtime more in line with your normal bedtime.

After completing a weekly schedule, examine it for the most dramatic variations in your daily schedule, and draw up a new schedule that has less variation. Don't make drastic changes that you can't possibly tolerate. Go slow. You can make additional adjustments later. Part of IPSRT calls for formulating goals and expectations for change. When your expectations are realistic, you leave less room for frustration, which itself can trigger mood problems.

Regulating your interpersonal and social rhythms

IPSRT also seeks to normalize rhythms in your relationships and social life. Studies show that relationship discord can significantly affect rhythms and daily routines, in addition to whipping your emotions into a frenzy. If you've ever had a big fight with a loved one just before bedtime, you know how the emotional stress and anger can disturb your sleep–wake cycle.

By tracking the amount of time you spend in high-intensity and low-intensity contact with family members and friends, you can often identify problem areas and begin to develop healthy relationships that keep your routines and emotions on an even keel.

My Daily Activities

Time of Day	Sunday	Monday	Tuesday	Wednesday	Thursday	Friday	Saturday
6 a.m.							
7 a.m.							
8 a.m.							
9 a.m.							
10 a.m.							
11 a.m.							
Noon							
1 p.m.							
2 p.m.							
3 p.m.							
4 p.m.							
5 p.m.							
6 p.m.							
7 p.m.							
8 p.m.							
9 p.m.							
10 p.m.							
11 p.m.							
Midnight							
1 a.m.							
2 a.m.							
3 a.m.							
4 a.m.							
5 a.m.							

Figure 8-1:
Record your daily schedule on this grid to determine your personal rhythms and needs.

If relationship issues cause a great deal of stress in your life, resolve the issues as soon as possible. Relationship counselors can help you and your loved ones develop more effective communication and problem-solving skills that can help not only with the current situation, but also with any future situations you may encounter.

Maintaining your rhythm in the midst of discord

You're finally in tune with the magical rhythms of the universe, and then you get the big one-two punch: Thanksgiving (ugh!) and Christmas (UGH!). In a matter of days, scheduling changes, crowded shopping malls, and your dysfunctional relatives trash your well-tuned circadian rhythm.

Therapists who specialize in IPSRT know that these events happen. Your kid's swim season starts, a temporary job you enjoyed ends, a close relative falls ill . . . you name it. Through therapy, you can practice techniques that help you anticipate such events and curb the effects of any unforeseen incidents. The following list provides some suggestions:

- ✔ **Plan ahead for holidays.** Don't let your family dictate the routines you follow. Someone else's rhythms may not coincide with yours.

- ✔ **Plan your weekends.** Unplanned weekends can leave you with nothing to do, which can be depressing, or leave you open to unrestrained spontaneity, which may lead to manic impulsivity.

- ✔ **Seek immediate treatment for any physical ailments.** Coughs, colds, night sweats, incontinence, and other illnesses can really foul up your sleep–wake schedule and other routines. See your doctor.

- ✔ **Resolve conflicts immediately.** Allowing conflicts and relationship issues to fester builds tension, which eventually finds some way to express itself. Seek counseling, if necessary.

- ✔ **Establish a 30-minute quiet time before bed.** No arguments and no exciting television shows or video games — in other words, nothing that may interfere with your sleep.

- ✔ **Outlaw arguments at dinnertime.** You can schedule a later meeting to deal with any issues that you need to address. This doesn't mean that you should stare silently at your plate — just avoid big blow-ups at the dinner table.

- ✔ **Provide sufficient time to get ready for work.** Keep your mornings as stress-free as possible.

- ✔ **Provide sufficient time at the end of your workday to unwind.** Having a smooth transition between work time and your time (or family time) can reduce stress.

Benefiting from IOT and RTCs

Many hospitals and mental health clinics offer intensive outpatient therapy (IOT), which typically consists of a half day or full day of therapy at the hospital or clinic. During IOT, the psychiatrist on staff typically meets with you to discuss your medication regiment. You also spend time one on one with a therapist, who may offer techniques from various therapeutic approaches, including cognitive behavioral therapy and interpersonal and social rhythm therapy. IOT often includes group therapy as well. One of IOT's main benefits is that it removes you from your daily surroundings, which can be quite stressful, and places you in an environment where you can focus on your mental well-being.

Resident programs, often referred to as resident treatment centers (RTCs), offer similar advantages, plus an alternative living arrangement. Such an arrangement is especially useful for providing long-term care for people who can't care for themselves and can't rely on family and friends for support. In addition to monitoring medications and providing psychotherapy, a resident program typically offers occupational therapy or job placement services and works closely with your employer to ensure success.

Fixing Us: Relationship and Family Therapy

Few people consider blaming the house when a tornado blows it apart, but when a person suffers a mental breakdown, people direct all their attention to fixing that person so it doesn't happen again. The patient's family dynamic, career, and finances may be swirling out of control and picking up speed, but no matter; as long as the doctors can patch up the patient, she should be able to withstand the tempest.

You may have an inherent vulnerability to bipolar disorder, but stress is often the catalyst for the reaction that produces the symptoms. Some stress may come from within, as in the case of distorted thoughts and beliefs (see the previous section "Fixing Me: Individual Therapy"), but stress can also come from dysfunctional family dynamics, relationship conflicts, your job, and other external sources. Furthermore, the disorder itself frequently triggers stressful life events and losses. People with bipolar disorder are most in need of reducing life stress, yet by definition they have more than their share because of the illness. Breaking the cycle at some point is a part of managing the illness and preventing recurrence.

In most cases, you can't reduce external sources of stress on your own — you need the cooperation and commitment of others, especially your loved ones. Through relationship and family therapy, you and your loved ones can reap the following benefits:

- ✔ **Relief:** Bipolar disorder can make everyone in the family feel as though they're walking on eggshells and wondering whose fault it is. Knowing that the disorder has caused at least some of these problems is often very comforting to family and friends.

- ✔ **Empowerment:** Knowledge not only empowers all those involved, but also reduces the fear of the unknown and alleviates anxiety about the future.

- ✔ **Improved communication skills:** You and your loved ones can team up to establish a healthy emotional ambience that benefits all involved.

- ✔ **Personal development:** Appreciating the unique gifts of a loved one and working together to overcome the challenges of bipolar disorder can deepen relationships and build character.

Repairing rocky relationships

You can run out to your local bookstore and fill a shopping cart full of books about relationship issues and ways to fix your marriage. To discover some very useful skills, check out *Relationships For Dummies,* by Dr. Kate M. Wachs, or *Making Marriage Work For Dummies,* by Dr. Steven Simring and Dr. Sue Klavans Simring. When you're in a committed relationship with someone who has bipolar disorder, you need all the expert advice in those books and then some.

In particular, you need a therapist who has experience working with bipolar disorder in committed relationships. Such therapists offer the following benefits:

- ✔ **Ability to recognize signs and symptoms:** An experienced therapist can tell when someone is overly confrontational due to mania or hypomania. During such times, therapy can be counterproductive, so the therapist may recommend that you postpone relationship therapy and seek individual treatment until your mood episode subsides.

- ✔ **Knowledge of common problems that arise in relationships due to bipolar disorder:** You want a therapist who's aware of the toll that depression and mania can have on a relationship. A therapist who knows common problems that can result from the impulsiveness of mania, for example — including unchecked spending, sexual promiscuity, and risky business ventures — can often provide suggestions for reducing the risks.

✔ **Awareness of how bipolar disorder affects family dynamics:** Bipolar disorder commonly runs in families, so other relationships outside of your relationship as a couple may affect and be affected by your relationship. A therapist who has experience with bipolar disorder can identify and help you address these peripheral problems.

✔ **Knowledge of how other couples in similar situations have successfully dealt with issues:** An experienced therapist has a deeper well from which to draw advice.

Attempting to solve relationship disputes when either or both of you are manic or depressed can make problems worse. In moments of mood instability, you're much more likely to be confrontational and defensive. Obtain individual treatment first and then work on repairing your relationship rifts.

If you and your partner experience occasional turmoil that you resolve within a few days, you're experiencing perfectly normal and even healthy relationship issues. However, if a particular issue continues to nag you or your partner or remains buried, festering a low-level chronic anger, you need to deal with it — the sooner, the better. You have two choices: Resolve the issue, or let it go. By "let it go," we don't mean bury it; make a conscious decision that it doesn't matter to either of you and will never again cause conflict.

Making bipolar disorder a family affair

A deep depression can draw the curtains on an entire household, stifling joy and affection. Mania can whip the same family into a frenzy of activity and enthusiasm, make everyone cower in fear, or transform a peaceful meal into a melee. When family members don't know what's going on, they may turn on one another in a vicious blame game that drives them further from any solution.

If bipolar disorder disrupts your family, any reaction is perfectly understandable. Everyone is geared to respond a certain way when symptoms of mania and depression generate turmoil. Sometimes your response is merely a self-defense mechanism to preserve your mental and emotional health. However, after your loved one receives a diagnosis, you can begin the process of acceptance, understanding, and recovery, and join forces as a family to prevent the disorder from ruling your lives.

Family therapy is very effective both in helping family members cope and in improving the prognosis for the person who has bipolar disorder. Therapy that includes the following components can help a family look forward to acquiring the knowledge and skills it needs to support one another:

✔ **Psychoeducation** initially focuses on assisting family members to come to terms with bipolar disorder, especially the most recent mood episode. As a family member, you reinforce that the illness is physical and that no one is to blame for its onset. Therapy fosters empathy and increases understanding of why the person with the disorder may resist treatment and intervention. You also find out what you can do to help and what to do in the event of a relapse.

✓ **Communication enhancement** assists family members in developing effective communication styles. Sessions typically involve some role-playing, in which you practice becoming a more active listener and phrasing your statements and requests in nonconfrontational language. Communication is the key to toning down the family dynamic and eliminating as many stressors as possible.

✓ **Regulating emotional intensity** helps keep emotional expressions in a healthy range. Family members tend to follow emotional patterns when expressing themselves. Loud and highly expressive styles can be entertaining and fun, but in a family with bipolar disorder, this style can be a powerful trigger for mood cycles. On the other hand, too much quiet and an inability to express appropriate feelings can yield emotional meltdowns. Chapter 16 discusses the importance of reducing the level of *expressed emotion,* a particularly harmful type of emotion.

✓ **Problem solving** encourages family members to identify problems and develop solutions instead of taking less effective measures, such as avoidance, blaming others or yourself, or trying to solve the problem entirely on your own and feeling bitter about it later.

Remaining cool when bipolar disorder turns up the heat can be quite a challenge. When experiencing a manic or mixed episode, a person may get right in your face and unleash a litany of caustic remarks and insults. Your first impulse may be to lash back at the person, but a negative reaction is like pouring kerosene on a blaze that's already out of control. Try your best to defuse the incident before it gets out of hand, and then do what you can to assist your loved one later. Chapter 16 provides additional advice and strategies.

Developing problem-solving skills

A knack for solving difficult problems reduces conflict in any family or close relationship, but problem solving is even more critical when bipolar disorder is involved. Mania and depression can team up to create insurmountable problems; mania creates the problem, depression magnifies it, and vice versa. And in addition to the normal issues people face, such as financial fiascos and time and household management, bipolar disorder introduces areas of potential disagreement:

✓ **Treatment management:** Which treatment option is best? Is the person receiving treatment adhering to the treatment plan? Are the medications working? When will things be back to normal? All these questions and more can generate anxiety and confusion, which can lead to conflict.

✔ **Work options:** When one person can't work, the burden of meeting financial needs falls on others. In addition, the decision of whether and when to return to work can cause tension.

✔ **Household responsibilities:** A serious illness always shifts household responsibilities to others in the family and shakes up the normal family dynamic. Problem-solving skills can help smooth the transitions.

Problem-solving skills focus on identifying problems that may seem insurmountable and then breaking them down into small, manageable units or steps, which you can then perform methodically. When you face such a problem, sit down as a couple or a family, and take the following steps to solve the problem:

1. **Identify the problem, and state it in one or two sentences.**

2. **Brainstorm potential solutions.**

   Don't evaluate solutions at this point; just throw everything down on a page.

3. **Pick the top solutions, based on which ones seem most realistic, most effective, and most do-able.**

4. **Brainstorm the benefits and drawbacks of each remaining solution.**

5. **Pick the best solution, or combine different ones to form an even better solution.**

6. **Draw up a plan made up of small steps.**

7. **Execute the plan to the best of your abilities.**

8. **Adjust the plan as needed to improve its effectiveness.**

When plans meet reality, reality often wins. A common mistake is to stick with a well-laid plan even when it fails to produce the desired results. If the plan fails, ditch it, cut your losses, and try something new. Don't be surprised if you need to problem solve three or four times before you discover an effective solution.

Chapter 9

Expanding Your Treatment Options

*T*he one-two punch of psychiatric medication and psychotherapy knocks out the worst symptoms of bipolar disorder for most people. But in some cases, medication proves ineffective, or it produces side effects that make the cure seem worse than the curse. In other cases, especially for pregnant women, the potential risks of medicine outweigh the benefits. The person with bipolar disorder may be so resistant to taking the required medication, for whatever reason, that doctors must consider other treatment options.

Electroconvulsive therapy (ECT) and light therapy are proven medical treatments that doctors use less frequently than medication and psychotherapy, but they have an important place in the bipolar toolbox. Herbal remedies and vitamin supplements also appeal to some patients. Anecdotal evidence and a few studies suggest that some herbs, vitamins, and other supplements may be somewhat useful, especially when used in conjunction with standard medications and therapy. Other studies show that the same treatments are completely useless or even dangerous.

Who's right? Who's wrong? How dangerous can an herb possibly be? Is St. John's wort as effective as my neighbor claims it is? Can I improve my mood in a tanning booth? Will electroconvulsive therapy grill my gray matter? This chapter sets out to answer all these questions and more.

Assessing the Risk-to-Benefit Ratio of Alternative Treatments

All treatments have a risk-to-benefit ratio that pits *potential risks* against *potential benefits.* We qualify our statements with the word "potential," because the risks and benefits vary in each case. One person may respond very favorably to lithium, but another may not respond at all. Lithium may cause weight gain and thyroid problems in one person and cause no negative side effects in another. The same is true of other treatments.

As a consumer, you work along with your doctor to evaluate the risk-to-benefit ratio for various treatment options. You and your doctor may want to consider alternative treatment options for any of the following reasons:

- **Nothing else works.** Sometimes, you have no choice; standard treatments have proved ineffective for you, so an alternative treatment is worth a try.

- **You can't tolerate the side effects of any other drugs on the menu.** If you can't handle the side effects of any of the prescription medications that your doctor recommends, an alternative treatment may help alleviate symptoms without causing dramatic side effects.

- **You want a second opinion from a different perspective.** A food allergy or nutrient deficiency that the standard battery of lab tests didn't examine may contribute to your mood swings. Approaching bipolar disorder from a different perspective may reveal other treatment options.

- **You're pregnant and concerned that prescription medication may be dangerous for the fetus.** If you become pregnant while being treated for depression or mania, your OB/GYN and psychiatrist need to discuss your treatment options together and with you. Especially in the first trimester, optional treatments may be able to alleviate symptoms with less potential risk to the fetus.

- **Your current treatment regimen isn't working well enough.** The addition of a dietary supplement may increase the effectiveness of a prescription medication.

Psychiatrists refer to any treatment or therapy intended to increase the effectiveness of your primary medications as *complementary* or *adjunctive* — fancy words for "add-on." For Bipolar I (see Chapter 2), psychotherapy is considered adjunctive treatment, but medicines or substances that increase the effectiveness of the main medications are also considered adjunctive or complementary.

Feeding Your Moods All-Natural Ingredients

Sometimes a home remedy, an herbal concoction, or a handful of dietary supplements can help lift depression and calm mania. Doctors and scientists are constantly on the lookout for the root cause of various illnesses, and occasionally they hit on something in nature that shows promise. After all, lithium is a naturally occurring element with a long history of stabilizing moods.

This section explores the pros and cons of some of the more promising "natural" treatments for depression and mania and lists some of their potential risks and side effects.

Assessing the safety of all-natural ingredients

People often think that vitamins and herbs are "worth a try." If you can get them at the store without a prescription, they must be safe, right? Well, not exactly. These so-called *nutraceuticals* carry their own potential risks and drawbacks, such as the following:

- **Unconventional treatments may cause you to forgo more effective treatments.** The most serious risk associated with trying alternative remedies is that they may keep you from obtaining the best treatments currently available. Always consult your doctor before you try an alternative treatment.

- **Unconventional treatments may not be cost effective.** If you've ever been to a holistic healer, you know that you can walk out with an armload of remedies and supplements that cost hundreds of dollars. A prescription for lithium or a generic mood medication may actually be less expensive and much more effective.

- **Insurance may not cover unconventional treatments.** If you load up your cart at the local health food store with megavitamins, nutritional supplements, and herbal remedies, your insurance company is unlikely to foot the bill.

- **Unconventional treatments can require high maintenance.** Some treatments require you to perform extensive colon-cleansing and liver-cleansing routines and then take high doses of dietary supplements and herbal mixtures. If you have trouble remembering to take your medication three times a day, unconventional treatments may pose an even more daunting challenge.

Even worse, drastic body-cleansing routines can raise the concentrations of some medications, particularly lithium, to dangerous and potentially lethal levels.

✔ **Unconventional treatments have negative side effects, too.** "Natural" substances work by changing your brain chemistry in much the same way that prescription medications do. Although some natural substances may be safer than prescription medicines, they may not be completely safe, and some can be downright dangerous.

✔ **Unconventional treatments are less strictly regulated.** The Food and Drug Administration (FDA) regulates the manufacture and distribution of prescription medications, ensuring that they meet quality standards. The FDA is less involved in regulating dietary supplements and herbs, so in many cases, you may not really know what you're taking.

✔ **Your doctor may not be well versed in unconventional treatments.** Most physicians and psychiatrists invest their time and research treating their patients with the most effective and harmless medications recommended by the medical establishment. They often have little expertise with less mainstream approaches.

Don't assume that your doctor is ignorant or averse to trying alternative treatments. Most doctors know something about them, are quite willing to discuss them with you, and can help guide you in making an informed and safe decision.

Fishing for a cure with omega-3 fatty acids

You may think that people subjected to a life of gnawing on whale blubber would be a little glum, but evidence proves otherwise. Studies have shown that in countries such as Finland and Iceland, where fish is a huge part of the national diet, the rates of depression are lower than in the United States and other parts of Europe. This fact led scientists to hypothesize that something in the diet makes the brain less susceptible to depression. What they discovered were omega-3 fatty acids — essential fatty acids (EFAs) found in fish and other foods — that show promise in preventing heart disease and in treating depression and autoimmune diseases.

One relatively limited study has shown that high levels of omega-3 (2 to 7 grams daily) can help prevent recurrence of mania and depression. Larger, more recent studies report that omega-3 doesn't reduce mania or mood cycling, but that in some cases, high doses of omega-3 fatty acids can improve the effectiveness of antidepressants.

Omega-3 is no replacement for your mood stabilizer or antidepressant, especially if you're treating extreme mood episodes, so don't flush your meds just yet. However, if you like anchovies, ordering them on your next pizza can't hurt, and in the long run, some extra omega-3 in your diet may help.

You can obtain omega-3 fatty acids from any of the following sources:

- ✔ Cold-water fish (including salmon, mackerel, herring, tuna, anchovies, and sardines)
- ✔ Wild animals (including deer, buffalo, and free-range chickens)
- ✔ Omega-3 enhanced eggs
- ✔ Dark green leafy vegetables (such as purslane)
- ✔ Flaxseed oil
- ✔ Walnuts
- ✔ Omega-3 supplements

Don't start eating three servings of fish a day so you can be health-smart. Some farm-raised fish are very low in omega-3, and wild fish can have high levels of mercury, which is hazardous to your health. Manufacturers typically filter out the mercury when processing their omega-3 supplements so you can obtain high levels of the essential fatty acids with fewer potential risks.

Unless you literally chew the fat with Eskimos, getting 2 or more grams of EFAs daily through your diet is tough, so you probably need to take supplements. Unfortunately, the FDA doesn't control omega-3 supplements, so check the label to make sure the supplement meets the following requirements:

- ✔ **Highly concentrated in omega-3.** Obviously, if you have a choice between a supplement with 30 percent omega-3 or 70 percent, pick the one with 70 percent.
- ✔ **High purity rating.** The label may not contain this information, but look for a product that's known to be pure. Filtering out mercury and other contaminants is important, both in terms of safety and effectiveness.
- ✔ **Less fishy aftertaste.** You may not want to keep popping omega-3 tablets if they make your tongue taste like a rancid sardine.

Many omega-3 supplements are derived from fish and can leave an unpleasant aftertaste, which many people find . . . well, distasteful. Buy small quantities of various brands to try before you purchase any in bulk. For more information about omega-3, including a selection of recipes, check out *The Omega-3 Connection* (Free Press), by Andrew L. Stoll, MD.

Pumping up your brain with vitamins and minerals

Insufficient amounts of vitamin C can cause scurvy. Too little iron can result in fatigue. A vitamin D deficiency can weaken your teeth and bones. Obviously, vitamins and minerals can have a significant impact on your overall health, but when the brain starts to malfunction, few people look to vitamins and minerals for answers.

In some ways, overlooking vitamins and minerals is understandable, especially in Western countries, where food is plentiful and enriched. In these countries, true vitamin and mineral deficiencies are rare, but low levels of these nutrients, even when the levels are not low enough to qualify as a deficiency, may be related to some depressive symptoms. Although we wouldn't suggest that any vitamin or combination of vitamins is effective for treating depression or mania, several vitamins and minerals can have a significant effect on brain development and function, including the following:

- ✔ **B complex:** B-complex vitamins consist of B1 (thiamine), B2 (riboflavin), B3 (niacin), B5 (pantothenic acid), B6 (pyridoxine), B7 (biotin), B12 (cobalamin), and folic acid (folate or folacin). Your body uses the B-complex vitamins to build cells, especially nerve cells. Taking them together in the appropriate relative concentrations is important, because too much of one can cause a deficiency of another.

- ✔ **B1 (thiamine):** Thiamine deficiencies have been known to cause fatigue, irritability, anxiety, insomnia, and loss of appetite. People who drink a lot of alcohol are susceptible to this deficiency. Your doctor may recommend additional thiamine on top of a B-complex supplement.

- ✔ **B6:** True B6 deficiency is rare, but older people, alcoholics, women taking birth control pills, people with poor diets, or children on the asthma medication theophylline are at risk of low B6 levels. B6 can be dangerous in high doses, especially when taken alone (as opposed to taking it as part of a B-complex supplement), so don't increase your intake of B6 beyond a traditional supplement unless prescribed by a physician.

- ✔ **B12:** A B12 deficiency is also rare, but strict vegetarians, older adults, people with certain stomach and intestinal illnesses, and people on certain medications, including those used to treat acid reflux and peptic ulcers, are at risk. The diabetes medication metformin (Glucophage) can also reduce B12 levels.

- ✔ **C:** Researchers continue to explore the link between vitamin C and a number of illnesses, including the common cold, heart disease, and cancer. How vitamin C relates to mood disorders is unknown, but some researchers suspect that it may play a contributing role.

✔ **E:** Some healers have touted vitamin E as a cure for everything from heart disease and cancer to depression, but large recent studies call these connections into question. True deficiencies are rare, and vitamin E may actually cause medical problems at high doses, so always consult your doctor.

✔ **Folic acid:** Folic acid is critical in the development of the human nervous system, so pregnant women must take folic acid supplements. People who abuse alcohol and people with certain illnesses who must take particular medications are at risk for folate deficiencies. Some research has connected low folate levels to depression, so checking levels and supplementing with folic acid may be part of treatment for depression, particularly in people in these high-risk categories.

✔ **Magnesium:** A magnesium deficiency is rare, but high-risk groups include older adults, people who abuse alcohol, diabetics, and people with a number of other medical conditions that require a variety of medications. Low body stores of magnesium may be related to a number of health problems, including mood regulation.

✔ **Calcium:** Like magnesium, calcium is a mineral that plays an important role in the formation of strong bones and teeth and in regulating the circulatory and nervous systems. Calcium is often combined with magnesium in supplements to improve the absorption of magnesium. Supplementation is often necessary for women, vegetarians, and people with lactose insufficiency.

✔ **Zinc:** Some clinical studies suggest that low levels of zinc may contribute to depression, but a well-balanced diet typically provides enough zinc. People who abuse alcohol and patients with chronic stomach problems that include diarrhea are at risk of zinc deficiency.

Your body can usually dispose of excess water-soluble vitamins, including vitamin C. Fat-soluble vitamins, including E and K, however, can build up in your system to toxic levels. Always consult your doctor before taking supplements, including vitamins and minerals.

Going herbal with St. John's wort and other supplements

Wouldn't it be great if you could cure bipolar disorder with something growing wild in your backyard? Maybe you could brew a batch of dandelion tea or eat a bowl of berries from that bush you're constantly trimming back. Nature provides a host of effective cures and treatments for common ailments, but does it serve up anything for bipolar disorder? Some people believe so, and they point to the following herbs and supplements as examples that support the claim:

- **St. John's wort:** Some limited studies, mostly performed in Germany, suggest that St. John's wort (a medicinal herb) is effective in treating mild to moderate unipolar depression. A relatively recent, extensive study performed in the United States, however, suggests that St. John's wort is about as effective in treating major depression as a lemon drop. Some doctors continue to recommend it, and some people with depression continue to sing its praises. Be careful, though; like most antidepressants, St. John's wort carries the risk of inducing mania. It can also interact with a number of drugs, so, as always, consult your doctor first.

- **Ginkgo biloba:** Some sound research supports the use of gingko biloba (a medicinal herb) in the treatment of dementia, including Alzheimer's disease. Its use in mood disorders isn't well established, but its effectiveness is being explored. At high doses, it can thin the blood too much and cause bleeding, so consult your doctor.

- **Black cohosh:** Marketed primarily to help women with night sweats and hot flashes, black cohosh (a medicinal herb) hasn't yet proven its effectiveness in formal research studies. Some studies have shown that black cohosh is downright dangerous, sometimes triggering an autoimmune response in the body that attacks the liver. Don't take this without first consulting your doctor about the potential risks.

- **SAMe:** Short for S-Adenosylmethionine, SAMe (a natural substance found in your body) has been proved to function effectively as an antidepressant in some studies. However, SAMe can induce mania at rates similar to the SSRI antidepressants (see Chapter 7), making it extremely risky for treating bipolar depression. Don't even think about using SAMe before trying all other standard treatment options and consulting your doctor. Another drawback — it isn't cheap.

- **GABA:** GABA (gamma-aminobutyric acid, an inhibitory of the nervous system neurotransmitter) has been touted as a treatment for mood disorders because it's related to depression, anxiety, and mania in the brain. However, GABA taken as an oral supplement doesn't cross the blood–brain barrier. It doesn't even get into the brain and is therefore useless. This particular "natural" cure is a fraud.

- **Taurine:** An amino acid, taurine helps regulate the electrical activity in the brain and may counteract the effects of excitatory neurotransmitters, including dopamine and norepinephrine. Some studies show that taurine levels are depleted in the brains of people with bipolar disorder, but no studies currently show that taking supplements will improve depression.

✔ **Melatonin:** Melatonin is a hormone that the brain uses in response to light and dark and is part of the body's sleep/wake machinery. Supplements may reduce insomnia for sufferers of some types of sleep problems. It's safe for short-term use, even in children. Check with your doctor before you use melatonin, however, because it can interact with some psychiatric medications.

✔ **5-HTP:** This supplement provides your body with the building blocks it needs to assemble serotonin, but no evidence proves that taking supplements of 5-HTP improves mood.

✔ **Valerian:** Valerian is an herb commonly marketed for the treatment of insomnia. Although studies are currently deemed inconclusive, some have reported positive results. Valerian appears to be relatively safe, but be cautious, especially if you're taking other medications or are pregnant or nursing.

✔ **Kava:** This plant/herbal product purportedly reduces stress and anxiety, but some reports have linked it to liver damage, so practice extreme caution.

Before ingesting natural substances, check with your doctor, and do additional research on your own. A reliable information source is the National Institute of Health's National Center for Complementary and Alternative Medicine (NCCAM). Check out its Web site at www.nccam.nih.gov.

Bathing Your Brain with Electricity, Magnetic Stimulation, and Light

Past practices in psychiatry instill a fear in some mentally ill patients. If they hear of any treatments designed to physically alter the structure or electrical activity of the brain, they may panic. "Lobotomy? Electroshock? No way! Nobody's scrambling my brain!"

Fortunately, lobotomies are no longer commonplace, and electroshock therapy isn't as shocking as it once was. In fact, many people with bipolar disorder have found that of all the treatment options currently available, electroshock (electroconvulsive) therapy is the safest and most effective option.

However, you should always approach any treatment with a healthy dose of skepticism and understand its potential risks and benefits. In the spirit of keeping you informed, the following sections describe three additional treatment options: electroconvulsive therapy, repetitive transcranial magnetic stimulation, and light therapy.

Zapping your moods with ECT (electroconvulsive therapy)

In the past, *electroconvulsive therapy* (ECT) was extremely traumatic, at least in the movies. A burly orderly would strap the patient to a gurney, shove a block of wood in his mouth, and stick a couple of electrodes to his temples. A devious doctor would saunter in, donning a virgin-white lab coat, and toggle the on/off switch, jolting the patient's brain with wave after wave of high-voltage current. Needless to say, it wasn't something that many people looked forward to.

Modern techniques have significantly reduced the trauma and the drama of ECT. Nowadays, the doctor uses sedatives to keep you sleeping through the procedure and muscle relaxants to loosen you up so you don't hurt yourself. The doctor applies a low-voltage current for only one or two seconds. The current triggers a seizure, although your body doesn't physically seizure because of the muscle relaxants. The repeated seizure activity, usually three times a week for about 12 weeks, is responsible for relieving mood symptoms. About 80 percent of patients experience significant relief from symptoms of both depression and mania and report relatively mild side effects, such as temporary memory loss and blood pressure changes. ECT is used commonly in elderly and frail individuals who can't tolerate antidepressants and antimanic medications. In these people, ECT has proven very effective.

Why would anyone consider ECT? The primary reasons include the following:

✔ Nothing else works for you.

✔ Your depression or mania is severe and requires fast relief of acute symptoms.

✔ You can't take antidepressants or antimanics, for some reason.

✔ You don't want to take medicine.

✔ You're pregnant, nursing, or plan to become pregnant, and you're concerned about the effects of various medicines on the fetus.

ECT's main side effect is memory loss, which is usually temporary. Other potential risks include reactions to the anesthetic or muscle relaxant and possible changes to heart rhythm and blood pressure. Your doctor will evaluate your health before treatment and monitor it during treatment for any signs of distress.

Researchers are experimenting with another electromagnetic treatment, called VNS (Vagus Nerve Stimulation), that has been used successfully to reduce epileptic seizures. An electronic implant that functions as a pacemaker for the brain sends electrical signals to a specific brain region through the vagus nerve for a few seconds each minute. Although VNS stimulation may be effective in treating depression, records show at least one reported case of hypomania occurring during this treatment.

Bringing Max back through ECT

Max was an 82-year-old gentleman with a long history of bipolar disorder. He had been on lithium for many years, but he could no longer take it due to his many other medical complications. He was a successful businessman and a widower with five children and numerous grandchildren. Max came to the psychiatric hospital with his oldest son after several weeks of declining mood and function. He had stopped eating and sleeping. He was disheveled and dirty, and he mumbled to himself during his first few days in the hospital. Eventually, Max was taken to the recovery room for ECT treatment. With his hospital gown open in the back, he slumped over in the wheelchair and tried to hide a cigarette and lighter that he had liberated from another patient in the unit while he headed down for his first treatment. Max received three treatments during his week in the hospital. He was then discharged and continued to come in for regular treatments.

Two months later, Max arrived for his treatment at 6 a.m. He was wearing a suit and a big smile. His son was with him and reported that the family was preparing to take him to the finest restaurant in town for a Father's Day celebration. Max told stories about his oldest grandchildren learning to drive, and he chatted easily with the nurses about their plans for the weekend. Max was back.

Moderating moods with rTMS (repetitive transcranial magnetic stimulation)

Powerful magnets, similar to those used in MRIs, may be able to reset your brain's electrical power grid with less trauma than ECT causes. Several studies have shown that *repetitive transcranial magnetic stimulation* (rTMS) may be just as effective as ECT at treating depression and carries less risk of memory loss. However, the research so far indicates that rTMS appears to be less effective at treating mania and may induce hypomania and mania in some patients.

The course of treatment typically calls for five half-hour sessions per week for six weeks. No anesthetic is required, and few patients report any pain, although some have reported a tightening of the skin, especially around the scalp and jaw, and a knocking sensation in the skull, which may be partially due to the sound of the machine. Very little risk of memory loss or seizure accompanies the procedure.

rTMS treatment is still in its early, experimental stage and is not yet an approved or widely available treatment. Researchers are working with the intensity and frequency of the magnetic pulses to reduce potential side effects.

Shining some light on depression

Bears hibernate during winter, perhaps because they know how grumpy they would be if they didn't. Humans, on the other hand, choose to remain active and often irritable throughout the winter. How depressed you become may have something to do with the amount of light you receive. Some moods, especially those of bipolar sufferers, are very responsive to light; too little light leads to deep depression, and too much light sparks mania.

Light therapy, also called *phototherapy,* can often boost your moods, especially for those whose moods are at the mercy of the seasons. But not just any light will do. Sitting in a tanning booth, for example, probably won't provide you with sufficient light at the right wavelength, and the bed may blast you with too much UV light. For safe, effective phototherapy, follow these guidelines:

- ✔ Consult your doctor, first and foremost.
- ✔ Proceed with light therapy only under the direction and supervision of a qualified professional. Time of day, frequency, and duration of treatment are critical factors.
- ✔ Use a device designed specifically for the purpose of providing phototherapy. Most light boxes use special fluorescent bulbs rated at 10,000 lux.

Therapy consists of sitting for 10 minutes to an hour facing the light box, but you don't need to stare directly into the light. You can read the morning paper, drink your orange juice, work a crossword puzzle, or do whatever you normally do, as long as you face the light.

Too much light can cause hypomania and mania, especially during seasonal changes when you receive more light from natural sources. You and your doctor need to monitor your intake of light just as carefully as if you were monitoring your dose of medication.

Part IV
Helping Yourself

The 5th Wave   By Rich Tennant

"Why don't we talk to your doctor about adjusting your medication and then see about building that underground railroad to all your friends' homes."

In this part . . .

Although your doctor, therapist, family, and friends may be willing to pitch in when you need them, you should work toward taking ownership of the situation and doing whatever you can to control your own destiny. But first, you need to find out what the heck just happened. After a major depressive or manic episode, making sense of what happened and taking inventory of the damage it caused in your life can be terribly difficult. We dedicate the first chapter in this part to helping you make it over this first hurdle.

After you begin treatment, the remaining chapters in this part help you paddle upstream on the river to recovery. We show you how to reclaim your life and restructure it to reduce stress, how to monitor and manage your moods, how to take care of yourself, and how to let other people lend assistance without becoming too intrusive.

Chapter 10

Surviving Your Current Crisis

· ·

In This Chapter

▶ Spotting the signs of a major mood episode

▶ Knowing when and who to call for help

▶ Giving your loved ones a wake-up call

▶ Landing softly after a mood episode

· ·

*W*ith most illnesses or injuries, you know exactly what to do, and if you're faced with an emergency you can't handle, you dial 911 and let the professionals deal with it. With bipolar disorder, however, you and those around you may not even notice that you're ill. Maybe you feel overly tired and achy, or perhaps you feel juiced up and more alert and productive. Others may perceive you as disinterested and confrontational or lively and captivating. But sick? Heck no. You look perfectly healthy. In fact, you may look and feel better than ever. So what's the problem?

When your moods begin to wield undue influence over your behaviors, interfering with your life, your relationships, and your ability to keep your thoughts and actions in check, you have a problem. All too quickly, the disorder can push your life into a tailspin that traumatizes your brain and body and often wreaks havoc on your life and the lives of those around you.

To survive during these times of crisis, early detection and aggressive intervention are the keys. The sooner you can recognize trouble, get help, and obtain effective treatment, the faster you can resolve the crisis and prevent collateral damage.

In this chapter, we help you identify the signs and symptoms of major mood episodes so you and your support network can intervene as quickly as possible. We tell you who to call when you first recognize the early warning signs and how to talk to people to make them listen. Finally, we describe some medical interventions that have proved successful in helping others make a safe, soft landing from a major mood episode.

Checking Your Mood Pulse

You're very ill. Or are you? To outsiders, you probably don't appear to have anything they would describe as an "illness." Friends and family members may sense that "you're not your normal self," but even close friends may hesitate to tell you that you seem overly tired or wired. Inside, you may feel too tired to do anything, too dispirited to care, or so incredibly good that you can't possibly conceive of yourself as being ill.

When the people around you don't provide honest or reliable feedback and your own mood meter is busted, how do you obtain an objective measure of your mood? Self-evaluation may not be entirely reliable, but by completing a survey or a depression or mania scale, you can obtain a clearer insight into how you really feel.

If you're feeling down but don't know if you should be concerned, complete the depression scale we describe in the following section. If you're feeling overly energetic, irritable, or active, skip ahead and complete the mania scale.

Self-diagnosis is no substitute for a professional psychiatric evaluation and diagnosis. If you're suffering emotionally or psychologically, or if you're having thoughts of death or suicide, seek professional help immediately. Use the depression and mania scales included here only for your own reference and to provide additional information to your doctor.

Rating your depression

To complete the depression scale (see Figure 10-1), circle T (true) or F (false) next to each statement based on how you've felt over the last two weeks. If you see several statements that apply, we encourage you to consult a doctor or therapist for a professional evaluation.

Measuring your mania

To complete the mania scale (shown in Figure 10-2), circle T (true) or F (false) next to each statement, based on how you've felt recently or how you've felt in the past. If several statements seem true and your thought processes or behaviors are interfering with some aspect of your life, we encourage you to consult a doctor or therapist for a professional evaluation.

The mania scale is intended to help you identify recent manic symptoms. But if you've *ever* experienced the symptoms described in the mania scale for more than a few hours while not intoxicated, you may have bipolar disorder. Consult a psychiatrist for a more thorough evaluation.

Depression Screening Questionnaire

Answer true (T) or false (F) to the following questions based on how you have been feeling over the last two weeks. You can take this information to your doctor and review it with her. No matter what this screening says, if you have concerns that you are depressed, contact your doctor or therapist right away.

I feel sad most days.	T	F
I cry frequently.	T	F
I have trouble falling asleep.	T	F
I have trouble staying asleep.	T	F
I wake up too early in the morning.	T	F
I am sleeping too much.	T	F
I have no appetite, or I have lost weight.	T	F
I eat too much, or I have gained weight.	T	F
I am having trouble concentrating.	T	F
Everything, even little things, feels hard to do.	T	F
I have no energy.	T	F
My thoughts feel slowed down.	T	F
My body feels slowed down.	T	F
I don't enjoy things anymore.	T	F
I have lost interest in sex.	T	F
Nothing matters to me anymore / I don't care about anything.	T	F
Nothing is interesting / I frequently feel bored.	T	F
I am worthless.	T	F
Things are hopeless / things will never get better.	T	F
I am a bad, horrible person / I do terrible things.	T	F
I feel guilty about everything.	T	F
I feel scared all the time.	T	F
I am restless or can't stop moving.	T	F
I think about death and dying a lot.	T	F
I want to die / I think about killing myself. *	T	F

Figure 10-1:
The depression scale helps you self-evaluate your moods from the prior two weeks.

*If you answer yes to this, contact a doctor, hotline, or friend immediately. Do not wait for an appointment to see someone.

Mania Screening Questionnaire

Answer true (T) or false (F) to the following questions based on if you've ever had a period of time in your life when you experienced the particular symptom for more than a few hours and not while intoxicated. During a manic episode, you may not be able to objectively evaluate your moods and behavior, so ask others to complete the questionnaire for you or take the questionnaire when you are not manic. You can take the completed questionnaire to a qualified doctor or therapist who can review it with you.

I felt so good/hyper that other people thought I was not myself.	T	F
I felt so good/hyper that I have gotten into trouble.	T	F
I've been so irritable that I shouted at people or started fights or arguments.	T	F
I felt much more confident than usual.	T	F
I wasn't sleeping as much as usual and I didn't miss it.	T	F
I was much more talkative than usual.	T	F
I was talking much faster than usual.	T	F
Thoughts raced through my head.	T	F
I couldn't slow down my thinking.	T	F
I was distracted and had trouble staying on track.	T	F
I had so many plans that I could barely do my job.	T	F
I had much more energy than usual.	T	F
I was much more active than usual and felt like I was accomplishing much more.	T	F
I was much more social and outgoing than usual.	T	F
I was more interested in sex than usual.	T	F
I was acting out of character, doing things that others might think excessive, foolish, or risky.	T	F
I spent so extravagantly that my family or I was in danger of significant financial problems.	T	F
I was driving faster and more erratically than usual.	T	F
I was planning projects or business ideas that I had neither the expertise nor resources to accomplish.	T	F
People kept telling me to slow down.	T	F

If you marked True for more than one of the above, have two or more of the above ever happened during the same time period?   Yes   No

How much of a problem have these thoughts and behaviors caused you in respect to work, relationships, family dynamics, finances, or legal issues? Select one:

No problem   Minor problem   Moderate problem   Serious problem

Figure 10-2:
The mania scale helps you assess your recent manic behavior.

Calling for Backup

Normally, your rational mind lounges on your shoulder and provides a running commentary of sage advice. It makes sure you take care of yourself, drive safely, spend wisely, and generally stay out of trouble. Depression and mania aim to knock that angelic voice off your shoulder, relinquishing your mind to the chatter of anarchy. At this point, you need a replacement. You need immediate help, or at least someone to keep you out of trouble until reinforcements arrive.

Who ya gonna call?

Luckily for you, help is only a phone call away. Stay put, and call someone on the following list:

- ✔ A reliable friend who can get you out of trouble rather than get you into more trouble.

- ✔ A family member who won't try to convince you that you're fine.

    Family members, particularly those who are caught up in the drama of the moment with you, may not be the best choice.

- ✔ Your insurance company, which may have a mental health line with an emergency number you can call for immediate assistance. Some companies even have mental health case managers who are trained to spot trouble.

- ✔ Your minister or the minister of any established church in your area.

- ✔ Your primary-care physician, who may be able to give you something for temporary relief.

- ✔ Your psychiatrist or therapist, who can counsel you through a crisis or adjust your medications.

- ✔ Other professional resources, such as 911, 800-SUICIDE (800-784-2433), or 800-273-TALK (800-273-8255).

When depression or mania strikes, the question isn't "Should I call someone for help?" but "Who should I call for help?" You need a reliable person on your side — someone who can keep a watchful eye on you, drive you around, and get you to professionals who can help. Depression and mania are dangerous and often lethal. Assuming that depression will eventually dissipate or that mania will burn itself out is risky, both to yourself and to those around you.

Why don't they listen to me?

If you were drowning in a lake, thrashing about in the water and screaming for help, anyone within earshot would come running and do whatever they could to save you. When you're depressed or manic and you cry for help, people stare at you as if your cell phone just rang in the middle of a movie. Some people just want you to shut up. Others actually try to convince you that you're okay, or they tell you to tough it out. Meanwhile, back in your head, you're starring in your own personal horror flick.

Why don't some people listen when a depressed or manic person cries for help? Several reasons come to mind:

- They can't see the immediate danger.
- They haven't been trained to identify the signs of depression or mania.
- They're unaware of the serious potential consequences of your manic or depressive behavior.
- They're too scared or intimidated (if your mania has made you angry or confrontational).
- They're angry with you, with themselves, or with the current situation.
- They really don't understand what you have to be depressed about, as if that matters.
- They hail from the days when people didn't talk about their feelings.
- They were raised to believe that people have complete control over their moods.
- They've never experienced dramatic mood swings.

Blaming people for not being empathetic does you no good. With a little education, the people who make up your support group can develop a deeper sense of empathy, but that takes time and effort. For now, that's not something you need to worry about. But you do need to know that some people are incapable of hearing your cries for help. Don't waste your time trying to convince them. Move on to the next name on your list of emergency contacts and call for help. Don't stop until you find someone who can hear you and provide the assistance you need.

Recognizing how it looks to outsiders and feels to you

Human beings are prone to judge behaviors, not necessarily to understand them. When you see someone who looks perfectly healthy lying in bed all day, you may think "lazy" rather than "sick." When you see a high roller, the life of the party, you think "fun" or "entertaining," not "ill." If someone gets in your face and batters you with insults, you think "jerk," not "patient." During a major mood episode, especially depression, you know better, because you know how you feel inside. But outsiders don't.

Sally's (not-so-) silent suffering

For several weeks, Sally's moods were flying higher and higher. At the school where she taught, she was on a mission to improve classroom behavior by handing out dozens of demerits and referrals daily. Her principal called her into the office several times to discuss the situation, and Sally argued that the school's disciplinary policy was too lax. One day when Sally complained to the other teachers, her principal wrote her up for insubordination.

When Sally returned home that night, she complained about her job and cried about the injustice at work. At dinner, she chastised her children for their poor table manners and corrected their grammar whenever they spoke. She turned on her husband for allowing the children to behave in such abominable ways. He told her to calm down and to realize how good she really had it. Sally spent the rest of the evening calling the parents of students who were causing problems in class. Her husband spent the evening drinking.

Sally stayed awake that night. It was her third night without sleep. Realizing that something wasn't right, she called in sick the next day and asked her husband to take her to the doctor. He was busy with his own work and upset from the night before, so he told her to drive herself.

At the doctor's office, Sally begged her doctor for a sedative, something to calm her nerves. When the doctor asked Sally questions, she became combative and demanded medication. She said that if her arm were cut and bleeding, they would do something to help, so why were they refusing to help her now? The doctor told Sally that until she calmed down, he wouldn't give her anything. She stormed out of the office.

On the way home from the doctor, Sally stopped at the grocery store. She became disoriented and collapsed somewhere near the public phones. An alert stranger rushed over and dialed a number in Sally's cell phone, the phone number of an old friend in town. Her friend drove over, picked her up, and took her to the hospital, where she was diagnosed with a severe manic episode and began treatment.

Keep in mind that other people really don't know how you feel. You can try describing your sensations, but even your lucid words are unlikely to convince most people — what they see and believe often trump whatever you tell them.

Communication also becomes strained because the extreme behavior of bipolar disorder tends to embitter your allies and make them less receptive to your needs. When depression saps your energy or makes you irritable, friends, coworkers, and family members typically carry a heavier load. When mania drives you to whip everything into a frenzy, your loved ones may become defensive and impatient. The only symptoms of this illness that your loved ones can observe are your behaviors. They can feel the pain that they themselves feel, but they can't feel the pain you feel. In the best of all possible worlds, family and friends have a mutual understanding that transcends the bad times, but the reality of bipolar disorder can drive a wedge between you and your loved ones.

Talking so they will listen

During normal mood cycles, asking for help when you need it is a no-brainer. You know when you need help, and you're coherent enough to ask for it. But when you're depressed or manic, especially before you've been diagnosed with bipolar disorder, you often have no idea what's going on. You feel lousy, you're mad about it, you don't want to feel like this, and you don't believe that anything or anyone can help you. So you do what any miserable person would do — rant, rave, cry, complain, slam doors, or lie in bed. And if you're feeling high, you spend loads of money, have tons of sex, and find any way possible to keep the good times rolling.

Few people interpret your actions as desperate cries for help. You need something more effective, more direct — something that accurately describes your inner turmoil and specifies the kind of help you need. When you call a friend, family member, or someone else for help (see the section "Who ya gonna call?" earlier in this chapter), supply the following three pieces of information:

- A description of how you feel physically and any inner thoughts and feelings you have

- Whether you're having thoughts of death or suicide

- The type of help you want (Do you need a ride to your doctor's office or the emergency room? Do you want the person to phone a family member? Do you need someone to go to the doctor with you?)

When asking a family member for help, pretend that you're asking a stranger. When you've known someone for 10 or 20 years, you tend to think that the person is or should be in tune with your needs and should know what you want. Unfortunately, this is rarely true. During a crisis, you need specific help, so make your request very specific.

Taking Immediate Action

After you find someone to help you, you need to act immediately to obtain a psychiatric evaluation and diagnosis and to start receiving treatment. Take the following steps:

1. **Seek medical help from a doctor or psychiatrist.**

   Medication is almost always required to end the mood episode, and sometimes brief hospitalization may help. Chapter 3 includes instructions and a checklist to help you prepare for hospitalization.

2. **Seek a stable living arrangement with someone who can help you.**

   If you live alone, ask friends or family members to move in temporarily, or ask if you can live with them. If your condition poses a risk to your safety or the safety of others, hospitalization may be necessary.

3. **If you work, call in sick, or have a friend or family member call for you.**

   All you need to say is that you're ill and can't come to work. Although your employer has no right to fire you when you're ill, calling in sick provides you with additional legal protection, just in case. (Chapter 13 provides additional advice for dealing with situations at work.)

4. **Have a friend or family member contact your health insurance company for details on how to proceed.**

   You don't want to get stuck paying a big bill when you get released.

If you're experiencing mania, you may want to give your car keys, credit cards, debit cards, and checkbook to your friends or family members until your moods stabilize. (See Chapter 17 for additional crisis-management suggestions.)

Battling Back from an Acute Attack

When experiencing a major mood episode — depression or mania — the first order of business, after identifying the problem, of course, is to stop it in its tracks. If left to run its course, a major mood episode can get you into all sorts of trouble and negatively affect the fragile balance of brain physiology and chemistry. In this section, we show how you can effectively knock out a raging mood episode with the one-two punch of medication and rest.

Making a safe landing from a manic episode

When mania hurls you out of orbit, and you first realize you have a problem, your first impulse is to turn the spaceship around and plummet back to the earth, but your re-entry can be just as traumatic as the dizzying heights of mania. You need to come down from the manic high as quickly as possible, but you don't want to be so doped up that you enter a tailspin of depression.

In response to a major manic episode, your doctor may prescribe one of the following medications:

- ✔ Lithium, a mood stabilizer

- ✔ An anticonvulsant, such as Depakote, that functions well as an antimanic

- ✔ An atypical antipsychotic, such as Zyprexa, Risperdal, Seroquel, Geodon, or Abilify, that also functions well as an antimanic medication

Avoiding chemical con artists

Alcohol, stimulants, and illicit drugs lure many bipolar sufferers into the self-medication (or, more aptly, self-destruction) trap. Alcohol, because it's both legal and readily available, is particularly alluring. With chemical properties similar to the makeup of sedatives, it tricks people by seeming to soothe anxiety and agitation. It can also make people feel less inhibited, leading them to believe that it eases the sadness and guilt of depression. But alcohol is a con artist. Although you feel better briefly, the chemicals continuously work to depress your brain and worsen your symptoms over the long haul.

During mania, many bipolar sufferers drink alcohol as part of their overboard behaviors, but they also frequently turn to stimulants or uppers.

Uppers seem to focus the racing brain and offer temporary relief from the manic mental whirlwind. But danger lurks here as well. Stimulants cause sleep deprivation, which worsens mania, and they can induce psychosis.

Self-medication can worsen symptoms, interfere with medications, and lead to dependency or addiction to the abused substance. These patterns fuel bipolar disorder rather than cool it, even if you seem to feel good at first. Although the prescribed medications may not feel as good initially, they're going to help, not hurt, in the long run. If you're currently self-medicating, talk to your doctor and your support group about your substance use, and make a decision to stay on track with the good stuff and avoid the bad stuff.

Medications vary in how fast they work. Some, like Depakote, can be "loaded up" so you jump right to your goal dose. Others take a few days to weeks to work up to the right dose.

Mood stabilizers rarely bring you down from a major manic episode immediately. You may experience ongoing symptoms for several weeks.

Depending on the severity of your mania and your additional symptoms, such as psychosis, your doctor may prescribe the use of two or more antimanic medications — often lithium with an anticonvulsant or atypical antipsychotic. Your doctor may also prescribe a sedative to help you sleep. Chapter 7 provides additional information on specific medications.

Follow your doctor's orders concerning sedatives. Overdosing on sedatives can be dangerous. Avoid any use of alcohol or other depressants, which can form a lethal combination when used with sedatives.

Lifting the darkness of depression

When depression drags you to the dungeon, you may turn to an antidepressant as the logical medication to help you climb back to the light, but when bipolar disorder is the dungeon master holding you down, an antidepressant alone can be risky business. Assuming your doctor suspects that you have bipolar depression rather than unipolar depression, he's likely to treat you with a mood stabilizer that has antidepressant qualities first, such as lithium, Lamictal, or Symbyax (a combination of Zyprexa and Prozac, the first FDA-approved medication for bipolar depression).

These mood stabilizers have proved effective in treating bipolar depression without triggering mania. The antidepressant Wellbutrin is also commonly used because it may bring less risk of inducing mania.

If your mood stabilizer alone is ineffective, or if your depression is extreme, your doctor may add an antidepressant — usually an SSRI (Selective Serotonin Reuptake Inhibitor), which we explain in Chapter 7. If psychosis or agitation layers the mix, your doctor may prescribe an atypical antipsychotic as well.

Attending to the "minor" details

Your train wreck of a mood episode has derailed the engine, and the passenger cars you've been pulling are barely hanging on to the rails. That's not your problem. You need to focus on getting your engine back on track. However, if you don't get the rest of the train back on track to prevent it from being rear-ended by other events, you'll have even more problems to contend with after your recovery.

The only solution is to delegate. Have the people in your support network handle the minor details. The to-do list you hand a lucky individual (or group) will probably contain many of the following items:

- ✔ Care instructions and tips for your children, if you have young children
- ✔ Care instructions for any pets
- ✔ A list of essential errands
- ✔ A reminder to let your boss know how long you'll miss work
- ✔ A reminder to check on your insurance coverage and to make sure premiums are paid
- ✔ Small reminders to check the mail, pay the bills, and stay in touch

Avoid the temptation to return to work too soon. Full recovery from a major mood episode can take several months. Chapter 11 provides some tips on how to ease back into your old life at your own pace. Chapter 13 offers additional tips on restructuring your life and dealing with issues at home and work.

Chapter 11

Healing at Your Own Pace

- -

In This Chapter

▶ Being selfish for the good of everyone

▶ Adhering to your treatment plan . . . when it works

▶ Hopping back on the saddle . . . when you're ready

▶ Managing the financial and legal fallout

- -

*B*attling bipolar disorder is like going 12 rounds against a world-class prizefighter. Everyone in your corner cheers you on as your pugilistic opponent pounds your puss. The cut man in the corner patches you up after each round, and your trainer offers a few words of encouragement just before sending you in for another three-minute bashing. You feel like throwing in the towel, but you're no quitter, so you hang in there and keep taking it on the chin.

All too often, people respond to a mood disorder this way. The doctor patches you up with medication; your therapist and support network offer some encouragement; and you step back into the ring, still reeling from the mental thumping you took during your previous mood episode. Not only are you weaker and more vulnerable than before, but you've also fallen behind at work and probably have a host of additional problems to deal with — the perfect setting for a relapse.

During your recovery, keep in mind that this is no prize fight and you're no Rocky Balboa. Push other people's expectations to one side, focus on your recovery, and retain your focus until you feel ready to return. Of course, this sounds easier than it is. You may have a job, a family, a home, bills — the list goes on. Without a full recovery, however, all these important elements in your life remain in jeopardy.

In this chapter, we encourage you to make a full recovery your number-one priority. We help you come to terms with the aftermath of a major mood episode and deal with the fallout. We also reveal the importance of focusing on your health and well-being first and show you how to retreat to a place that's more conducive to convalescence. And when you're ready, we provide instructions on how to smoothly transition back to your family and job.

Making Recovery Your Number-One Priority

Long-term recovery requires long-term solutions, including medication management; individual therapy; relationship therapy; and, in many cases, family therapy. You may be tempted to try solving it all at once, especially if you're coming down from a manic high. In most cases, however, you have a better chance of moving forward by taking smaller steps and initially focusing on your own health and well-being, a process we discuss in this section.

Coming to terms with what just happened

After your doctor quells the most severe symptoms, you may feel as though you've just woken up from a bad dream. You look back at the episode and wonder what just happened. Well, what just happened is that your brain seriously malfunctioned for some reason, driving your mood up or down to an intolerable level.

That's what happened to your brain, but what happened as a result of your brain's mutiny may encompass much more than your personal anatomy and inner thoughts and feelings. The fallout, especially from a manic episode, may strain your relationships, career, finances, and social status. And if you performed any illegal acts during the mood episode, you may need to contend with court dates, fines, parole officers, and even jail time.

Although these issues may cry out for your immediate attention, avoidance is often the most prudent maneuver for now. After you fully recover, you can begin to focus on any fallout (see the section "Reclaiming Your Life When the Time Is Right," later in this chapter, to begin picking up the pieces).

BIPOLAR BIO

Bernard's Vegas nightmare

Bernard had lived a driven, energized life as a young man. He played college football and went on to become a successful investment banker. He had an episode of depression right after college, but he experienced no other symptoms from that point on. He married his college sweetheart, and they had four sons together. Life was good.

Around the time of his 15th wedding anniversary, Bernard began to believe that he didn't need to work anymore because he was going to write a best-selling novel. He didn't start writing or taking courses; he just knew in his heart that he was a great writer and would be famous and wealthy very soon. He began skipping work and taking trips to Las Vegas, almost every week, "for research." He slept little, gambled and drank a lot, and started a relationship with a casino waitress. He regaled his comrades at the high rollers' tables with tales of his novel writing and sexual prowess.

With each trip, Bernard stayed longer and longer, and his family became increasingly frightened, panicked, and angry about his absences and their rapidly dwindling bank accounts and investments. His colleagues at work were fed up with covering for him, so they divided up his accounts among themselves, leaving Bernard jobless. The next week, he brought his girlfriend from Vegas home to New York and took her out to dinner with his sons.

Sarah, Bernard's wife — like many people in similar situations — didn't make the connection between her husband's behavior and bipolar disorder. She was enraged at first, but gradually she began to recognize the manic symptoms because her father had suffered from bipolar disorder. She rallied their families and friends and began coaxing, cajoling, and bribing Bernard into treatment. The journey was long and difficult for everyone. When the dust finally settled, and he returned to his old self, he was devastated. He had lost his job and almost lost his family, and his son was applying to colleges, but he had no way to pay for them. Bernard, with the help of his doctor and family, worked on putting the pieces back together, including a change of careers that allowed for more down time and a slower pace. The family adjusted — not always easily — to a change in financial status. Bernard struggled with feelings of guilt about what he did to his family, but he and his family gradually came to understand that it was the illness that had hurt them and not Bernard.

Knowing what to expect

How fast and fully you recover from depression or mania depends primarily on the severity of the mood episode and how well you respond to treatment. You may be one of the lucky few who respond within days of treatment, or you and your doctor may spend weeks or longer trying to find the right mix of medicines and therapy.

As your body adjusts to the medications and your mood begins to stabilize, you may experience one or more of the following effects:

- ✔ **Memory difficulties:** You may not recall periods of time during the mood episode, especially during a manic episode. Some medications or treatments, such as ECT (see Chapter 9), can also cause memory loss, making it difficult to function at 100 percent.

- ✔ **Increased/decreased energy:** Antidepressants and other medications may pep you up, and antimanic medications and sedatives may drag you down. Don't be surprised if you need significantly more sleep after a manic episode — your body and brain need time to recuperate.

- ✔ **Anxiety:** Some medications can increase anxiety, so be sure to report any increase in anxiety levels to your doctor. In addition, people frequently and understandably become anxious after a mood episode due to worries about family, work, relationships, bills, and other facets of their lives that may be in upheaval.

- ✔ **Confusion:** A major mood episode and the medications used to treat it can muddle your thinking. You may wonder who you really are and how the medications will affect you. Until you know more about bipolar disorder, you may realize that something's not right, but you don't know exactly what's wrong.

Many of these symptoms are most prevalent when you begin taking a medication, but they diminish over time. If the symptoms are intolerable or persist for more than a week, contact your doctor.

Antidepressants often take as long as three to six weeks to become fully effective. Don't stop taking them just because they don't have an immediate effect. Also, don't stop taking any medication just because you begin to feel better. Always consult your doctor before making any medication changes.

Mastering the art of selfishness

People who suffer from mania and depression are often the movers and shakers of the world. They're working nights and weekends, taking care of the kids, and volunteering for neighborhood service. They focus on meeting the needs of others. But when you ask these Type-A personalities what they need, they can't give you a straight answer, because most of them don't know. They don't pause long enough from their busy schedules to take a personal inventory of their needs, and even if they did, they probably wouldn't ask for help.

If this sounds like you, a mood episode may signal the time for a change — a time for you to become more aware of your needs and more assertive in meeting them, a time to begin working on developing the fine art of selfishness. During your recovery, you need to look out for number one.

Assessing your needs

The first step in mastering selfishness is to figure out what *you* need and how to ensure that *your* needs are met (either by you or someone else). To assess your needs, try the following exercise:

1. **Write down five to ten needs, starting with your most immediate need.**

   For example, "I need help getting the kids ready for school in the morning."

2. **Brainstorm ways to have each need met, including the names of people who can help, such as friends or family members.**

   You may be able to meet some needs on your own, such as taking an hour at the end of the work day to wind down.

3. **Take the best idea for meeting each need, and draw up a plan for executing it.**

4. **If you need assistance, write a detailed description of the type of help you need and the amount of time required.**

   Contact the people who can help, and request their assistance.

5. **Put your plan into action.**

Getting used to saying "no"

Mastering the art of selfishness requires you to become sensitive to your needs and to avoid overcommitting your time and energy. In short, learn how to say "no." If you have trouble saying no, try the following lines:

- ✔ "I would love to help, but I really have too much on my plate right now."

- ✔ "I'm sorry, but I really want to spend more time with my family."

- ✔ "I haven't been feeling quite like myself lately. Can you call me back next year?"

- ✔ "I'll have to check my schedule and get back to you on this. What's your number again?"

- ✔ "I'm sorry, but we've donated all we can this year."

- ✔ "We have a policy of donating only to educational institutions."

- ✔ "Excuse me, I think someone is calling in on the other line."

- ✔ "Oh, dear, my cat just tipped over the trash."

Caller ID costs a little extra, but it can help you screen out the most annoying callers. Or you can let your answering machine pick up and then return the call later. If telemarketers are infringing on your peace and tranquility, consider having your name added to the National Do Not Call Registry. You can do this online at www.donotcall.gov.

Retreating to a safe, quiet place

The most obvious place to recuperate from a major mood episode — your home — isn't always the best. If you live alone, the solitude may aggravate your symptoms, and without the watchful eyes of a support person and some human interaction, you may slip back into depression or mania. If your home is tense or you live with unsupportive family members, the environment can be downright toxic. You want a safe and quiet place, a structured environment with the right combination of the following elements:

- **Tranquility:** Peace and quiet are essential in relieving anxiety, especially after a manic episode.

- **Activity:** Although rest is important, too much rest can lead to depression.

- **Interactivity:** Remaining connected to friends, family members, and colleagues provides additional social support.

- **Support:** Somebody should be available to help you follow your treatment plan and to remain on call if you need assistance.

- **Routine:** A structured routine with regular wake times, bed times, meals, and activities can help the recovery from both depression and mania.

Living arrangements that meet these criteria may include staying with a friend or family member or, if necessary, going into a hospital, halfway house, or other temporary residence. Having a friend stay with you can sometimes provide support and companionship if you live alone or supply an ally and advocate if you live with family members who don't get it. Remember not to stray too far from your medical and personal support networks when looking for places to stay.

If your family situation has deteriorated, avoid the impulse to move out on your own. Solitude can often deepen depression and unleash your manic impulses. Some degree of personal support almost always improves the treatment outcome.

If you decide to return home with family members, we strongly encourage your family members to learn more about bipolar disorder and make any necessary adjustments to ease your transition. Family therapy can play a critical role in your successful recovery, as we explain in Chapter 8. At the very least, you and your family should plan on making the following adjustments:

- **Regulate schedules.** Set times for waking up, eating meals, and going to bed.

- **Ease your workload.** Your family must pick up the slack during your recovery.

- **Crank down the volume.** Total silence isn't required, but if you have to shout over the stereo and television, lower the overall decibel level.

- **Create a retreat for yourself.** Designate a quiet place where you can escape during times of stress.

- **Outlaw criticism, demand, and judgment.** These patterns are the most common sources of conflict and stress, and families frequently don't even realize how much conflict goes on.

- **Avoid conflict.** Eventually, all families must address problems that arise, but during the recovery period, everyone must avoid serious conflict as much as possible.

You don't necessarily need to move out in order to cultivate a safe, quiet place. With the support of friends and family, you can usually create such a place right at home.

Following your doctor's orders

Your doctor will give you an earful about the importance of taking your medications as directed and sticking with your treatment plan, so we won't bore you with another lecture. What your doctor may omit, however, are instructions about what to do if your medications don't work or if they produce undesirable side effects. Here are four simple rules for sticking with your treatment plan and making adjustments if the plan doesn't produce the desired results:

- **Give it time.** Some medications take several days or several weeks to become fully effective. During the adjustment period, most negative side effects taper off.

- **Keep a record.** Take notes whenever you start a new medicine or change your dosage so you can provide your doctor with detailed feedback on how the medicine affected your feelings and behavior. Chapter 12 provides a mood chart and sleep log with note-keeping areas for logging medication changes.

> ✔ **Communicate your concerns.** Feeling just okay is unacceptable. If you experience negative side effects, contact your doctor for suggestions on how to minimize them. If your doctor seems insensitive to your concerns, find a doctor you can work with.
>
> ✔ **Consult with your doctor before making any changes.** Don't play doctor, and don't stop taking a medication without your doctor's approval.

Treatment for bipolar disorder is highly individual; what works for one patient won't necessarily work for another. Team up with your doctor to discover the most effective treatment plan for you. Your job is to clearly communicate the way you feel so your doctor has the information she needs to make well-informed decisions and adjustments.

Close, timely communication with your doctor is essential, especially when you're starting a medication or changing medications. If your doctor doesn't provide a timely response, you need to find another doctor who does.

Reclaiming Your Life When the Time Is Right

You found the perfect place to recover — a private little beach in Bora Bora, two blocks down from your psychiatrist's grass hut. You're resting in your hammock and reading this book without a care in the world.

We hope you have a good vacation, but eventually, you need to sail back to reality — return to your family and friends; deal with your problems; and, unless you're independently wealthy, find some gainful employment that's not too stressful.

In this section, we help you determine when you're ready to board your cruise ship home, and we provide some tips to ease the transition.

Knowing when you're ready (the preflight checklist)

When you dislocate your kneecap, your doctor doesn't pop it back in place and send you on your way. He probably recommends a couple weeks of anti-inflammatory medication, coupled with keeping your knee elevated, followed by several weeks of physical therapy. Only then can you make a slow transition back to your normal activities.

Recovering from a major mood episode requires a similar approach, in which you first stabilize your medications and moods and then slowly transition back to your normal activities. To prevent relapse and ensure a smooth transition, make sure you meet or exceed all criteria in the following checklist:

✔ Your medications are stable.

✔ Your moods are stable. (You may not be the best judge of your mood stability. Rely on your support group, doctor, and therapist for more objective feedback.)

✔ You're getting sufficient sleep.

✔ You're thinking clearly.

✔ Your support group is in place.

✔ Your doctor/therapist believes you're ready.

Don't divorce your spouse, quit your job, or make any other major life decisions while your moods are unstable. Mania, depression, and anxiety can often push you to make rash decisions you later regret.

Returning to friends and family

A mood episode doesn't always physically remove you from your family and friends, but it does almost always drive a wedge between you and your loved ones in some way. Mania can dramatically damage relationships, especially if it contributes to acts of infidelity, physical or verbal abuse, overspending, or substance abuse. Depression harms a relationship in more subtle ways — by diminishing energy and the ability to show affection. If the depression leads to a suicide attempt, it can make other family members feel guilty, inadequate, or embittered.

The first step is to stop beating yourself up over whatever may have unfolded during the mood episode. Sure, you're ultimately responsible for your words and actions, but you're not responsible for the mood episode that enabled you to say and do the things you said and did. The next step is to encourage everyone to work together; this is the tough part, because it takes understanding, empathy, and the ability to forgive and forget.

To build understanding and empathy and to enable forgiveness, take the following steps:

1. **Find out how you may have hurt each person in your family, and apologize.**

   It's natural to be unaware that you hurt someone and how you hurt that person, especially during a mood episode.

2. **Encourage family members and friends to learn more about bipolar disorder.**

   The more they know, the easier it is for them to understand that bipolar disorder isn't a product of your volition. Chapter 6 provides a list of informative sources.

3. **Involve family members in your therapy to a degree that you and they feel comfortable.**

   Chapter 8 provides details of how family therapy can help.

4. **Give family members specific instructions on how they can help support you.**

   By becoming involved, family members often feel empowered rather than victimized.

You may meet some resistance from family members or friends who feel as though *you* have somehow victimized *them*. What they need to realize is that bipolar disorder has victimized your entire circle, and *you* most of all. You're doing your part by seeking treatment, managing your medications, and attending therapy sessions. Now it's their turn to step up and contribute.

When you apologize for something you said or did, accepting the apology is entirely up to the other person. By taking responsibility and offering your apology, you've done all you can do. If the person doesn't accept your attempts, you may need to let it go.

Dusting off your briefcase and returning to work

Is your job making you sick? Do you break out in hives just thinking about returning to the daily grind? Is your boss a self-serving control freak? If so, returning to your old job may not be conducive to your mental health. But if you hacked away at your old job for 20 years, you may be reluctant to change careers at this stage in your life. What do you do?

Weighing your options

You must first look at and evaluate your options. They basically boil down to the following three:

- ✔ **Return to work.** Return to your job just as if you had never left. If you have a low-stress job, this may be the perfect solution, but if your job is a major stressor, this option carries significant risk.

- ✔ **Work the system.** Return to work on your terms, taking full advantage of your rights as an employee. Under the Americans with Disabilities Act

(ADA), your employer is legally obligated to provide you with reasonable accommodations. *Reasonable* means that the accommodations don't cost the company too much or require excessive adjustments. In other words, you may be pushing your luck by requesting a new supervisor, but time off for doctor's appointments, a more structured work schedule, additional training, fewer hours, and additional time to complete tasks are all reasonable requests.

Under the Family and Medical Leave Act (FMLA), you can take up to 12 weeks' unpaid leave with health coverage each year (you still have to pay your portion of the health insurance premiums). For details about your rights, turn to Chapter 13.

✔ **Cut and run.** Quit your job, and find a new one. If you choose this option, be fully aware of what you risk losing: a stable income, the personal satisfaction that comes with being productive, a portion of your retirement, built-up sick days or vacation time, and so on. Also, if you quit, you may not be eligible for unemployment or disability benefits. If you're considering jumping ship, refer to Chapter 13 for information on restructuring your life and finding rewarding work.

Consult your doctor and therapist before quitting a job to make sure you're not making your decision when your moods are cycling. Also, before you make a final decision, list all the benefits and drawbacks of your current job so you can accurately assess the cost-to-benefit ratio of quitting.

Returning to work with (the greatest of possible) ease

Assuming you decide to return to the job you had at the time of your most recent mood episode, here are a few suggestions to help ease the transition back to work:

✔ **Meet with your doctor before your return.** You may need a doctor's release to return to work. In addition, your doctor may offer some helpful suggestions concerning how to handle your medications in the workplace.

✔ **Set up a doctor's appointment for the end of your first work week.** By setting up an appointment in advance, you can return to work knowing that if anything goes wrong, you can get in to see your doctor soon.

✔ **Discuss your return with your supervisor.** You're not required by law to disclose your diagnosis or treatment, but if you feel comfortable disclosing this information, it may make your supervisor a little more understanding and flexible. If you request reasonable accommodations under the ADA, you must disclose the reasons why you need special accommodations. Your employer can't fire you for having bipolar disorder.

You can often predict how your supervisor may react to your diagnosis by thinking back to actions he performed or words he uttered in the past. How accommodating has your supervisor been regarding other illnesses and absences from work? Has he ever made unkind remarks about people who were "nutjobs" or "headcases" on the job? Look for clues from the past.

✔ **Discuss your return with one or more coworkers you trust.** Again, you have no obligation to disclose your diagnosis or treatment. In fact, a disclosure may not always be the best idea. But if you have coworkers you trust, a support person on the job can help you watch for early warning signs and avoid potential conflicts.

You may need to submit medical forms and other paperwork to receive sick pay or other benefits, but keeping up on all the paperwork can be quite stressful and difficult when you're feeling depressed or overwhelmed. Get help from a family member or friend, a union representative, or your employer's human resource department. Union representatives and HR workers are typically very knowledgeable about your rights and dedicated to making sure that your employer follows the proper legal procedures.

Facing your financial frets

Money can't buy happiness, but excessive debt can purchase a warehouse full of misery that visits almost everyone who suffers from bipolar disorder. Expenses stemming from missed work, medical costs, and therapy quickly add up. Roll in the cost of that Lamborghini you purchased during your last manic episode, and you have all the makings of a financial Molotov cocktail.

Taking control of your money and your debt

Facing your financial problems and solving them require determination, discipline, and at least a few of the following techniques and tips:

✔ **Budgeting:** List your sources of income and your expenses so you know how much money is coming in, how much is going out, and where it's going. When you get organized, start cutting expenses. Chapter 13 offers some tips on trimming expenses and simplifying your life.

✔ **Limiting credit card use:** Cut up your credit cards, or at least most of them. Call your credit card companies, and lower your credit limit. Allow a friend or relative to take your credit cards, debit card, and checkbook when you begin to cycle.

✔ **Consolidating debt:** You may be able to roll all your personal debt into a single account so you have only one payment to make per month. However, depending on your situation and the debt consolidation company you use, this may cost you more in the long run.

Before you choose a debt consolidation company or credit counselor, ask your bank, credit union, family, and friends for referrals. Many companies, even those that advertise as not-for-profit, charge exorbitant fees. For more information about finding legitimate organizations, check out the Federal Trade Commission's Web site at `www.ftc.gov/bcp/conline/pubs/credit/fiscal.htm`.

✔ **Finding affordable healthcare:** Chapter 20 provides a list of 10 ways to save money on treatment and find affordable health insurance for you and your family.

✔ **Filing Chapter 7 bankruptcy:** With Chapter 7 bankruptcy, the government takes most of your belongings, except for exempt property (such as your pension), which varies from state to state. It sells your stuff, divides the money up among the people you owe, and then forgives you any remaining debt. You can file Chapter 7 bankruptcy only once every six years.

✔ **Filing Chapter 13 bankruptcy:** Chapter 13 bankruptcy generally lets you keep your home and car, assuming you can make the monthly payments. The state requires you to pay monthly installments to pay off a reasonable portion of your debt over a three- to five-year period, after which any remaining debt is forgiven.

Bankruptcy remains on your record for up to 10 years, fouling up your credit rating and making it difficult to secure loans.

Handing control of your finances to someone else

In extreme cases, you can relinquish control of your finances and other important matters to a trusting friend or relative through the courts:

✔ **Power of attorney** allows a friend or relative to make legal and financial decisions for you when you're physically or mentally incapacitated.

✔ **Legal guardianship** enables a relative to act as your guardian, making that person responsible for your health and well-being.

✔ **Financial guardianship:** If you've had many manic episodes and are left with limited resources that must last the rest of your life, you may be able to seek financial guardianship. Some financial institutions will create guardianships for people with illnesses even if they don't meet the institution's usual minimum for such services.

Giving a trusted relative power of attorney or legal guardianship strips you of much of your freedom and legal rights and can often lead to bitter feelings. Make the decision only when your moods are stable, and choose a person whom you completely trust to do what's best for you.

Locking up your legal issues

People rarely break the law during spells of depression. They may do some uncharacteristic things, like leaving a stack of dirty dishes in the sink or frowning at Disneyland, but nothing that calls for jail time. Mania is depression's evil twin, the insidious instigator who tugs on your puppet strings and encourages you to perform all manner of lewd and immoral acts. It handcuffs and gags your conscience, so you act without inhibitions. Sure, a manic state can make you more spontaneous and creative, but it can also push you past the boundaries of what's socially acceptable and legal.

If you get caught breaking the law, the legal system can complicate your life and increase your stress level by subjecting you to court dates, legal fees, fines, parole officers, and possibly even jail time. You rarely have the option of whether or not to deal with these inconveniences, but you may be able to diminish the negative effects they have on your life. Here are a few suggestions:

- **Keep quiet.** When you're manic, keeping your mouth shut may not be a realistic option, but it's always good advice to defer to your lawyer when questioned. Remember, you do have the right to remain silent.

- **Obtain legal representation.** You have the right to a court-appointed attorney if you can't afford a private attorney. You can also seek help from advocacy groups. NAMI (National Alliance for the Mentally Ill) has a legal center you can contact by calling 703-524-7600 or e-mailing legal@nami.org.

- **Inform the court of your bipolar diagnosis.** Lawyers, judges, social workers, and correctional officers should be well aware of the effects mania has on behavior, and they may be more flexible knowing that you've been diagnosed and are receiving treatment.

- **Add your parole officer to your treatment team.** If the court assigns you a parole officer, encourage communication between the parole officer and your doctor and therapist. In addition to fostering understanding and empathy, the team effort can assist in your recovery.

- **Seek assistance with any substance-abuse problems.** Alcohol and illicit drugs can often exacerbate mood symptoms and lead to illicit behavior. If you have a substance-abuse problem, make sure your doctor and therapist know about it. Alcoholics Anonymous and other support groups can help you stay clean and sober.

If you need to call the police to deal with a friend or relative who's currently suffering a major manic attack, inform the dispatcher that the person has bipolar disorder. Most officers are trained to confront an alleged perpetrator directly, which is the worst approach for dealing with someone experiencing full-blown mania. NAMI and other organizations are working hard to train police on how to defuse tense situations and get mentally ill people to treatment rather than to jail. If your friend or relative is arrested and jailed, officers won't allow the person to take medication, so you need to call the doctor and perhaps a lawyer in order to convince the justice system to pass along the medications to your friend or relative.

Dealing with Setbacks

The best strategy for maintaining your health is to follow your doctor's orders, reduce stress, and avoid any surprises that could throw off your rhythm. If you adhere to this strategy, you're likely to proceed for a much longer time without experiencing symptoms than if you don't make the adjustments. However, being a "good little patient" doesn't provide you with a money-back guarantee that you'll remain symptom free. In the real world, variables, such as the following, can have a tremendous influence over the course of the illness:

- Medicines can lose their effectiveness over time.

- Job changes can increase stress.

- Family events and crises can trigger mood fluctuations.

- Other health problems can cause mood swings.

Knowing that setbacks are normal helps keep them in perspective so you don't feel as though your treatment has failed when something goes wrong. The key is to remain vigilant, identify problems as early as possible, and address those problems quickly and aggressively:

- **Monitor your moods.** Keep track of your moods, and note any significant changes, as we explain in Chapter 12. As soon as you notice a change, meet with your doctor or therapist.

- **Meet regularly with your doctor.** Review your medications with your doctor every few months — more frequently if you're just recovering from a mood episode or your doctor has recently adjusted your medications.

- **Meet regularly with your therapist.** Even when you're stable, you should visit regularly with your therapist. She's your ally in monitoring your moods and recognizing early warning signs. She can offer support and strategies for all the issues in life that can trigger a mood cycle.

- **Check in with your caregivers when you experience a major life event.** Meet with your doctor or therapist as soon as any stressful event occurs — a job change, divorce, child moving away or back home, death of a loved one — even if you think you can handle it just fine.

Chapter 12

Identifying Your Triggers and Mapping Your Moods

*W*ant to try an explosive experiment? Seal a pot of water good and tight, set it on the stove, and crank up the heat. In a matter of minutes, your pot will blow its lid. The same is true with people. Although each person has a different boiling point and can handle varying amounts of pressure, if you apply enough heat without providing some way for the pressure to escape, everyone will either explode or implode. Pressure always finds a release — in the form of anger or violence, a flurry of activity, a depressive meltdown, or some other discharge of pent-up energy and angst.

Medication regulates your mind's reaction to stressful events and raises your internal boiling point, but it can't reduce or eliminate the heat — the external sources of stress. Tense situations, personal conflicts, unresolved family matters, and even major shifts in your daily routine all contribute stress that can eventually upset the sensitive balance of your moods.

Of course, you can't eliminate all the stress in your life (nor would you probably want to), but you can identify the major stressors and mood triggers and remove or reduce the effects of enough of them to keep the pressure at a manageable level.

This chapter empowers you to rid your environment of the events, conflicts, and structure-busters that commonly aggravate moods. Here, you find out how to identify the main stressors and triggers in your life and begin to address them. We show you how to monitor your moods, energy levels, and sleep patterns. And we help you build an early warning system so you can react to depression and mania before they take control.

Pinpointing (and Dealing with) Your Stressors and Triggers

What makes you tick? What ticks you off? What makes the back of your neck tingle? What inspires your deepest passion, enables you to forgo meals and sleep, and drives you to lose track of self and time?

If you're like most people, you haven't given such questions much thought. And if you didn't have bipolar disorder, you could live the rest of your life in blissful ignorance of the answers. But because you have bipolar disorder, you have a responsibility to yourself to become aware of your environment and the factors that influence your emotions and moods.

People, places, jobs, events, seasons, and even holidays can play a significant role in your mood stability. By identifying your mood triggers and the primary sources of stress in your life, you can begin to remove them, or at least diminish the toxic effects they have on your moods. This section initiates the identification process by describing some of the more common stressors and triggers.

Your job

Your job can be an obvious source of stress, especially if you're overworked, underpaid, and have a knucklehead for a supervisor. But your work can be just as tense if it features some of the following, more subtle, characteristics:

- **Monotonous:** Although routine can be comforting, too much of a good thing can become tedious. Breaking up your work day with variations in activity may be what you need.

- **Cushy:** An easy job can be just as stressful as one that's too demanding, especially if your mind tends to turn on itself when you don't challenge it.

- **Unrewarding:** Working for money and benefits is perfectly acceptable, but at some point in your life, you may find that money isn't enough. You feel like you really need to do something you believe in.

- **Noisy:** Loud machinery, music, or talking can be unnerving, especially if you're ultrasensitive to sounds.

- **Disruptive:** Focused individuals often become anxious and frustrated when interrupted. For example, a teacher who's very detail oriented may find interruptions from students nerve racking.

- ✔ **Deadline-focused:** Deadlines often present goals that motivate some people and improve moods, but tight deadlines may increase anxiety.

- ✔ **Irregular hours:** Alternating shifts and irregular work hours are hard on everybody but potentially toxic to someone with bipolar disorder.

- ✔ **Unpredictable:** When your workload can change at a moment's notice — emergency room nursing, for example — the adrenaline surges can be a real drain on the nervous system.

- ✔ **Constrained:** Responsibility without the necessary power and resources is a formula for failure and chronic stress.

Only you can decide whether or not the benefits of your job outweigh the drawbacks, but if you find that you can't perform your job or that any attempts to return to work result in a major mood episode, you should seriously consider your alternatives. As we discuss in Chapter 13, under the Americans with Disabilities Act, you can ask for reasonable accommodations to enable you to successfully perform your job duties. If that doesn't work, consider changing jobs or filing for disability. Staying in a job that aggravates your illness is rarely the best choice. Chapter 13 provides some suggestions for finding and securing a job that's more conducive to your mental health.

Lover quarrels

When a steamy romance morphs into a cauldron of conflict, the bipolar brain begins to boil. And what's most startling, perhaps, is that the bipolar brain often seeks out conflict in order to feed its insatiable appetite for stimulation. To compound the problem, bipolar disorder tends to trigger relationship trouble and then that trouble in turn aggravates the illness.

In romantic relationships, several elements often contribute to producing the ideal setting for conflict:

- ✔ Loss of interest in sex, sometimes as a result of antidepressants and other medications

- ✔ Increased sexual desire, making the person seem sexually insatiable or leading the person to seek sexual gratification elsewhere

- ✔ Inability to show affection

- ✔ Lack of interest in anything

- ✔ Lack of desire to socialize

- ✔ Inability to have fun

✔ Overspending

✔ Inability to work

✔ Refusal to adhere to treatment plan

✔ Desire for conflict

✔ Avoidance of any conflict

Just because your partner has been diagnosed with bipolar disorder doesn't mean that you can blame every disagreement on the disorder. You and your partner can expect to have differences of opinion; you are, after all, two different people. However, because heated arguments can significantly affect moods, you need to work on keeping the intensity down and resolving your differences as quickly, rationally, and completely as possible. Chapter 16 offers additional suggestions on supporting a loved one with bipolar disorder.

Couples therapy can often help you and your partner develop the communication and problem-solving skills you need to keep disagreements from spinning out of control. See Chapter 8 for details.

Family fiascos

Families are as unique as the individuals who comprise them. Some families are so calm they seem comatose. Others resemble ant farms, in which every family member busily carries out an assigned chore. And some are so competitive that you wonder if they fit the dictionary definition of "family" (which includes some clause about shared goals and values). Every family has problems, but when personality conflicts and other issues become insurmountable and trigger mood episodes, you need to recognize the risks to your mental health and take action:

✔ **Identify and resolve issues as a family.** The faster you identify and resolve conflict, the less effect it has on all family members, especially those who suffer most in the presence of emotional instability. If your family can't resolve a serious issue on its own, you need to look into the next option.

✔ **Seek family counseling, if necessary.** Family counseling improves the overall understanding of bipolar disorder, increases support from family members, and enhances communication skills, as discussed in Chapter 8.

✔ **Limit family contact, if all other options fail.** If your family refuses to learn more about bipolar disorder and make necessary adjustments to aid in your recovery, you may need to limit family contact. Don't martyr yourself for the good of the family.

Be aware of others in the family who may have bipolar disorder or something similar. When multiple people in the family have symptoms, the fallout is often even more damaging.

Happy (?) holidays

For many people who suffer from psychiatric illnesses, the holidays deliver a double dose of dysfunction: They disrupt a carefully structured routine and frequently place you in contact with family members, some of whom may be quite irritating. Planning for the holidays requires that you strategically prepare for your holiday survival and remain committed to:

- ✔ Sticking to your established schedule
- ✔ Adhering to your treatment plan
- ✔ Avoiding tense situations

If you know that a particular holiday or season destabilizes your moods, plan ahead for it. Your doctor may recommend a short-term medication adjustment or a limited prescription for a sedative. In addition, you may want to limit the amount of time you spend on the road or with your extended family. If you usually host the holiday celebration and find it stressful, you should plan on celebrating at the home of another friend or relative.

Jet lag can seriously disrupt sleep-wake cycles and cause problems with mood cycles and medications. Consult your doctor about how to manage meds if you have to cross time zones. Avoid the temptation to self-medicate with alcohol or sedatives. Your doctor may prescribe sleep medicine to assist with your adjustment to the new time zone if he thinks the transition may be too stressful.

Mood-altering people

Instinctively, you avoid your most annoying acquaintances, but some pests may be unavoidable, and others may alter your moods in less noticeable ways. An old high school buddy, for example, may influence you to overindulge in alcohol or party too late. One of your children may test your patience with passive-aggressive behavior. Perhaps a parent or other authority figure chips away at your self-esteem with subtle innuendos or "good-hearted" teasing.

The world is only so big, so you probably can't avoid all the annoying and hurtful people in the world. If you identify who they are and what they say and do to irritate you, however, you can begin to take control of how you feel in their presence. After you identify the source of the problem, you have several options, including the following:

- ✔ **Blow it off.** If the person is of little consequence, and you're pretty sure he doesn't care about how you feel, why should you care? Admittedly, letting it go is easier said than done.

- ✔ **Open up.** Describe to the person how what he says or does affects you. This reveals the negative effects of his words or actions and is often enough to make him stop. People can't argue with how you feel, so express your feelings as "I" statements — for example, "I feel like a failure as a parent when you criticize my children."

- ✔ **Ask the person to stop.** If you tell the pest that something he says or does hurts you in some way, and he continues behaving and speaking in the same manner, ask him to stop.

- ✔ **Attach a consequence.** In other words, if the person doesn't stop, what do you plan to do about it? Pick something realistic and not too terribly cruel — perhaps simply leaving the room. Don't offer an ultimatum unless you're fully prepared to carry it out.

Clashing temperaments

The Odd Couple made great humor out of the temperamental mismatching of neat-freak Felix Unger and his slob of a roommate Oscar Madison, but such pairings in real life result more often in tragedy than comedy. Each person is born with a unique temperament that remains consistent through the course of a lifetime. When temperaments click, the meetings often result in deep and lasting friendships. When they don't, the confrontations can wreak havoc on personal relationships, work interactions, and student–teacher connections. Certain temperamental traits, including the following, are more prone to create friction:

- ✔ **Tempo:** Each person has an identifiable tempo. Some people thrive in high gear all the time, and others proceed at a more measured pace.

- ✔ **Intensity:** Energy levels shift a great deal, but everyone has a baseline intensity level that you can usually detect when a person enters the room. Some people are dynamos, beaming heat and electricity, and other individuals may be low-wattage types, generating a cooler, less-concentrated light.

- ✔ **Need for order:** People seem wired to be either slobs or neatniks — at least to some degree. You may be totally oblivious to the stacks of clothing lying on the floor, but your wife notices every speck of dust in a room. Humans can be trained somewhat, but natural tendencies are stubborn and resist change.

✔ **Need for predictability and consistency:** Some people need their lives to remain pretty much the same on a day-to-day basis. They plan for the future and take the steps necessary to execute their plans and achieve their desired outcomes. Others throw all caution to the wind and go with the flow. They ride life's ups and downs like surfers ride waves. Each approach has its benefits and risks, but trying to get two people with opposite tendencies to work together can be a nightmare.

✔ **Social style:** Look around the room at the next party you attend, and you'll see variations in social styles that range from garrulous extrovert to mousy introvert. Although neither style is right or wrong, better or worse, differences in social style and one's desired amount of social contact are a common source of relationship conflict.

✔ **Reactivity:** You may get frustrated with your husband's lukewarm response to your headline news, but his internal reactor may be wired a little differently. People vary greatly in how quickly (or not) their emotional charges get juiced up. People with bipolar disorder tend to land in the more reactive end of the spectrum.

Remember that temperamental differences are just that: differences. One style isn't inherently superior. Tolerance for someone else's innate way of being can reduce most conflicts. Big temperamental differences can be difficult to negotiate, but awareness of these issues is a good start to navigating situations that may otherwise create enormous stress.

Uncomfortable situations

Do you go ballistic waiting in your doctor's office? When you stop at a gas station for a fill-up and find out that your pump is prepay? When some joker at the table next to you lights up a stogie? Situations such as these are often unavoidable, so the most effective way to deal with them is to change your thinking and behavior toward them, which can be quite a challenge. Chapter 8 explains ways to alter your thinking patterns through cognitive behavioral therapy. If the source of your discomfort involves an annoying person, and changing your thinking isn't an option, skip back to the previous two sections for some advice.

Downtime

Moods often ride waves of activity. When you have plans and the resources to carry them out, you often feel motivated and energized. Without plans, or without a reason to wake up in the morning, you may feel lost. Perhaps this is why so many people with bipolar disorder experience their first major mood episode in college, when frenetic finals are followed by extended breaks.

Developing temperamental tolerance

Maggie worked at a television station and loved every minute of it. She was up at the crack of dawn every day and never stopped moving until she crashed into bed at night. Her husband, Hal, was slightly less energetic, but he worked at a similar pace. Together, they adopted Sam at birth. He was a loving, gentle baby with big brown eyes, but as Sam grew, he puzzled them. They scheduled plenty of exciting activities for him — baseball, music lessons, rock climbing, and astronomy classes. They wanted him to have everything, see everything, and do everything. But Sam would have none of it. He protested every trip to the hockey rink and every round of tennis. He fussed and sometimes even exploded when it was time to go anywhere. He liked to stay home reading, coloring, watching TV, or playing with blocks. He rested a lot and enjoyed quiet "thinking time," as he called it. Maggie and Hal cajoled, they wheedled, they screamed, and they threatened, but nothing changed.

When Sam was 13, he was diagnosed with bipolar disorder. Therapists and doctors explained to the family that their high-intensity demands often triggered Sam's explosiveness; to successfully manage his bipolar disorder, this cycle had to stop. The emotional intensity was creating more and more mood episodes for him. Maggie and Hal were devastated. They kept thinking that more activity would help Sam's bipolar disorder, but it kept backfiring. When discussing this with his doctor, they were told that Sam probably had a different temperament — different tempo and energy patterns — than they did. They were stunned to imagine that other people and families in the world didn't operate at their level of activity. When they realized that his temperament wasn't a bad thing, but a different way of being, they began to feel less anxious about his low energy and instead learned to use it as part of his life structure to minimize mood episodes.

If periods of downtime make you feel depressed, try to avoid downtime by planning more carefully, regulating your workload, and looking for rewarding activities. Here are some suggestions to get you started:

- ✔ **Schedule your days.** Plan ahead for tomorrow so you go to bed knowing that you have specific tasks to accomplish the next day. This allows you to wake up with a purpose.

- ✔ **Schedule your weeks.** You don't have to pack your week full of activities, but plan one or two special activities so you have something to look forward to.

- ✔ **Plan a project.** If you have a project around the house or even outside your home that will take at least a couple days and possibly require some extra supplies, start planning for it. This often provides just the motivation you need to start executing your plan.

✔ **Plan an outing.** Do you like to camp? Go to the theater? Take rides in the country? The anticipation of a pleasant activity can often lift you out of the doldrums.

✔ **Create a to-do list.** You don't need a Martha Stewart to-do list, but having a few things jotted down helps structure your day.

✔ **Set a realistic goal.** A simple goal, such as walking outside for 10 minutes a day, can give you something specific to do and provide you with a sense of accomplishment.

✔ **Take up a hobby.** What do you like to do even when you don't get paid to do it? Paint? Write? Sew? Build model airplanes? It doesn't have to be an expensive hobby, just something you enjoy doing on a regular basis.

Chapter 13 provides additional suggestions for achieving mood stability by restructuring your life.

Monitoring Your Moods

Every few years, mood rings become "the thing." When you slide one over your finger, you can glance at the colors throughout the day to determine if you're happy or sad, angry or calm, passionate or indifferent. Too bad the rings don't work, because if they did, they would be great accessories for people with bipolar disorder. One look at the ring would tell you whether your moods are stable or if you're on the verge of a nervous breakdown. You could even get a mood dot to stick on your forehead like a Hindu bindi to let others know when to back off.

Until mood rings are perfected, however, you must rely on your perceptions and charting expertise to monitor your moods. Mood monitoring offers the following benefits:

✔ Increases your awareness of your moods and fluctuations

✔ Functions as an early warning system against impending mood episodes

✔ Records the affects of medication adjustments on moods

Figure 12-1 provides a sample mood chart that enables you to record your mood for each day on a scale of "Who Cares?" (extremely down) to "Yeehaa!" (extremely up), with "Groovy" as your baseline or normal mood level. Simply place an X in the box that best represents your overall mood level for each day. The notes area at the bottom provides space for you to log any medication changes or significant events that may affect your moods on any given day.

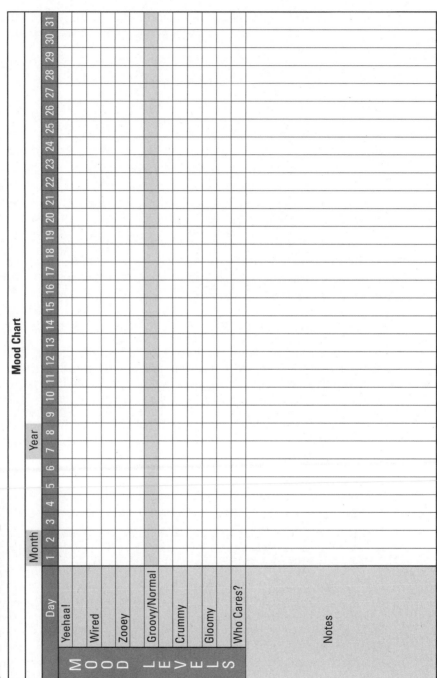

Figure 12-1:
Mood charts allow you to monitor your moods to track variations over time.

Share your mood charts with your doctor and therapist. The information your charts provide can help tremendously in identifying your stressors and triggers, managing your medications, and tracking the success of your treatment. When your doctor or therapist asks you how you've been doing since your last appointment, you can provide concrete data.

Charting Your Sleep Patterns and Energy Levels

A mood chart (see the previous section) contains subjective data; it provides a record of how *you* perceive your moods during any given day. But as people with bipolar disorder know, you can't always trust your perceptions. A mood rating of "Zooey" may indicate that you're feeling only a little high, even though you're not sleeping and you're beginning to exhibit manic symptoms. You can often obtain a more objective measure of your moods by charting your sleep patterns and energy levels — how much sleep you're getting, when you're getting it, and how energetic you feel.

Figure 12-2 provides a sleep log you can use to track your sleep data and energy levels. Simply mark the hours you sleep each day, including naps, and record your energy level for that day on a scale of –5 to +5. (You may find that your energy level is pretty much in line with your overall mood rating for the day.) The notes area provides space for you to log any medication changes or significant events that may affect your moods.

Your sleep log can help you identify early warning signs and patterns that you may need to attend to for optimum mood stability. At the end of each day, examine your sleep log for the following patterns and warning signs:

- ✔ **Increasing need for sleep:** If you have an increasing need for sleep, and your energy levels are sinking, your mood may be on the downswing.

- ✔ **Decreasing need for sleep:** If your energy levels are climbing, even though you're getting less and less sleep, you may be working yourself up to a manic episode.

- ✔ **Variations in sleep patterns:** Are you sleeping in on weekends? Taking long naps during the day? Unable to sleep when you normally go to bed? If so, you may need to work on regulating your sleep patterns. Sleep regulation is one of the primary goals of interpersonal and social rhythm therapy (IPSRT), which we discuss in Chapter 8.

Significant changes in your sleep patterns and energy levels can be a sign of an impending mood episode. If you're having trouble falling asleep or sleeping through the night, refer to Chapter 13 for suggestions.

Sleep Log

Month	Year							
Day	Time you went to bed	Time you fell asleep	Time you woke up	Times you woke during the night	Nap time (total)	Total sleep time	Energy Level +5 to -5	Notes
1								
2								
3								
4								
5								
6								
7								
8								
9								
10								
11								
12								
13								
14								
15								
16								
17								
18								
19								
20								
21								
22								
23								
24								
25								
26								
27								
28								
29								
30								
31								

Figure 12-2: Your sleep log helps you relate your sleeping patterns to your moods and keep track of your energy levels.

Can sleep deprivation cure depression?

Can you sleep-deprive your way out of a depressed episode? Some researchers think that it may be possible. Using a technique called TSD (total sleep deprivation), researchers subjected depressed bipolar patients to three cycles of sleep deprivation, each consisting of a 36-hour period of sleeplessness followed by a 12-hour sleep-in. After the sessions, over half the participants reported feeling less depressed.

The trouble is, TSD runs about a 10 percent risk of kicking a bipolar sufferer into hypomania or

mania — about the same rate as SSRI antidepressants. In addition, the positive effects of TSD generally wear off as soon as you return to your normal sleep/wake cycle. Researchers continue to study the potential benefits of TSD when used in combination with other therapies, but the only solid conclusion that researchers have reached is that TSD is definitely not something you should try on your own.

Logging Confrontations

How many arguments did you have this week? And the week before that? Your answers can warn you about a looming mood episode or simply point to the fact that you happened to lock horns with some really annoying people during the last couple of weeks. After all, your sister doesn't know how to raise her kids, and your boss needs to bone up on his people-management skills.

But placing blame isn't your goal here. You just need to determine an accurate fight count and intensity level for comparison purposes. That way, if you usually have one or two minor disagreements a week, and the number suddenly jumps to five or six major blow-ups, you can easily tell that you may be becoming a little more sensitive or irritable. And telling yourself you're being a little more sensitive and irritable is certainly less irritating than hearing it from someone else.

You can log your confrontations in any number of places, including the following:

- ✔ Your personal calendar or day planner
- ✔ In the notes area on your mood chart (see Figure 12-1)
- ✔ In the notes area on your sleep log (see Figure 12-2)
- ✔ In your journal

 Consider using a secret code or color and marking the intensity of the altercation on a scale from 1 to 5, with 1 being mildly upset, 3 indicating the use of insults and foul language, and 5 being all-out war.

Keeping a Journal

When most people hear the term "journal," they think "diary" — an honest description of events, feelings, perceptions, and impressions. As such, journaling can be very therapeutic, especially if you have nothing to hide and nobody to hide it from. For the less fortunate, journaling is the equivalent of offering up a full confession to the state prosecutor. Sure, you can log your feelings and perceptions, but unless you're sure that you can keep other prying eyes out of your journal, you probably don't want a written record of your thoughts and feelings on public display.

For the purpose of tracking moods, medications, and other data, your journal need not be so personal. A daily entry can contain the following details:

✔ Medication adjustment

✔ Missed medications

✔ Overall mood rating

✔ Amount of sleep you obtained

✔ Special activities or events

✔ Whether or not you exercised

✔ Recent problems or resolved issues

Of course, if you want to take a more personal approach, we encourage you to do so. Journaling enables you to express your thoughts and feelings without fear of negative repercussions. It provides you with a way to look back on how you were feeling and what you were thinking at a specific point in time, which allows you to witness your progress and development as a person. And it can help you identify recurring issues that are calling out for your attention. You can hand-write your journal, type it as a document in your word processor, or even use a tape player to narrate it.

Many people choose to share their journals online in the form of a blog. *Blog* is short for *Web log* — a Web page that typically contains a daily record of an individual's thoughts, feelings, observations, insights, and whatever else the person wants to spill on a page. A couple of good places to learn the ropes are Blogger, at www.blogger.com, and LiveJournal, at www.livejournal.com.

Chapter 13

Restructuring Your Life

*W*hen you survive a major mood episode, receive your bipolar badge, and begin effective treatments, the whole experience can scrub the sleep out of your eyes and impart a clarity of vision. It can burn away all the petty, insignificant nonsense in life and reveal what's really important. The experience plasters a big red arrow on your lifeline that says "YOU ARE HERE," and that's all that really matters.

You can now measure your life in eras: BBD (Before Bipolar Diagnosis) and ABD (After Bipolar Diagnosis). The BBD era is over. All your past mistakes and indiscretions instigated by your bipolar disorder are finished. You may have to deal with some fallout and aftershocks, but the words and deeds are done, and you can't do anything to undo them. Nor can you get rid of your condition. Some of your old dreams may be finished, too. You may not be able to retire at 50 or take a year off work to explore the Amazon rainforests.

Now is ABD time. You're a different person. You've been reborn in a way, baptized by fire. Your current situation is different — not better or worse, just changed. After a period of mourning for the passing of your old self, you may find this time somewhat liberating. It provides an opportunity to start anew — to reinvent yourself, create a life that's both more manageable and rewarding, and paint new dreamscapes.

That's what this chapter is all about. Here, we lead you through the process of determining what's really important. We assist you in identifying and stripping away the trivial, irrelevant gunk that muddles your life. Finally, we provide suggestions on how to restructure your life in a way that helps you maintain your mental health and achieve a meaningful, rewarding existence.

Budgeting Your Time and Resources

People tend to accumulate stuff. We fill our houses with furniture and appliances, our budgets with expenses, our calendars with appointments, and our free time with commitments. Occasionally, we clean house to remove a few broken and nonessential items, and when finances get tight, we examine our budgets to trim discretionary spending. But few of us budget our time and resources. Have you ever sat down and figured out where you're spending your time? Have you tabulated your energy expenditures? Perhaps you should.

Time and resources, like money, tend to trickle away unless you keep track of where and how you spend them. And now that you've been diagnosed with bipolar disorder, you need to manage your time and resources more carefully so you have enough left for yourself and your friends and family, as well as for doctors' appointments, therapy, and support groups.

Re-allocating your time

If you feel like you're under a constant time crunch, go back to Chapter 8, and use the form there to record your daily schedule for the week. Better yet, make four copies, and track your schedule over the course of a month. Take a highlighter and mark any discretionary time expenditures. Be on the lookout for the following flab:

- ✔ Television time
- ✔ Video-game playing
- ✔ Internet access, including e-mail, chat, and instant messaging
- ✔ Unnecessary telephone time

After highlighting potential time-wasting activities, you can begin to trim the fat to free up time you can invest in more productive and rewarding endeavors, such as problem solving, date nights, weekend outings, and exercise.

Downtime is an essential part of a healthy mental diet, so don't eliminate time-wasting activities altogether. Clear out excessive wastes of time, but keep a few mindless interludes to remain refreshed. Just as you have to allow for a few indulgences in a financial budget to reward yourself for sticking to it, you dangle some mental "treats" in front of your nose to help you adhere to your time-management plan.

Another way to overcome time-crunch issues is to pay yourself first, as financial advisors often recommend to clients concerning their investments. Consider that you have 168 hours a week, and calculate from there:

> 168 hours a week
>
> – 56 hours for sleep (8 hours a day)
>
> – 44 hours for work (40, plus commuting time and so on)
>
> – <u>30 hours for household chores (cooking, cleaning, eating, paying bills)</u>
>
> = 38 free hours a week

Now take those 38 hours, and pay yourself and your loved ones first. Whatever remains, you can blow on TV, movies, the Internet, volunteer work, card games, or whatever else commands your interest.

Conserving your energy and resources

According to comedian George Carlin, at the end of the game of life, the guy with the most stuff wins. That may be true, assuming you really like your stuff and have the time and resources to maintain your belongings properly. But if you try to maintain a lifestyle of the rich and famous on a Homer Simpson budget, your mental health is likely to pay the bill.

Less is often more. You may be able to add to your life by subtracting from it, thus saving time, money, and aggravation. The options for streamlining your life are limited only by your imagination and commitment to change. When negotiating lifestyle changes, consider everything that takes your time, energy, and resources, including

- ✔ Home ownership
- ✔ Career
- ✔ Social commitments
- ✔ Kids' sports and school activities
- ✔ Cars and other vehicles
- ✔ Pets

Focus not only on the costs of maintaining your lifestyle choices, but also on the value they return to you. If the costs outweigh the values, you've identified prime candidates for trimming.

Perfecting imperfection

Nowadays, everyone needs to be perfect: the super mom, the beauty queen, the sensitive male hunk, the successful investor, the apprentice, the swan. And if you don't quite stack up to what society and culture expect from you, you'd better get to work. Head to your neighborhood bookstore, load up on all the self-help books and videos you can carry, and pile on a few magazines while you're at it. And don't forget to turn on the television to get blasted with more messages that you're not good enough, smart enough, or talented enough to make it. Our society and our media glorify perfection, and people doggedly pursue it, often to the point of self-destruction. Families can't just be made up of loving individuals who hang out together; they have to be "amazing" and achieve some incredible goal. A loving, available mom doesn't quite make the cut unless she has a hot body and the right clothes and makeup to complete the package.

Learning to accept yourself, imperfections and all, is the only key to achieving genuine satisfaction and peace. People with bipolar disorder discover more quickly than others that you can't keep trying to do more and be more. You have to evaluate what you need to do and what you love to do and then carefully sort through everything else that gets piled onto your plate. The word "no" must be become your mantra, because people always ask you to do one more "little" thing. If you're a working mom, you probably can't make it to every school function. If your spouse has bipolar disorder, you may have to decline a few dinner invitations. Maybe you can't have your children in organized sports because you don't have the time to get them there. Perhaps you can't take on a promotion that will saddle you with ridiculous hours. Only you can make these decisions and live with them. But whatever you choose to do, don't let society define perfection and set unrealistic goals for you. "Doing it all and doing it well" isn't a realistic option for most people, let alone people with bipolar disorder.

Establishing Healthy Routines

Bipolar disorder thrives in an atmosphere in which it calls the shots. When you're depressed, it saps your energy, discourages you from visiting friends and family, and keeps your hand hovering over your alarm clock's snooze button. When you're manic, it revs your thoughts, lifts your inhibitions, and instills a sense of omniscience and omnipotence or irritability and anger that can get you into trouble. In either case, bipolar disorder creates a self-perpetuating, self-destructive mindset that typically discourages sufferers from taking the necessary action to break the cycle.

By establishing healthy routines and making a commitment to stick to them, you can take control and often prevent depression and mania from establishing a foothold. If you're committed to being in bed only eight hours a night and up and about the rest of the time, for example, no matter how you feel, you may prevent some mood episodes or reduce the severity of them when they do come. Your routines help keep the sleep and energy changes of depression and mania down to a dull roar.

In this section, you find out how to regulate your sleep and schedule social activities to gain more control over your moods.

Regulating your sleep

Show us a person with bipolar disorder, and we'll show you a person who sleeps too much, not enough, or not deeply enough. The disorder messes with your sleep patterns, and your disrupted sleep patterns often aggravate your moods. If you want to remain healthy, you need to get some sleep. The following suggestions can help you establish a regular sleep schedule:

- **Go to bed at the same time *every* day.** Refer to Chapter 8 for suggestions on how to build a structured schedule. People with bipolar disorder are commonly night owls, which is okay as long as you commit to a specific bedtime each and every day.

- **Wake up at the same time *every* day.** Yes, even on Saturdays and Sundays.

- **Don't nap.** Napping is like snacking: It can ruin your appetite for sleep.

- **Don't fight insomnia.** Ordering yourself to sleep is usually counterproductive. Use some of the centering exercises in Chapter 8 to bring your thoughts into the moment or engage in a quiet activity, such as reading.

- **Avoid caffeine and other stimulants.** Yeah, we know this is a duh! suggestion, but you wouldn't believe how many people who complain about lack of sleep guzzle coffee or chain-smoke during the day. Sleep specialists say that any caffeine after noon influences your sleep. If you have sleep problems, keep this in mind. Also avoid spicy foods, alcohol, decongestants, and other enemies of sleep.

- **Turn off the television.** If you have a TV or computer in the bedroom, consider moving it out. If you simply can't miss an episode of your favorite show, record it to watch later. If music helps you fall asleep, great; otherwise, turn off the radio or CD player, too.

- **Transition to sleep mode.** Avoid all stimulating input for one full hour before bedtime — phone calls, TV shows, work or schoolwork, and computer activities are all stimulating. Reading, listening to quiet music, and other soothing activities should be the only things you do for the hour prior to bedtime.

✔ **Turn on a fan or other hummer.** Monotonous noise, commonly referred to as *white noise,* helps some people sleep. It may also block out more disturbing noises, such as dogs barking, cars honking, or neighbors bickering.

✔ **Don't exercise before bedtime.** Unless, of course, you consider sex exercise. If you don't have a particular problem with being awake all night after engaging in intimate acts with your significant other, intimacy is usually encouraged. Regular exercise often acts as a stimulant, so try moving exercise time to earlier in the day.

✔ **Get family support.** If your significant other begs you to stay up to watch David Letterman, and your son tramps through the house at 1 a.m. trying to find something to eat, they aren't doing much for your sleep regulation. Everyone in the house needs to get on board. If your cat jumps on your face in the middle of the night, you may need to do something about that, too.

✔ **Work with your doctor.** Ask about changing the time you take your medications, adjusting dosages, or switching/adding medications to help with sleep. If your medications don't put you to sleep soon enough or leave you groggy in the morning, you may need to take them earlier in the evening.

The Depression and Bipolar Support Alliance is so aware of the mental health benefits of regular sleep that it launched a campaign called "Sleepless in America." For more information, check out its Web site at `www.sleepless inamerica.org`. The site provides some additional suggestions for getting a restful night's sleep.

Scheduling social activities

Remaining social as bipolar disorder ravages your life can be quite a challenge. When depressed, you may shun company. After a manic episode, you may hesitate to mix it up with your usual circle of friends, especially if you said or did something embarrassing during your last episode. However, forcing yourself to maintain social contact on a regular basis often delivers some valuable benefits, including the following:

✔ Regulates your schedule

✔ Connects you with others who can often lift your mood

✔ Widens your support network

✔ Provides a social context that enhances your perspective

Not everyone is a social butterfly, so don't feel as though you need to pack your schedule with social occasions. Some people value their time spent alone much more than others. But do try to get out of the house, even if it feels a little painful at first.

Leaving room for spontaneity

Some people think the perfect vacation is to ride around on a tour bus, visiting main attractions. Others prefer to ramble about on their own, searching for hidden gems. And some are content to sit in one place and watch the world go by.

If you enjoy a more freewheeling lifestyle, a rigid routine may feel like too much starch in the collar. To loosen up your lifestyle, program some unplanned time into your schedule. Put regulations on your sleep, work, and meal times, but leave the remainder of your schedule open.

To ensure successful long-term changes, consider making minor adjustments over an extended period of time. You're unlikely to follow through on dramatic changes that don't align with your temperament.

Building Healthy Relationships

Relationships can contribute significantly to stabilizing moods. A friend who's more gregarious than you may encourage you to get out more and become involved in activities that lift your moods. A companion who's calm and stable may act as a metronome, providing you with a steady rhythm and pace that keep your mania in check.

Whether you want to work on improving a current relationship or building a new one, remain aware of the following aspects of a relationship that can affect mood stability:

- **Healthy shared interests:** If your shared interests consist of drinking, smoking, or taking drugs, consider structuring your relationship around healthier activities. Many people who suffer from substance-abuse problems face the difficult choice of having to dump some of their friends in order to make healthier lifestyle adjustments.

- **Acceptance and understanding:** Accepting and understanding bipolar disorder is difficult for you, but it can be even more difficult for friends and relatives who don't have first-hand experience with it. However, if they criticize you for it with words or through their body language and behavior, the criticism only adds to your burden. By becoming more informed about bipolar disorder, the people in your life can learn acceptance and understanding.

✔ **Appreciation:** The people who love you and find you attractive do so not only despite your bipolar disorder, but also frequently because of it, or at least partially because of it. When building new relationships, look for people who appreciate your unique attributes and talents. Be careful of people who appreciate your extreme highs and lows too much; they may encourage unhealthy lifestyle choices for their own entertainment, even though they may be completely oblivious to the effect of their actions.

✔ **Support:** Stabilizing your moods requires extra work on your part. You need to manage your medications, make lifestyle adjustments, and possibly even face periods of unemployment and diminished cash flow. During times of crisis, you need supportive people around you to meet both your physical and emotional needs.

Every so often, evaluate your current relationships to determine if any of them are undermining your mood stability. If you spot potentially harmful relationships, decide whether they're valuable enough to save or if you would benefit from ending the relationships and investing your time and energy in new, potentially productive connections.

Criticism, demands, judgment, and abuse (both physical and verbal) have no place in a healthy relationship. Through therapy, you can often identify these elements and root them out, assuming all parties involved are committed to improving the relationship. If you're in an unhealthy relationship, and the other party refuses to negotiate, you face the difficult choice of remaining in the relationship and risking your health or leaving the relationship.

Making Your Job Work for You

Sometimes, a job is just a job — something you do between the time you wake up and the time you eat dinner. It puts some cash in your bank account. But a job is usually much more than that. It can deliver bountiful benefits, including the following:

✔ **Security:** Your employer may provide you with health and life insurance and retirement benefits.

✔ **Independence:** Supporting yourself financially provides independence and freedom. You don't need to live according to the rules and regulations imposed by people who support you.

- ✔ **Identity:** You're not just you; you're also a lawyer, a cook, a custodian, a nurse, a singer, a butcher, a baker, or a candlestick maker. Losing a job can make you wonder who you are, which isn't always a good thing.

- ✔ **Sense of accomplishment:** Being a productive member of society can fill you with a sense of accomplishment and pride.

- ✔ **Community:** Your colleagues and coworkers make up a community of people with shared experiences. Even when you're griping about low pay or an overbearing boss, you're bonding with others, which can help stabilize your mood.

- ✔ **Structure:** Assuming you have fairly regular work hours, your work schedule can help structure your life (see the first section of this chapter).

Bipolar disorder threatens to rob you of all these benefits by making tasks more difficult to perform, complicating your life with medication and doctors' appointments, and increasing your sensitivity to the pressures inherent in your job. In some cases, bipolar disorder may convince you that you can no longer function as a productive worker, which is usually bunk.

As a human being, you have the right to work and the right to reap the benefits of a good job. The trick is to find an enjoyable and rewarding job that doesn't destabilize your moods. Finding such a job is no easy task, but this section offers some suggestions, techniques, and tips that can help you succeed.

Hunting for a rewarding job

Some people change jobs as effortlessly as they change their socks. Others are so entrenched in their career paths that any change seems insurmountable; they've been working as a teacher, investment broker, emergency nurse, or whatever for 15 years and can't imagine doing anything else. Or maybe after 20 years on the job, they have too much to lose by packing up and moving on. If your current job is contributing to mood instability, however, you may need to make some adjustments; think of it as supplemental mental health insurance.

The prospect of any major change in your life can leave you feeling overwhelmed and curtail any attempts to generate a list of alternatives. Step back, take a deep breath, and look at your situation one small step at a time — a strategy that reduces the massive anxiety associated with looking at a big task all at once. You climb a mountain one step at a time by using equipment to keep you from falling. A major life overhaul requires the same systematic approach. And don't be hesitant to get help and perspective from a loved one or therapist.

So, what are your options? They basically boil down to the following five:

- **Improve your current job situation:** Do you think you'd have the ideal job if it just weren't for this or that? Perhaps you can make a few adjustments to find this *and* that. Refer to the following two sections for details.

- **Change positions:** Your employer is great, your supervisor is a doll, but you just can't imagine doing the same task you've been doing for the past few years. One option is to seek out a different position in the same company — maybe something that's less stressful.

- **Change employers:** If you enjoy your work but find your work environment unbearable and unfixable, consider looking for another employer in the same business.

- **Change careers:** Some careers are pressure cookers, destined to trigger mood episodes. If you're an emergency medical technician, air-traffic controller, police officer, 911 dispatcher, grave-shift worker, or on another job with irregular hours or a high level of stress, tabulate the toll that your job takes on your mental health, and consider changing careers.

- **File for disability:** If you need to work with your healthcare providers before you feel well enough to return to work, you can file for disability benefits, which we explain at the end of this chapter.

Changing careers can be a monumental task, but it can also be fun to find out what other people do to make money. If you're considering a career change, check out *Cool Careers For Dummies,* by Marty Nemko, Paul Edwards, and Sarah Edwards, and *Changing Careers For Dummies,* by Carol L. McClelland, PhD (both published by Wiley). These books list some of the more interesting careers available and impart solid advice on how to execute a successful career change.

Negotiating a healthy schedule

You probably devote about 40 hours of your 168-hour week to your employer, and that total may not be negotiable. How you serve your 40 hours a week, however, may be negotiable, and under the Americans with Disabilities Act, your employer may be legally obligated to accommodate schedule adjustments. What sort of adjustments can you request? The following list provides some suggestions:

- **Start and end time of your work day:** Changing the time of day you work may be necessary for establishing a healthy circadian rhythm and for accommodating the side effects of your medications. Some employers offer flex time to all employees — for example, employees must work eight hours a day sometime between the hours of 7 a.m. and 7 p.m.

- **Break frequency and times:** You may need more frequent breaks during the day or breaks at specific times to take your medicine.

A good job gone bad

At 30, Renee was on the fast track to a successful career in nonprofit management — a career that fed her passions and showcased her talents. She loved the social activities — the parties, the fund-raisers, the presentations — and she would spend hours at home designing and building presentations to wow her audiences.

That was before her full-blown manic attack. It crept up on her gradually and unnoticed, because she was always a high-energy person, but when it hit, it hit hard. Her condition eventually sent her to the hospital. Over time, the mania subsided, but it transitioned into a deep depression that kept Renee from working for several weeks.

With treatment, Renee was able to return to work and pick up where she left off, but when she returned, her focus and drive were diminished. Smiling to clients and pressing the flesh with potential donors quickly sapped her energy, and she no longer had the get-up-and-go to work long hours on her slide-show presentations after work. Thinking that her medications were diminishing her energy level, she stopped taking them, only to experience an inevitable relapse and several more weeks off work.

Renee discussed her situation and feelings with her family, doctor, and therapist. She knew deep down that the nature of her job was contributing to her illness, but she felt that changing careers at this point wasn't an option. Finally, Renee hit on a solution. She used her relationships at her current job to connect to a smaller organization where she could do more desk work and less partying. Renee sometimes missed her old life, and she still struggled with her moods and medicines, but with her new job, she had one less enemy to battle.

- ✔ **Time off for doctor and therapy visits:** Your doctor and therapist may have office hours that conflict with your work schedule, in which case you need additional time off during weekdays.

- ✔ **Part-time employment:** If you can't work full time, request part-time work, although this may affect your benefits.

- ✔ **Telecommuting opportunities:** Depending on the nature of your job and the flexibility of your employer, you may be able to work all or part of the week at home.

Work closely with your supervisor and your company's human-resources department to establish a schedule that's healthy for you and productive for your employer. If your employer refuses to make the necessary accommodations, submit your request in writing, accompanied by a note from your doctor or therapist. The following sections provide additional information about your rights as an employee.

Knowing your rights

Most people who suffer from bipolar disorder are dedicated employees. When they miss work due to a mood episode, they're not trying to stick it to their employers. More often than not, they feel guilty for missing work and for any inconvenience or disappointment they may have caused. They may even consider themselves a burden and quit in order to relieve their employers of the responsibility.

We can't tell you whether you should stay in your current job or leave, but we do encourage you to carefully consider your options before you make a final decision. Keep in mind that when your employer hired you, the company made a commitment to you that it can't break simply because you happen to be ill. As an employee, you have certain rights that your employer is legally obligated to honor. It's your responsibility to know your rights and to become aware of the potential risks and benefits of disclosing information about your condition so you can negotiate from a position of power. The following question-and-answer session leads you through the basics:

Q: What information, if any, am I legally obligated to provide?

A: You may need to provide a letter or note from your doctor to excuse an absence and make yourself eligible for sick pay. You're not legally obligated to disclose any information about your diagnosis or treatment. People can ask for information, but only you decide whether or not to provide details.

Q: Can my employer fire me for having bipolar disorder?

A: Legally, no. The Americans with Disabilities Act makes it illegal to fire an employee due to a physical or mental disability. If you choose to inform your supervisor, do it in writing, and keep a record of it. To find out more about your rights under the Americans with Disabilities Act, visit www.ada.gov or call 800-514-0301.

Q: What are the potential benefits of disclosing my condition?

A: Many employees with bipolar disorder find that disclosure relieves the stress of trying to keep a secret. In addition, when your supervisor and one or two coworkers know that you have bipolar disorder, they can help you monitor your symptoms and provide appropriate assistance when you need it most.

Q: What are the potential drawbacks of disclosing my condition?

A: Your supervisor may view you as a liability and overlook you for promotions or even try to force you out without actually firing you. Ill-informed, closed-minded colleagues may avoid you or mistreat you. You can, however, choose to fight back by refusing exile and by carefully logging incidents of unfair practices and treatment that follow the disclosure of your diagnosis. However, keep your eye on the time and energy required for this and how it affects your overall mental health.

Q: Can I request special accommodations?

A: Yes. Under the American with Disabilities Act, you have a right to *reasonable* accommodations. Reasonable accommodations may include extra training for specific tasks, the assistance of a mentor or job coach, partitions or headphones to help minimize distractions, written as opposed to verbal instructions, and the reassigning of minor job duties to others so you can focus on your primary responsibilities.

Q: If I take time off, will my job be available when I return?

A: According to the Family and Medical Leave Act, you can take up to 12 weeks of unpaid leave with health coverage each year. If your employer must hire someone to fill your position, your company must offer you a comparable job when you return. You have to fill out and submit the appropriate paperwork, and smaller companies may not be subject to this law. For more information, visit the U.S. Department of Labor Web site at www.dol.gov/esa/whd/fmla/ or call 866-487-9243.

Q: What should I do if I have a relapse?

A: If you feel overwhelmed after you return to work, resist any impulse to quit, which can be very strong during an episode. Report your ill feelings and go home for the day. If you think you need to see your doctor or therapist, make an appointment. As long as you don't quit, you're still an employee with certain rights. Don't make any major life changes or decisions during a major mood episode or even early in recovery. Maintain the best mood you can with what you have, but don't quit your job or take a new one while you're depressed or manic.

Q: Can I get my job back if I quit during a mood episode?

A: Maybe. You have a much better chance if you request your job back within six months from the time you quit and if you can document that you've been receiving treatment. Approach your employer first and then contact ADA (visit www.ada.gov or call 800-514-0301) if your employer needs additional prodding. If you can't pursue this right now, ask one of your support people to help you. Of course, your employer may decide to hire you back, whether or not she's legally obligated to do so.

When returning to work after an extended leave of absence, touch base with your doctor and therapist at least once every two weeks until you adjust to your work schedule. Having a doctor or therapist appointment set up at the end of your first week back is always a good idea.

Filing for disability benefits

The Social Security Administration (SSA) treats mental and physical disabilities equally. That's the official party line, anyway. In reality, mental disabilities are more difficult to prove. If you can walk into a Social Security office, talk to the receptionist, and fill out the paperwork, uninformed bureaucrats usually conclude that you're quite able to work. Here are the hoops you must jump through to meet the guidelines and gain approval.

Meeting the guidelines

When you file for disability because of a mood disorder, the Social Security workers evaluate whether or not you can still perform "work-related tasks." Using a set of guidelines referred to as the RFC (Residual Function Capacity) evaluation, the SSA checks to make sure you meet the following conditions:

✔ **You meet clinical criteria for bipolar disorder:** Your doctor may be able to provide the necessary information to enable the SSA to make this determination. The SSA may also require that you see one of its recommended doctors for a second opinion.

✔ **Your disorder results in at least two of the following:**

- Significant restriction of everyday activities

- Significant social difficulties

- Deficiencies in concentration that result in failure to complete tasks on time

- Recurring episodes of deterioration at work that cause you to withdraw from situations or that worsen your symptoms

Disability doesn't have to be forever. Leaving your job and filing for disability may be painful or make you feel like a failure, but remind yourself that you're doing what you must to regain your health and prepare yourself to be a better employee in the future.

Improving your chances of approval

If bipolar disorder prevents you from holding down a job right now, consider applying for disability immediately, no matter how unsure you are about your chances of approval. Here are some suggestions that may improve your chances of success:

✔ **Consult your doctor and therapist:** Their approval, support, and assistance are critical to helping you establish the fact that bipolar disorder prevents you from working and that any work during this stage of your illness can worsen your symptoms. If you're not currently seeing a doctor for treatment, the SSA is very unlikely to approve your claim.

✔ **File immediately:** Disability claims can take several weeks to months to process and often require that you file multiple appeals. In the meantime, you may go through your savings and face some real financial hardship. The sooner you file, the better. Most disability lawyers won't even talk to you until you've filed a claim and been denied, so don't waste your time consulting a lawyer at this point.

✔ **Appeal:** If the SSA denies your initial claim, which it does 60 to 70 percent of the time, consult a lawyer or other legal representative to file an appeal. A judge can override the SSA's original decision, but you may need to appear at a hearing, in which case you should have a qualified legal representative. You may need to appeal several times.

✔ **Keep your doctor appointments and health records:** Seeing your doctor regularly provides you with documented proof of your bipolar disorder and keeps your doctor in the loop, ensuring that she will support your appeal. You can't expect your doctor to cooperate if she hasn't seen you in three months. Use the mood chart provided in Chapter 12 or a journal or Depression and Bipolar Support Alliance personal calendar (www.dbsalliance.org) to keep track of the ways your disorder affects your moods and life. Documented evidence can help your case.

✔ **Have your doctor complete an RFC form for you:** Your doctor's evaluation of your ability to perform work-related tasks often carries more weight than your personal opinion. Usually, the SSA has a form that it sends to your doctor as part of the process of applying for disability, so you may not have to request it from your doctor.

✔ **Be nice:** Whenever you want something done, you need to treat the people involved with courtesy and respect. Most SSA employees are inundated with paperwork and phone calls — giving them grief can only hurt your case, not help it. Give yourself time to cool off before calling if you're angry or hurt about needing to appeal or not receiving a response as quickly as you'd like.

✔ **Keep copies:** Copy everything before submitting it.

✔ **Follow up:** Wait a few days after you mail your claim and any pertinent paperwork before you call to make sure that the SSA received the documents. If you can establish a good relationship with an individual at your local SSA office, you have a better chance of keeping everything straight.

Don't give up. The SSA may seem to be doing all that it can to discourage people from filing for disability benefits, but persistence often pays off, and the SSA is becoming more sensitive to the fact that bipolar disorder and other mental illnesses can be as debilitating as physical disabilities. If you can't work for a while because of your disorder, you have every right to receive benefits.

Chapter 14

Working Out and Eating Right

. . . .

In This Chapter

▶ Exercising your way to mood stability

▶ Moderating your moods through yoga, T'ai Chi, and meditation

▶ Feeding your moods a balanced diet

▶ Steering clear of easily accessible stimulants and depressants

. . . .

*Y*ou know that diet and exercise are important, because you can feel it. When you eat a heavy meal and double-dip on dessert, you feel like a beached blob of blubber. When you take a brisk walk or work out for an hour at the local gym, you feel pumped up and energized. But in the process of juggling your medications, doctor appointments, therapy, job, family, and everything else in your life, you can easily overlook the most obvious and basic components of your mental health: diet and exercise.

Can a healthy diet and exercise cure you? Not in and of themselves, but they can act as low-cost, healthy complementary therapies, especially for bipolar depression. A healthy diet combined with a sensible exercise program increases the efficiency of your cardiovascular system, improves digestion, and releases mood-enhancing endorphins. A healthy lifestyle can also help you maintain steady energy levels and fend off the mind rot that commonly accompanies a sedentary life.

In this chapter, we increase your awareness of how diet and exercise can affect your moods and mood medications. We explore the benefits of cardiovascular exercises, such as walking and running, and reveal the mood-stabilizing effects of centering exercises, including yoga and T'ai Chi. We introduce you to foods that boost your moods and warn about those that sap your energy. And we confront the evil consumables — caffeine, alcohol, and other stimulants and depressants — that are well-known mood destabilizers.

As you read this chapter, keep in mind that your brain is part of your body, and anything you can do to improve the condition of your body will likely enhance your moods.

Sweating Out Your Bipolar Depression

You're probably aware that aerobic exercise is good for both body and mind, but you may not know about the unique benefits exercise offers people with bipolar disorder:

- **Exercise improves depression without inducing mania.** Because most antidepressants carry a risk of inducing mania, especially when taken without a mood stabilizer, exercise provides an effective alternative. If exercising late in the day keeps you from falling asleep, however, consider moving your exercise routine to an earlier time slot.

- **Exercise helps control weight gain, which commonly accompanies the use of antipsychotic medications and mood stabilizers.** Antipsychotic medications and some mood stabilizers, including lithium and Depakote, potentially have the negative side effect of causing weight gain. Exercise can help minimize this effect.

You don't need to down protein shakes and pump iron every day to get in shape. If your primary goal is to regulate your moods, a 15- to 20-minute daily walk is all you really need. Sure, you can do more, but if your current exercise program consists of *thinking* about going running, you're more likely to follow through on a modest commitment, and you can immediately begin to reap the mood-stabilizing benefits of aerobic exercise:

- Fresh air and sunshine

- Increased ability to sleep (in many cases)

- Improved digestion

- Increased energy levels

- Sense of accomplishment

- The feeling that you're playing an active role in controlling your moods

Consult your doctor before you begin any strenuous exercise program, especially if you're taking a mood stabilizer like lithium. When you perspire, you lose fluids, which can increase the levels of these medications in your system. In the case of lithium, increased levels can create a potentially fatal condition. Your doctor can recommend ways to reduce the risks.

Centering Yourself through Yoga, T'ai Chi, and Meditation

Throughout the day, people tend to focus on external stimuli — the work that sits in front of you, the people who bump into you, car horns beeping, telephones ringing, kids yelling, and so on. Your brain and body react to these stimuli in subtle ways that you may not even notice. When you concentrate on a project, your breathing becomes more shallow, your stomach tenses up, and you squint. These reactions can affect your overall physiology and influence your moods in negative ways. In some cases, the increased tension can ultimately build up to levels that induce full-fledged depression or mania.

By increasing your *mindfulness* — your awareness of how you feel at this moment — you can often counteract the negative effects of your body's unconscious reactions and learn to relax more completely. Several disciplines can increase your mindfulness, including yoga, T'ai Chi, and meditation, which we cover in the following sections.

Yoga

In addition to increasing your flexibility (so you can twist yourself into a pretzel), yoga's primary goal is to increase your mindfulness. The distinctions among mind, body, and soul melt away, opening you up to the moment and enabling you to experience your connectedness to all being. And yoga feels good, too.

You can probably sign up for Yoga 101 at your neighborhood YMCA or community center, but be aware that several types of yoga are available, including Hatha, Karma, Kundalini, Raja, and Tantric. Different types of yoga appeal to different people:

- ✔ **Hatha yoga** uses the body, through postures and breathing, to control the mind and senses and to release psychic and physical energy. Hatha is one of the most common beginning-level yoga disciplines. Teachers generally encourage students to develop at their own pace.

- ✔ **Kundalini yoga** focuses on poses and intense breathing exercises designed to awaken the six *chakras,* or main energy centers of the human body. Breathing exercises are central to many therapies designed to reduce anxiety, which is often associated with bipolar disorder.

For additional information about the various forms of yoga and specific instructions, check out *Yoga For Dummies,* by Georg Feuerstein, PhD, and Larry Payne, PhD (Wiley), or follow along with a videotape, such as *Basic Yoga Workout For Dummies* with Sara Ivanhoe.

T'ai Chi

T'ai Chi is an ancient Chinese martial art that people are currently practicing both as exercise and meditation. Many practitioners describe it as "moving meditation." Its slow, controlled movements and breathing can reduce stress, tension, anxiety, anger, depression, and fatigue and sharpen mental acuity and focus. Because T'ai Chi isn't a strenuous exercise, you can perform it during your lunch hour without getting all hot and sweaty.

T'ai Chi For Dummies, by Therese Iknoian (Wiley), is an excellent beginner's guide to the philosophy and practice of T'ai Chi.

Meditation

Although ancient Eastern practices have a certain romantic aura to them, you don't need to sign up for yoga or T'ai Chi classes in order to become more mindful. You can increase your mindfulness simply by making a conscious effort to be more aware of what you do every day. The following exercises can help you practice mindfulness:

- When you're stuck in traffic, focus on your breathing or on the music that's playing instead of thinking about where you want to go or what you need to do later.

- When you lie down to go to sleep, focus on your breathing, the feel of the pillow and sheets, and the darkness around you.

- Stop and note what you're thinking and feeling several times during your day at work. If you find yourself worrying about a deadline or a problem, try to bring your thoughts and feelings into the moment, and focus on the task at hand.

- Make a trivial task into a ceremony to become more mindful of it. Whether you're washing your hands, preparing a meal, brewing a pot of coffee, or scrubbing dishes, focus on the moment, and become aware of all the sensory stimulation around you.

The more you practice mindfulness and meditation, the easier they become. By remaining committed to becoming more aware of the moment, you make the process second nature. A bonus is that worries, time crunches, and financial problems may become less overwhelming, and you can start to tackle them effectively.

Serving Up Healthy Foods in the Right Portions

You can't pour soda into your car's gas tank and expect it to purr; likewise, you can't pack your body with junk food and expect to feel energized and alert. Your body requires the proper mix of nutrients for optimum performance.

It needs carbohydrates for energy, proteins to form muscle and supply the amino acids that your body requires to produce some neurotransmitters, and a collection of vitamins and minerals to enable your body to carry out its many physiological processes.

When you're feeling depressed or manic, your diet is likely to suffer. You may overeat to feed your mood, fast because food just doesn't appeal to you, or crave only foods that are high in sugar and starch. Following some basic nutritional recommendations can improve your overall mood stability in the long run:

✔ Eat regularly — three full meals a day or several small meals throughout the course of a day.

✔ Don't skip meals — especially breakfast.

✔ Eat a well-balanced diet.

✔ Consume coffee and alcohol in moderation, if at all.

The following sections provide specific recommendations to help you evaluate and improve your diet.

How do you feel after you eat?

One of Mother Nature's cruel jokes is that we often crave the foods and substances that can do our moods the most harm — caffeine, alcohol, sugars, and starches — and avoid those that carry the greatest benefits — complex carbohydrates and protein.

What effect do the foods you eat have on your moods? To find out, keep track of what you eat and how you feel after eating certain foods. Here are some simple steps:

1. **Jot down how you feel just before eating.**

   Do you feel normal, tired, or full of energy?

2. **Eat your meal or snack.**

3. **Jot down how you feel 30 minutes and then 60 minutes after eating.**

   Do you feel normal or tired? Is your heart beating significantly faster or harder? Do you feel full of energy, light-headed, or wobbly?

If a certain food makes you feel terrible, you may have an intolerance for that food. Symptoms of food intolerance can include stomach pain, nausea, diarrhea, gassiness, and headache. When your body isn't feeling well, your mood generally follows, so try to limit or avoid foods that cause discomfort.

Food allergies are a different story. A true food allergy can cause skin reactions, shortness of breath, rapid heart rate, and jitteriness. More severe allergic reactions include swelling of the mucous membranes and a potentially life-threatening closure of the airways. These side effects are medical emergencies. Only about 2 percent of the adult population has a true food allergy.

Alternative-medicine experts argue that many hidden food allergies contribute to all kinds of negative symptoms, including emotional and behavioral reactions, but well-designed research studies don't support this idea. Most medical experts agree that if certain foods bring discomfort, they can contribute to a dip in mood, but so far food doesn't appear to be a primary cause of psychiatric symptoms. If you suspect that you may have a food allergy, consult a specialist for a thorough evaluation, but question any claims that you can fix your bipolar disorder solely through nutritional management.

The amount and type of food you consume can also influence how you feel after a meal. If you get tired right after lunch, try eating more protein and vegetables and less sugar and other simple carbohydrates (see the following section). Also, try eating smaller meals. Having the equivalent of a turkey dinner for lunch can deplete your energy for the rest of the afternoon.

Sugar and other simple carbohydrates

Need an energy boost? For a quick fix, sugar and starch usually do the trick. A soft drink, a doughnut, a snack cake . . . pick your poison. Do they work? You bet. Not only do they inject you with a quick boost of energy, but they also elevate your serotonin levels. But sugar and simple carbohydrates have a dark side. Foods such as white rice, potato chips, cookies, crackers, and pasta often take your body on a roller-coaster ride of sugar highs and lows. You may feel an initial energy surge, but watch out later. In about 30 to 60 minutes, you crash as your blood-sugar drops, leaving you drained and craving your next sugar fix.

The reason that a sugar buzz doesn't last is that it triggers a dramatic boost in blood-sugar levels that your body must respond to in order to survive. As your blood-sugar rises, your pancreas dumps insulin into your system to convert excess sugar to fat for storage. With a large rush of insulin, your blood-sugar drops, making you feel sleepy or cranky and often hungry for more sweets.

To steady your moods, cut down on junk foods, including soda, cookies, candy, and cake, and avoid simple carbohydrates, including most breads and pastas, potatoes, and highly processed foods. Whole-grain products, vegetables, and fresh fruits contain complex carbohydrates that enter your system gradually, preventing extreme fluctuations in your blood-sugar levels.

Chocolate, glorious chocolate

Considered by some to be the perfect mood food, chocolate has several ingredients that contribute to mood alteration: a dash of sugar to increase energy and serotonin levels, a pinch of phenylethylamine (a brain chemical that your body releases when you fall in love), smidgens of theobromine and magnesium to enhance brain function, a touch of caffeine to make you more alert, and a few grams of protein to boost the excitatory neurotransmitters.

Of course, too much chocolate can give you a bellyache, which is a definite downer. Hershey Kisses or a handful of M&Ms in moderation, however, may be just the morsels you need to get over that midafternoon speed bump.

Protein

When you hear the word "protein," you probably think "muscle." But protein contributes to many other areas of the body as well. The basic building blocks of proteins are amino acids, several of which act as neurological regulators. When you consume protein, your body immediately breaks it down into amino acids so it can transport them to where your body needs them. One of these amino acids, tyrosine, is a building block of excitatory neurotransmitters — dopamine and norepinephrine — that can increase energy, make you feel more alert, and improve performance.

We don't recommend that you follow the Atkins diet and eat only protein and vegetables, but obtaining sufficient protein can help stabilize your moods. Meat provides the easiest way to obtain the nine essential amino acids that comprise complete proteins, but vegetarians can get their protein by combining complementary food items, such as beans and rice, beans and corn, and whole wheat and peanuts. Vegetarians should also monitor their intake of essential vitamins and minerals (especially B-complex vitamins and selenium); refer to Chapter 9 for information about supplements.

Fruits and vegetables

Open your fridge and take a quick inventory of the fresh fruits and vegetables you have on hand. Chances are that your stock is woefully inadequate. Most people in the United States subsist on a steady diet of sugar, fat, and protein. Fruits and vegetables serve as garnishes to make the meat and potatoes look better.

To improve your moods, at least indirectly, increase your daily consumption of fresh fruit and fresh or frozen vegetables. These food items offer some unique benefits you can't find in most processed foods:

- ✔ **Fiber,** which improves digestion
- ✔ **Vitamins and minerals** commonly lacking in meat, pasta, and breads
- ✔ **Complex carbohydrates** that provide a steady flow of sustenance and energy throughout the day (rather than the highs and lows associated with sugary and starchy foods)

Avoiding the Not-So-Good, the Bad, and the Ugly

Caffeine, nicotine, diet pills, alcohol, marijuana, and other uppers and downers form a veritable cornucopia of legal and illegal mood manipulators. If you wash down your antianxiety medication with an energy drink and head out for a night of bar-hopping with your buddies, you may be doing more harm than you can possibly imagine. Although these substances may seem innocent enough, they can wreak havoc on your carefully crafted medication combination and attempts at improving your diet and exercise.

The following sections introduce a few of the most common and available drugs and substances that can cause problems. The list isn't exhaustive; we don't include plenty of dangerous street drugs, including methamphetamine and cocaine. Such illicit drugs are so wrong in so many ways, we've deemed them too obvious to mention.

Caffeine, nicotine, and other uppers

Getting jacked up on coffee, tea, or soda can be a thrill. The chemical reactions pump you up and make you feel a little less groggy in the morning and after lunch, and the drinks taste yummy, too. For an added boost, you can light up a cigarette. Unfortunately, these stimulants can bump up your heart rate and blood pressure and accelerate both your brain and body. They can magnify mania, irritate a depressed brain, and join forces to undermine the efforts of your mood stabilizers.

To minimize the negative effects of these socially acceptable mood boosters, consider taking the following actions:

✔ **Eliminate caffeine, or monitor your intake and reduce consumption.**
Some studies show that ingesting small amounts of caffeine throughout the morning and afternoon may be more beneficial and less harmful than consuming large quantities at a single sitting.

✔ **Stop smoking, or cut back on the number of cigarettes you smoke.**
This applies to tobacco chewers and cigar aficionados, too.

✔ **Avoid any other stimulants — especially amphetamines.**
Amphetamines are intensified versions of caffeine and nicotine and can easily trigger full-blown manic episodes or psychosis. If you have a problem with amphetamine use, speak to your doctor or seek out community resources, such as Narcotics Anonymous (www.na.org), to get help right away.

Quitting caffeine or nicotine use cold turkey can be extremely difficult. Withdrawal symptoms include headache, fatigue, and irritability. Taper off your use gradually, or remain vigilant of any significant mood shifts if you decide to quit cold turkey. Your doctor should be more than happy to help you develop a cessation program to alleviate withdrawal symptoms.

Alcohol, marijuana, and other downers

When you're under emotional and psychological duress, a bottle of booze, a bag of weed, or a couple of downers may seem like welcome relief. That's one of the reasons why so many people with bipolar disorder self-medicate with these substances. Although drugs do provide temporary relief, the negative long-term effects and the potentially dangerous interactions they can have with prescription medications far outweigh the benefits.

In and of itself, alcoholism is destructive; it's a potentially deadly illness that tears apart families and shatters lives. In combination with bipolar disorder, alcohol can be a life-stopper, causing the following problems:

✔ **As a depressant, alcohol cranks down your brain energy.** In high concentrations, it poisons the brain and can cause death. It can actually make you feel more depressed over time.

✔ **Alcohol reduces impulse control.** In people with mania, it can enhance dangerous behavioral patterns. In a depressed person, alcohol can take away the hesitation to commit suicide. Completed suicides are very often related to alcohol intoxication in a depressed person.

✔ **Alcohol can interact in dangerous ways with some of the medications used to combat bipolar disorder — particularly lithium.** It can change blood levels of medication, and it can cause increased sedation and slowed thinking — more so than alcohol or medicine alone. In some combinations, such as with tranquilizers like Valium, alcohol can cause you to stop breathing.

The after-school message here is that alcohol and bipolar disorder don't mix. If you don't have an alcohol dependence, stop using it. If you have an alcohol problem, get help right away. Talk to your doctor or contact Alcoholics Anonymous (www.alcoholics-anonymous.org). Talk to your family. Alcohol abuse presents a life-threatening problem. Don't wait.

Toking a joint or gobbling up a batch of marijuana brownies can also calm your nerves — at least temporarily — but marijuana is another potentially dangerous agent, especially when you're working hard to maintain mood stability. If you self-medicate with marijuana, strongly consider the following reasons to stop:

✔ Although marijuana can generate feelings of euphoria, it can also trigger paranoia and anxiety.

✔ Because marijuana is unregulated, its active ingredient, THC, varies in concentration with each batch. You never know what you're really getting.

✔ Like alcohol, marijuana can decrease inhibitions and increase your chances of getting in trouble.

Smoking marijuana when you have bipolar disorder is like injecting an unknown fuel into a high-performance engine. You've spent time, money, and energy tuning up your mental performance with medications, therapy, and lifestyle changes. Don't fry your engine on a fleeting joyride.

Weight-loss and energy supplements

Popping a diet pill or gulping an energy drink may seem innocent enough when you're in good health, but many diet pills and energy tonics are laced with potentially dangerous stimulants — some that are just as dangerous as nicotine or caffeine. Some diet "doctors" even hand out bona-fide amphetamines and amphetamine-like substances to help their patients shed a few pounds. Taking pills to keep your weight down is particularly tempting if your doctor just put you on a medication that causes you to gain weight (like lithium).

We're not telling you that you have to live with weight gain, but you can take safer steps to keep your weight in check:

✔ **Consult your psychiatrist.** He or she may be able to suggest an alternative medication that doesn't cause weight gain or add a medication to safely counteract that side effect. Your psychiatrist can monitor your glucose and cholesterol levels for some medications. Use this information to help plan your dietary strategies.

Janice's diet compromise

Janice was a young woman who had struggled with a major weight problem throughout her life. As a teenager, she lost over 100 pounds and had maintained her lighter weight during her first few years of college. The summer before her senior year, however, she developed an agitated depression that evolved into a manic episode. Her medication trials were difficult, but a combination of an SSRI (Selective Serotonin Reuptake Inhibitor) and lithium proved effective. The only problem was that she regained almost all the weight she had lost. She started eating more when she first became depressed, and the lithium seemed to pile on more pounds daily.

After a few months of stability, Janice became so frustrated with her weight gain that she stopped all her medications abruptly. She immediately crashed into a profound depression and was hospitalized. Eventually, she returned to lithium — at the lowest possible dose — with a commitment to exercise more and consume less junk food. Although she didn't return to her ideal weight, Janice did manage to shed most of her extra pounds and accepted the fact that a stable mood is more important than 30 extra pounds.

✔ **Consult your family physician or a qualified nutritionist to develop a sound weight-loss program.** Messing with your appetite and weight without help isn't advisable when you're working hard to keep your body and brain comfortable and in balance.

Drastic dieting — fasting or following extreme low-calorie regimens — can be as dangerous as diet medicines when it comes to your bipolar treatment. Medication levels and effects change with body weight and metabolism, so dramatic or rapid body changes can do damage when you're trying to stabilize your moods and medications.

Over-the-counter medications

How do you find out which everyday medications are safe with your bipolar meds? Check with your doctor, of course. In the meantime, consult the following list of common medications that are high up on the no-no list:

✔ Avoid pain relievers such as ibuprofen and Naprosyn when you're on lithium. Your kidneys clear these meds, and they can potentially cause kidney damage.

✔ Decongestants such as Sudafed (and any others that contain pseudo-ephedrine) are stimulants and can exacerbate mania or depression or worsen symptoms, even when calming agents are on board.

✔ Avoid Dextromethorphan, a cough suppressant, when you're taking SSRIs. This drug is abused in some cases; people take very high doses of the cough suppressant to induce euphoria. Read the labels and choose a cough suppressant that doesn't use Dextromethorphan.

✔ Avoid over-the-counter sleep aids unless your doctor gives you the thumbs-up.

Herbal and so-called "natural" products can also botch your bipolar treatments. Many herbal medications, although they may sound no more harmful than salt and pepper, can be quite powerful. Here are a handful you should watch out for:

✔ Ephedra and its more recent substitutes are stimulants to be avoided.

✔ Valerian is a powerful sedative, but it can have numerous interactions with psychiatric medications and symptoms.

✔ Melatonin can be a useful sleep aid, but it may be harmful in combination with some antidepressants.

✔ Kava, marketed as a calming agent, can cause severe liver damage.

✔ St. John's wort can make birth-control pills ineffective.

Chapter 9 covers herbal and natural products in greater depth to help you weigh the potential benefits and risks, but you should always consult your doctor before adding another substance to your brew. By keeping your doctor informed, you facilitate the process of arriving at a medical treatment that's safe and effective for you. Most psychiatrists are comfortable talking about these compounds with patients and will look into possible interactions.

Chapter 15

Battling the Urge to Fly Solo

· ·

· ·

*I*ndependence is what people generally value most. It's one of the few rights in life that people are willing to risk their lives to attain. When you receive your bipolar diagnosis, it can make you feel completely dependent at first — on your healthcare providers, family, friends, and other concerned individuals. In the midst of a mood episode, you may not even be able to trust your own perceptions and judgment.

Although a loss of freedom may not seem like it's worth it, what are your options? You basically have two choices:

✔ Get professional treatment and, with the help of others and the right medications and therapy, regain control over your life.

✔ Relinquish your fate to bipolar disorder, in which case you risk ruining your relationships, career, finances, and other aspects of your life that create your identity.

When faced with these two choices, a surprising percentage of people with bipolar disorder choose the second option when first diagnosed. Why? Well, that's the subject of this chapter. Here, we reveal several reasons why you may want to resist medical treatment. We do this to validate any apprehensions you have and to help you overcome any natural resistance you may want to put up. We explain the risks of not adhering to your treatment plan, provide tips to help you manage your medications, and offer advice on how to team up with your doctor and support network. Throughout this chapter, you discover how to take the necessary steps to regain your sense of independence by accepting and mastering the mood-management tools at your disposal.

"Why I Don't Take My Meds"

Head over to the nearest all-you-can-eat buffet, and ask the diners waddling back to their tables with heaping portions if they're following their doctors' orders and acting in the best interest of their overall health. Dig through any medicine cabinet (just don't get caught!), and count the unused portions of medications that have specific instructions to take the medicines until they're used up. The tendency to ignore doctors' orders and avoid taking medication doesn't apply only to people with bipolar disorder; the rebellion is universal. People just want to enjoy their lives, unfettered by diet restrictions, medications, and "helpful" advice.

The resistance to medical intervention is even more prevalent in people with bipolar disorder, and for good reason — actually, for several good reasons. In this section, we explore some of the most common reasons that people with bipolar disorder stop taking their medications, and we provide rebuttals to convince you to continue taking your medications, as prescribed, even when you prefer not to.

They don't work

Aspirin and Tylenol can alleviate pain in a matter of minutes. Decongestants typically start to work in less than an hour. Depakote, a very effective mood stabilizer, takes about 10 days. Prozac and other SSRI (Selective Serotonin Reuptake Inhibitor) antidepressants commonly require three to six weeks to achieve their full therapeutic effects. No wonder why someone suffering from depression or mania stops taking the medications; having to wait over a week for relief is torture, not treatment.

The following suggestions may help you endure the delay and possibly shorten it:

- ✔ **Ask your doctor up front how long each medication should take before it begins to work.** Sometimes, knowing that a medication may take a week or three weeks to start working, rather than 15 minutes to an hour, can reduce your anxiety. Mark the days on your calendar.

- ✔ **Ask your doctor what to expect when the medication starts working.** Sometimes, doctors prescribe medications without offering a thorough explanation of how they're supposed to help. Knowing the potential long-term benefits of medications can often encourage you to keep taking them, even when you don't see immediate benefits.

✔ **Expect some ups and downs during the initial recovery.** You probably won't wake up one day feeling cured. You can expect good days, not-so-good days, and bad days. The goal is to string together more good days than bad.

✔ **Contact your doctor and ask if you can do anything to feel better faster.** Your doctor may be able to add a medication to the mix on a temporary basis and then pull it back when you begin to feel better.

✔ **If you don't feel better in the time period that your doctor specifies, contact her immediately.** You may need a medication change, extra time, or a higher dose.

They work great — I'm fine now

Taking medication when you feel fine may seem about as rational as putting a bandage on unharmed skin — what's the point? The point — actually, two points — is *maintenance* and *prevention*. Maintenance means that the medicine has to stay on board for you to continue feeling better. When you treat a mood episode, the episode doesn't melt away — the medicine suppresses it. The episode has its own lifespan, and if you stop the medication too soon, the symptoms will bubble back up to the surface. Basically, you feel better because of the medicine; stop the medicine, and you stop feeling better.

The other primary goal of medication is prevention. Doctors often prescribe mood stabilizers as prophylactics. As such, the medicine doesn't just make you feel better when you become ill; it reduces the likelihood of a recurrence of symptoms. By preventing symptoms, you reap the following benefits:

✔ Avoid potential fallout from mood episodes, such as broken relationships or loss of employment

✔ Reduce the frequency and intensity of mood episodes

✔ Improve the course of the illness

✔ Avoid a stay in the hospital

The side effects are scary

Because so many antipsychotics and mood stabilizers cause weight gain, doctors may prescribe yet another medication to reduce weight or appetite. One such medication is topiramate (Topamax), which sometimes causes fuzzy thinking. In other words, you get a choice: You can be fat or stupid. Many of the medications for treating mood disorders offer similar choices:

✔ Depakote controls mania but can result in weight gain.

✔ Lithium stabilizes moods with the potential risk of causing weight gain, kidney damage, or thyroid dysfunction.

✔ Prozac, Paxil, Zoloft, and other SSRI antidepressants alleviate depression at the risk of inducing mania and causing negative sexual side effects.

✔ Lamictal helps control depression without inducing mania but may cause a potentially lethal rash, although the risk can be reduced significantly by gradually ramping up the dose at the beginning of treatment.

✔ Antipsychotics can cause weight gain, sedation, changes in sugar or fat metabolism, and other side effects.

Potentially negative side effects accompany all medications, even aspirin. If the medications are powerful enough to work, they're powerful enough to have side effects. Always discuss potential side effects with your doctor so you know what to look for and what to do if you experience one or more negative side effects.

Your doctor may offer suggestions, such as the following, on how to alleviate the most bothersome side effects:

✔ **Ramp up dosages gradually.** Many negative side effects occur when you start taking a medication. Your doctor may be able to increase the dosage gradually to avoid or diminish the intensity of the side effects.

✔ **Change medication times.** If you typically take a medication in the morning, for example, and it makes you too drowsy for work, your doctor may recommend that you take it in the afternoon or evening.

✔ **Switch to an extended-release version of a medication.** Many medications come in extended-release tablets that release the medication to your bloodstream in a gradual manner. Consult your doctor concerning your options.

✔ **Add another medication to counteract the negative side effect.** For example, if you experience weight gain on Depakote, your doctor may prescribe Topamax to reduce weight gain.

✔ **Change your medication.** If a medication causes intolerable side effects, your doctor may wean you off your current medication and prescribe a new medication that's less likely to produce the side effect you experienced.

Some side effects, such as drowsiness or digestive problems, go away after you take the medication for several weeks and your body adjusts to it. If you don't want to wait, or if the side effect interferes with your life, insist on receiving help.

I forget to take them

When you feel well, you have better, more important things to attend to than your medications — work, relationships, kids, golf. But when you have bipolar disorder, managing your medications should become a priority, or at least a well-ingrained habit.

To stay on top of your daily medications, try the following techniques:

- **Record your medications on an index card.** Keep the index card in your wallet or purse, or stick it to the side of your refrigerator for quick reference. Update the record whenever your doctor adjusts your medications.

- **Use a seven-day pillbox.** A seven-day pillbox has a compartment for each day of the week so you know exactly what you need to take each day. You can even affix a sticker to the box that lists the times of day for taking each medication.

- **Store your medications where you can see them.** This provides you with a visual reminder to take your medication.

- **Link your medication to daily meals or events.** Remembering to take your medications when you wake up, before you go to bed, or at mealtime may be easier than setting a specific time, such as 10 a.m.

- **Assign the task to a responsible family member.** If you simply can't remember to take your medication on time, ask a family member to remind you.

Having a family member or friend remind you to take your medication isn't always the best idea. The person you choose may be worse than you at remembering. In addition, if you're the type of person who doesn't like reminders from others, you may begin to perceive gentle reminders as nagging, which can be reason enough to resist.

Normal is boring

The alternative to the extreme highs and lows of bipolar disorder is normalcy. How dull is that? You get to be like everyone else — the people who find small talk intriguing, who've never experienced the utter loneliness of depression, and who remain unfazed by a world gone mad.

Your mania may have given you new insights and ideas, a vivacious personality, and a high energy level. With medication, you may feel like the color has gone out of your life and that your mind is dull and gray; you may be bored and feel like time has slowed down; and you may wonder how you'll be able to enjoy life without mood-induced drama and excitement.

If your medications have flat-lined your moods, try the following:

- ✔ **Realize that your muted mood probably is a temporary condition.** You may need several weeks to recover from a full-blown mood episode; the medications may take several days or weeks to begin working; and the negative side effects usually wear off as your moods begin to stabilize.

- ✔ **Consult your doctor.** As your depression or mania settles down, your doctor may be able to tweak your medications so you can experience more acceptable mood fluctuations.

- ✔ **Accept that your recovery is a process.** Side effects and medication trials can cause some people to get worse before they get better. Your healthcare providers will do everything in their power to prevent this, but it does happen. Don't assume that you'll never get better, even if your first few treatments make you feel dull, slow, or sluggish or worsen your mood symptoms. Stay in close contact with your doctors, and keep them informed about all your symptoms. Continue asking for more treatment options until you find an option that works.

I just want to be me

When you've lived with bipolar disorder for most of your life, separating it from your personality can be difficult. Some people are fine with it. They knew all along that something wasn't right, and when the wild mood swings are gone, they finally feel some balance. Other people miss themselves. They feel like some very essential qualities of their personalities have been extracted. They've lost their mojo, and they want it back . . . without the sleepless nights, ruined relationships, unpaid bills, and other inconveniences, of course.

Give yourself time to mourn your losses — the life you used to have — adjust to your current condition, and embrace your future prospects — a life without debilitating mood episodes. You're still you. Medication doesn't take away your creativity, energy, and zest for life. With a stable mood, you have the power to discover things you really enjoy and go after them. Therapy can help you through the transition (see Chapter 8 for info on therapy options).

I can control my moods without medication

Some people claim that they can successfully control their bipolar symptoms through diet, exercise, therapy, and the cooperation of family and friends, just as some people can control some types of diabetes by making dramatic lifestyle changes. Is this possible? Think of it this way: You can survive a free fall from 100 feet, but you'd have a much better chance strapped to a well-anchored, 50-foot bungee cord. Controlling bipolar symptoms without medication is extremely risky; the medical community advises against it, and we certainly don't recommend that you actually try it.

Bipolar disorder does, however, have several degrees of severity. Some milder forms can be amenable to *less* medical intervention, just as you can manage some types of diabetes with lifestyle changes (whereas some require insulin treatment). You should never attempt to reduce or eliminate your medications without discussing the situation with your doctor. You need to know how severe your bipolar disorder is and your chances of recovering and/or maintaining stability with less medicine. The following conditions also need to be in place:

- ✔ Your moods are currently stable.
- ✔ Your doctor approves and agrees to supervise your attempt — *slowly* decreasing doses of your current medications.
- ✔ You and your family have received some solid therapy, especially cognitive behavioral therapy and family therapy, which we explain in Chapter 8.
- ✔ Your support network is cooperative and well informed.
- ✔ You and your support network have a system in place to carefully monitor your moods.
- ✔ You have a solid backup plan in case something goes wrong.

Even under these conditions, withdrawing your mood medications entirely is extremely risky. Consider working out compromises with your doctor and therapist. With additional therapy, you have a chance to manage your moods with *less* medication rather than *no* medication. Think in terms of making minor changes over several months or years rather than major changes in a short period of time.

Other people need them more than I do

Are you a human dreaming you're a butterfly or a butterfly dreaming that it's human? Are you a sane person in a mad world or a mad person in a sane world? For centuries, thinkers have wondered what's real and what's surreal, who's sane and who's not, who's paranoid and who's just a little more perceptive than the average Joe.

People with bipolar disorder live with similar questions and doubts. "Am I depressed or just more perceptive and sensitive than those around me? Am I irritable because of my mania or because the world is too slow and stupid? Can it be possible that I really am psychic?"

We can't answer those questions, but even if we could, we're not sure the answers would do you any good, because the reality of your situation is what's important:

- ✔ Your mood swings exceed safe limits.
- ✔ Your depression and mania are negatively affecting your life.
- ✔ Any attempts at controlling your moods without medicine haven't worked.

Perhaps the world is a mess. Maybe others around you need to deal with their own issues. You may be smarter and more perceptive than others. You may even have a genius IQ. But right now, you're the one with the diagnosed illness, and you're the only person you have control over. A combination of medication, therapy, and support currently offers the greatest hope for relief. Even if the people around you need medication more than you do, getting your own treatment can help you deal with them.

Bottom line: It's a control thing

Not adhering to your treatment plan by not taking your prescribed medications is basically a control issue. People like to feel as though they can control their destinies without the assistance of foreign substances. Almost every reason you can give for not taking your medication boils down to control:

Reason: The meds don't work.

Translation: My meds can't control me.

Reason: The meds work great — I'm fine now.

Translation: I can control myself from this point on.

Reason: The side effects are scary.

Translation: I have no control over what the medications do to me.

Reason: I forget to take them.

Translation: I control when I take them and when I don't.

Reason: Normal is boring.

Translation: When I was in control, life was more interesting.

Reason: I just want to be me.

Translation: The medications control my personality.

Reason: I can control my moods without medication.

Translation: I can control my moods.

Reason: Other people need them more than I do.

Translation: Don't try to control me.

Not adhering to your treatment plan provides a false sense of control. By relinquishing some control to medications and to your doctor, therapist, family, and friends, you gain much more control over your life and your destiny.

Weighing the Risks of Nonadherence

Every "either/or" choice has potential benefits and drawbacks. To weigh the benefits against the drawbacks, you stack the benefits on one side and the drawbacks on the other and then decide if the potential benefits are worth the risk. Making a decision can be as simple as that.

Listing the benefits of stopping your meds

On one side of the scale, you stack the potential benefits of not taking your medications:

- $avings from prescriptions
- Freedom from popping pills
- No nasty side effects
- Creative, energetic highs of hypomania

Listing the drawbacks

On the other side of the scale, you stack the potential drawbacks of not taking your medications:

- Strained or ruined relationships
- Lost employment
- Debilitating depression

- ✔ Risky behavior that leads to illness, injury, and possibly death

- ✔ Legal problems

- ✔ Financial problems

- ✔ Masochistic and suicidal behaviors that potentially lead to death or permanent disability

Making your choice

After stacking the pros on one side of the scale and the cons on the other, see which side carries more weight. Most people with bipolar disorder eventually decide that not taking medication is far too risky, but only you can weigh the factors and decide what's best for you.

You should also keep in mind that stopping one or more medications often carries more risks than if you never took the medication in the first place:

- ✔ Withdrawal symptoms can make you feel temporarily better, causing you to believe that the medication caused problems that it didn't actually cause.

- ✔ Withdrawal can induce mania or depression.

- ✔ If you decide to go back on the medication later, it may no longer work for you.

People who choose to ditch their medications tend to focus on one factor, such as a particularly nasty side effect. When faced with the decision of whether or not to take your medications, carefully evaluate *all* the potential benefits and risks and discuss them with your doctor and therapist. An honest, open discussion may be just what you need to stay on course.

Avoiding Self-Medication and Self-Regulation

Every home is equipped with a thermostat that regulates its temperature. You set the thermostat to the desired temperature, and it maintains that temperature throughout the day. People who don't quite grasp this concept like to fiddle with the dials. When they feel a chill, they crank their thermostats up to 80°F. An hour later, they feel hot and sweaty, so they crank them down to 60°F. If they feel cold again, they crank the dials back up to 75°F. This happens throughout the day, to the consternation of other family members who actually understand the concept of temperature regulation.

> ## Janette's jam
>
> Janette was a beautiful and talented musician, described by family and friends as temperamental with a flair for the dramatic. She and her husband, also a musician, lived the artist's life — late-night jams, unwinding into the early morning, sleeping late each day, dabbling in substance abuse, and spending plenty of time on the road. Such was their life before Janette's first major depressive episode slammed it into reverse. She could barely drag herself out of bed in the morning, let alone rehearse or even consider performing. She became agitated, anxious, and suspicious of everyone.
>
> Her doctor started her on a combination of antidepressants and antipsychotics, and within days she felt better — so much better that she began flying into mania. Her husband immediately called the doctor, and she bumped down
>
> the antidepressant and upped the antipsychotic a bit. Two days later, Janette experienced episodes of despair that alternated with her improved mood. She and her husband wanted to add more medications right away to balance out her moods. Instead, their doctor suggested a low-dose tranquilizer to ease the acute discomfort while Janette waited for the "big-gun" medications to settle in and do their thing. The doctor also encouraged Janette to take a break from work (especially the late nights) to give her brain and body a genuine chance at recovery and repair. Within a couple of weeks, Janette's moods began to settle down, and she was sleeping through the night, although it took a full six weeks before she felt consistently like her old self.

People with bipolar disorder who self-medicate and self-regulate to feel immediate comfort essentially play with their mood thermostats. The temptation is understandable. When you feel ready to work, you want to feel alert and creative. When you want to party, you try to feel sociable and engaging. When you're ready to sleep, you want to feel tired. But most mood medications don't work that way. They're designed to reach a therapeutic level in your brain, establish a comfortable baseline, and prevent wild mood swings, not to boost you when you want to be up and calm you when you need some downtime.

Self-medicating and self-regulating often result in overcorrections that increase mood cycling. To maintain a more stable mood, work with your doctor to adjust your medications gradually. Avoid the temptation to self-medicate with feel-good drugs and other nonprescription substances and to self-regulate by adjusting doses on your own.

Teaming Up with Your Caregivers

At most bipolar support-group meetings, you're likely to hear at least one person griping about a psychiatrist. Most complaints center on availability;

the psychiatrist is unavailable during a time of crisis, doesn't return a phone call or e-mail message, or is out of the office for an extended period of time. Other complaints focus on communication issues; the psychiatrist doesn't listen, refuses to make the requested medication adjustments, or fails to fully explain the diagnosis and treatment plan. In most cases, the people feel like they must make a medical decision alone. Whether this feeling is justified or not doesn't really matter. What matters is that the situation is unacceptable and needs to be resolved.

The relationships you establish with your psychiatrist and therapist contribute significantly to your treatment outcome. If you feel that your caregivers are unreceptive to your concerns and unavailable when you need them most, your relationships may become adversarial, creating a situation in which you and your caregivers work against one another. On the other hand, if you establish relationships built on trust, you're much more likely to adhere to your treatment plan and communicate your concerns and feelings honestly and openly.

The following suggestions can help you establish a more productive, collaborative relationship with your healthcare providers:

- ✔ **Commit to full disclosure.** Let your caregivers know when you haven't taken your medication and when you've attempted to self-medicate. What they don't know can hurt you.

- ✔ **Follow their expert advice.** You wouldn't take your sputtering car into the shop and then refuse to have it tuned up, so don't seek psychiatric care and then refuse treatment.

- ✔ **Ask questions.** If you have a question about your diagnosis or treatment, ask. Your insurance company may allocate only 15 minutes for your psychiatrist to evaluate your medications and make adjustments, so have your questions written down and ready.

- ✔ **Voice your concerns.** When you experience a negative side effect, let your doctor know about it. If you're upset that your doctor didn't return a phone call or that you couldn't get an appointment when you needed to, mention these concerns as well. Ask for what you need.

- ✔ **Offer suggestions.** If you hear or read about a treatment option or new medication that you want to try, bring it up to your doctor and ask for advice. Your doctor may know more about the medication and how effective or ineffective it is.

Finding the perfect doctor is like finding the perfect spouse: impossible, because the perfect doctor doesn't exist. You need to find a doctor who's good and then work on communicating your needs so the doctor can effectively serve you. Too many people with bipolar disorder bounce around from doctor to doctor, never settling on a consistent, integrated treatment plan.

Leaning On Others

Independence is highly overrated. Teenagers crave it until they actually get it and then it isn't fun anymore. As you get older (and wiser), you begin to appreciate *interdependence* — serving other people's needs and having others serve your needs. That's what family, community, and society are all about, and that's what individuals strive for, consciously or not.

When bipolar disorder hits, it makes you dependent. And whatever age you are, dependence stinks. You no longer feel like an equal. Other people and other things have control. What bothers people most is that they can't (at least temporarily) reciprocate. They feel like they're going to a pitch-in dinner without a casserole.

The psychological burden of being dependent can be tough to bear, but the following realizations may help lighten your load:

- **Bipolar disorder is an illness.** When you're in bed with a cold and people bring you chicken soup, do you feel guilty?

- **People need to be needed.** When you need help, you fulfill other people's need to be needed. Don't you feel good about helping your friends or relatives?

- **People need you.** You're an individual with unique insight, skills, and vision. People need you; they want you to be well; and they want to invest in your recovery.

- **Your instability is temporary.** You may be looking at a lifetime of medication, but your moods will stabilize; you'll regain control of your life; and you'll be able to contribute to your community.

No matter what you're going through, you can benefit from the support of people who've been there. After diagnosis and treatment, the support of others is vital. Support groups, like those we describe in Chapter 6, can provide you with a "been there, done that" community of caring individuals. Don't overlook this tremendous resource.

Part V

Assisting a Friend or Relative with Bipolar Disorder

In this part . . .

After you discover that a loved one has received a bipolar diagnosis, you may experience a flurry of emotions ranging from relief and hope to guilt and despair, but regardless of what you feel, your loved one needs you now more than ever. Your job, as a friend or family member, is to build empathy, lend a hand, and avoid the temptation of becoming too overbearing, all without letting the disorder drag you down. Supporting a friend or relative who has bipolar disorder can be a daunting challenge, primarily because the person wants your help the least when he or she needs it the most.

We've been there, and in this part, we reveal what we've learned in the trenches. Here, you find out what you can do to support your loved one, when you should step in, and when you should step back. We provide advice on how to plan ahead for a crisis and how to keep your eye on the ball when bipolar throws you a curve. And in the final chapter of this part, we explain some of the challenges of diagnosing, treating, and supporting a child or adolescent with bipolar disorder.

Chapter 16

Supporting Your Loved One

· ·

· ·

*L*ives are interwoven. They overlap, intersect, and ignite one another like passing flames. If you have kids, you know how heartbreaking it is when you hear them cry and how joyous you feel observing their talents and achievements. When a friend or family member experiences a loss, it drags you down. When you feel excited and elated, everyone around you lights up.

When bipolar disorder afflicts a friend or relative, the disorder afflicts you, too. Symptoms can confuse and bewilder you, strain your relationship with your loved one, and leave you physically and mentally drained. You want to help, but how? What can you possibly do to remedy a "chemical imbalance" in the brain? What can you say to your loved one when he loses all hope? What can you do when your friend seems determined to blow her retirement money and ruin her marriage? And how can you help when your loved one resists your attempt to intervene and answers your well-intentioned advice with arrogance and condescending anger?

In this chapter, we confront the confusion and the sense of helplessness that friends and family members of people with bipolar disorder commonly face. We explain the cold, hard facts about bipolar disorder to prepare you for the struggles ahead; we provide exercises to steer you clear of any tendencies you may have to blame yourself or your loved one for what has happened; and we reveal what you can and can't do to help your loved one on the road to recovery. We also offer suggestions on how to properly care for yourself and find support so that you and your loved one can step out from the shadow of bipolar disorder and into the light of a hopeful future.

Establishing the Right Mindset

Becoming an effective caregiver and support person has as much to do with what you think as it does with what you do. If you approach your role with false expectations and misunderstandings, you may be more apt to say and do all the wrong things, become easily frustrated, and blame yourself for situations and events that are completely outside your control. By establishing the right mindset, you can function more effectively as a support person and maintain your mental health.

In this section, you find out how to establish the right mindset by adjusting your expectations, realizing that the disorder is something that your loved one can't control, and continually reminding yourself that you're not responsible for your loved one's condition.

Forming realistic expectations

We all need hope, but false hope can lead to disappointment and frustration. It can also cause you to let down your guard. In the case of caring for a loved one with bipolar disorder, you may begin to think your problems are fixed, the illness is cured, and that you've "put all this behind you." If you do, you're likely to drift back into old patterns that create fertile ground for mania or depression to take root. You forget about the medications. You become less vigilant of the warning signs. You get careless. And bam! You're right back where you were, watching your loved one battle a major depression or a manic episode.

To help your loved one win the battle against bipolar disorder, you first need to establish the right mindset and confront the realities of the disorder:

- ✔ Your loved one is and will remain vulnerable to future mood episodes.
- ✔ Your loved one can't will himself or herself to overcome the illness.
- ✔ Preventive medication is required to prevent relapse and control symptoms.
- ✔ Even with preventive medication, symptoms may recur.
- ✔ You and your loved one may need to adjust your future expectations and your lifestyles to improve the prognosis.
- ✔ Your loved one may not want your help at times, but he or she always needs your love and understanding.

We don't want to be the messengers of gloom and doom. You and your loved one have every reason to look forward to remission and a wonderful life, but your loved one needs to stick to the treatment plan, and you both need to remain vigilant when times are good so you can short-circuit escalating moods.

Disassociating the disorder from the one you love

Your loved one personifies bipolar disorder for you. The disorder expresses all its negative symptoms through your loved one's actions and words, making it very tempting to associate the disorder with the person, to identify the victim as the perpetrator, and to blame your loved one for any problems that the disorder may have caused.

To successfully battle the disorder, you and your loved one need to form an alliance, and to do so, you need to disassociate the disorder from the person who has it. In the midst of a major mood episode, disassociation is easier said than done, but when you have a moment to contemplate, try the following exercises:

- **Think back to a time before the first major mood episode disrupted your lives.** Did the person you love seem different? In what ways? Can you associate any specific behaviors with the disorder?

- **Look at photographs of pleasant times that you and your loved one experienced together.** Did you notice any symptoms back then? What has changed? Name some ways that the disorder affects your loved one's behavior during a mood episode.

- **List all the words and behaviors that seem out of character with the person you love.** Would your loved one say and do the same things if he or she were healthy? What would be different?

Be careful not to go too far when disassociating the disorder from your loved one. You may be tempted to attribute *every* negative behavior to the disorder, even behaviors that are consistent with your loved one's character. By attributing too much to the disorder, you diminish the importance and value of your loved one's personality and ability to think on his or her own, which can be just as damaging as attributing too little to the disorder.

Learning not to take it personally

When you're on the receiving end of an angry tirade, and when nothing you do seems to please your loved one, you may react by taking it personally and becoming defensive. This reaction is perfectly natural, especially when you're in a close relationship with someone you love. Your happiness and the happiness of your loved one may be intricately intertwined, and when one of you is unhappy, the other suffers as well. You begin to think that if you could just figure out the right way to act and the right words to say, the situation would improve. When it doesn't, frustration and bitterness often follow.

To overcome the common trap of taking it personally, try to *depersonalize* your loved one's hurtful words and deeds. Depersonalizing consists of coming to terms with the fact that much of what your loved one says or does has very little to do with you. Your loved one's feelings, thoughts, reactions, words, and actions can arise from multiple sources, including the following:

✔ Depression that makes your loved one overly sensitive, dejected, or pessimistic

✔ Mania that makes your loved one impatient, irritable, or unable to rein in behaviors

✔ Distorted thinking and paranoia secondary to depression, mania, or mixed states

You can't sit down with a calculator to determine what percentage of your loved one's responses are valid reactions to something you say or do. But by knowing that the disorder and other factors often contribute significantly more to your loved one's behavior than anything you say or do, you can blow off some of the reactions and become less defensive.

Don't blame yourself. Don't blame your loved one. Blame the disorder.

Knowing What You Can and Can't Do to Help

You stand by and watch the drama unfold. The doctor diagnoses and prescribes, the therapist counsels and educates, and your loved one wrestles with mood swings. You wander backstage like a lonely understudy, wondering if you'll have a role to play and something to contribute.

Naturally, you want your loved one to get well, but the situation is totally new to you. Should you get out of the way so the doctor and therapist can do their jobs? Should you take control? What would be most helpful? And how can you avoid making matters worse? The first step in becoming an effective support person is to determine what you can and can't do to help, and that's what this section is all about.

What you can do

Your presence, patience, understanding, and willingness to help are perhaps the most valuable gifts you can present. Beyond that, you can offer many types of help, but keep in mind that if your loved one is an adult, he or she has the option of accepting or rejecting your offers or limiting your level of involvement. Being too pushy or overbearing can cause feelings of resentment and additional resistance to treatment. Here are some ways you can help:

- ✔ Learn about bipolar disorder and its symptoms and treatments, which you're already doing by reading this book.
- ✔ Keep in touch, especially during the rough times.
- ✔ Provide unconditional love and encouraging words while setting boundaries to keep your emotional reserves intact (such as "I need you to only call me three or four times in one day").
- ✔ Reassure your loved one that with the proper treatment, she will eventually manage the symptoms.
- ✔ Encourage your loved one to seek professional help when necessary (but don't nag).
- ✔ Assist in locating a qualified doctor and therapist.
- ✔ Assist in following up on insurance coverage and claims.
- ✔ Assist in tracking moods and medications and watching for signs of impending mood episodes.
- ✔ Attend appointments with your loved one's doctor and therapist, if you're welcomed by all parties.
- ✔ Call your loved one's employer to report illness, being careful not to pass along any details that your loved one may not want to share.
- ✔ Keep other friends and family members posted as directed by your loved one.
- ✔ Perform basic household tasks, such as grocery shopping, watching the kids, and paying bills.
- ✔ Remain patient.

What you can't do

Bipolar disorder has stricken your loved one, not you (directly, that is). Through research, communication, and therapy, you can develop a feeling of empathy for your loved one, but you can never fully understand what she experiences or how she views this illness in the context of her life. Moreover, you can't control how your loved one chooses to deal with it. If your loved one is an adult, you can't force her to take medication, attend therapy, or even get sufficient sleep. If you attempt to take control, you risk taking ownership of a problem you can't fix.

You can and should step in at times when the illness makes your loved one incapable of making the right decisions, but the rest of the time your job is to let go and allow your loved one to manage on her own. Your loved one needs to take responsibility for sticking with the treatment plan:

- ✔ Making and keeping doctor's appointments
- ✔ Making and keeping therapy appointments
- ✔ Taking the mood medications as prescribed
- ✔ Avoiding mood-altering substances
- ✔ Getting sufficient sleep
- ✔ Asking for help

You didn't cause your loved one to get bipolar disorder, nor can you cure it. Don't feel guilty for the onset of bipolar disorder, and don't think that you have the power or the resources to fix the problem on your own.

What you shouldn't do (or say)

If you feel confused, hurt, helpless, and alone, multiply that by 10, and you still can't begin to approach the level of psychological pain and frustration that your loved one feels. Many of her emotions and behaviors are out of her control; most of the people she deals with on a daily basis don't understand; the condition significantly affects both her personal and professional life; and she's continually adjusting to the fact that she has a chronic, often unpredictable condition. This burden understandably makes your loved one much more sensitive and vulnerable to any words and actions pertaining to the illness, so try your best to avoid doing or saying anything to cause additional pain. For instance:

- ✔ Don't assume that the disorder or a missed medication causes every argument.
- ✔ Don't nag. (You can remind your loved one of a doctor's appointment or a medication dose, but only if you both agree that this is an acceptable role for you to play.)
- ✔ Don't tell your loved one how she feels or *should* feel. You don't really know.
- ✔ Don't talk to your loved one's doctor or therapist behind her back, except in the case of an emergency (you fear that your loved one will harm herself or others).
- ✔ Don't joke about the disorder unless your loved one accepts your joking, and then joke about it only to your loved one, not to friends or other family members.
- ✔ Don't assume that just because your loved one didn't want or need help one day that she doesn't want or need help another day.

✔ Don't expect your loved one to be mentally sharp at all times. Some of the medications can slow her thought processes and negatively affect her memory.

✔ Don't hesitate to ask questions. Most people who have bipolar disorder are willing to discuss it with people who show a genuine interest in learning more and helping.

✔ Don't try to live your loved one's life for her. She can make her own decisions, although you may need to help during times of crisis or when she asks. Encourage her to own her illness and its treatment, and instill a belief that she'll be able to manage her life better as she recovers.

Treat your loved one like you treat anyone else you love and respect. Trust your loved one to make the right decisions concerning her life and her treatment, step in when she can't make decisions for herself, and ask questions when you don't understand.

Cultivating a Healthy Home Environment

If your relative or friend with bipolar disorder lives with you, your home becomes his sanctuary, and everyone in your home becomes a caregiver. No, you don't need to dress in scrubs and talk in hushed tones. All family members just need to get up to speed on bipolar disorder and work together to create an environment that's more conducive to your loved one's recovery and to the mental well-being of the entire household.

In this section, you discover various ways to structure your schedule, tone down the emotional volume, set and enforce house rules, and strengthen relationships that suffered through the course of the illness and from other contributing factors.

Educate all household members

Everyone in your home, from Grandma to your toddler, should know the basics of bipolar disorder, how it affects your loved one, and what the family can do to help. If everyone is on a different page, you often see people working at cross-purposes and undermining any potential progress. If you have people in the household who "don't believe in medication," for example, they may make offhand comments that discourage your loved one from taking his medication.

Encourage open communication. A common mistake family members make is to begin discussing issues without involving the person who has bipolar disorder. You shouldn't create a secret society with the goal of protecting your loved one. This can make him feel as though everyone wants to gang up on him — as if he's the family problem. You enjoy much more success if everyone is involved in the discussion and has an opportunity to ask questions and voice concerns. Consult your loved one with bipolar disorder to determine the best time and the most effective way of opening the discussion and presenting the information. Having other household members read this chapter is a good way to start.

Establish a structured schedule

People who have bipolar disorder are much more sensitive to schedule variations. You may have no problem going to sleep at 10 p.m. one night and midnight the next or pulling an all-nighter on Saturday and sleeping in on Sunday. These same variations can flip a person with bipolar disorder into mania, with or without the protection of medication.

Some households can function quite well with individual family members following different schedules, but if the person with bipolar disorder tends to depend on the rhythms of other family members, the entire family may need to work together to establish a schedule and routine that works for everyone. If Junior likes to have his buddies over on Friday night to play video games until 2 a.m., but it disturbs the rest of the household, he may need to move the party to a friend's house or reschedule it for earlier in the evening.

Crank down the volume

Some households have a decibel level that rakes the nerves. As a visitor, it can make you feel like you're sitting in front of the high school band's cymbal player, just waiting for the crash to resonate between your ears. Thrilling? Maybe, but it also increases stress to a level that begins to negatively affect mood stability.

You don't want to turn your home into the neighborhood "SHHHH!" zone, but everyone should be aware of how their voices, stereos, and televisions affect the person in the house who's most sensitive to them. Crank down the stereo, the TV set, the computer speakers, and other noise producers; limit the shouting from room to room; and avoid slamming doors, banging pots and pans, and bouncing balls off the walls.

Reduce the level of expressed emotion

The emotional tone of a family resonates with all its members, and family members who are vulnerable to depression or mania are particularly sensitive to the tone. In fact, some studies show that in families that have high levels of expressed emotion, people who have had a major mood episode are much more likely to suffer a relapse.

Expressed emotion is defined as levels of criticism, hostility, and emotional overinvolvement directed toward the person with the mood disorder. It can take form in the following types of communications:

- ✔ Criticism
- ✔ Blame
- ✔ Sarcasm (even when mumbled incoherently)
- ✔ Eye rolling
- ✔ Sighs
- ✔ Door slamming

Any emotional expression that can make a loved one feel nervous, anxious, angry, frustrated, or guilty (for having the disorder) is an expressed emotion. Every family member must be a caregiver to some degree, so all family members must work together to establish a healthier emotional tone. The following three approaches can contribute significantly to cranking down the volume of expressed emotion:

- ✔ **Learning more about the disorder** typically increases empathy for the afflicted family member, thus reducing any expressions of criticism, blame, and emotional overinvolvement.

- ✔ **Improving communication skills** helps family members express themselves in healthier ways. You discover how to listen to one another and express yourselves in a peaceful manner.

- ✔ **Enhancing problem-solving skills** enables you to resolve issues logically and rationally.

Lowering the level of expressed emotion doesn't mean sucking all emotion out of the family. The goal isn't to transform your family into zombies, but to enable you to express your emotions in healthier, more positive ways. (For more on keeping things fun, see the section "Have some family fun" later in this chapter.)

Avoid conflict by setting limits

You can eliminate many areas of conflict by having family members set clear limits. As a caregiver, you can specify the types of language and behavior that you refuse to tolerate from other family members, including the person who has bipolar disorder. The person with bipolar disorder can also benefit by defining the type of help he wants and the language and behavior he can tolerate.

Setting limits and communicating those limits offers several advantages, including the following:

- ✔ **Reduces confusion.** All parties know the rules and what happens if someone crosses the line.

- ✔ **Eliminates nagging.** Your loved one knows what you expect, so you don't need to remind him.

- ✔ **Eliminates criticism.** You don't need to criticize family members for not respecting your limits; you simply react with the previously agreed-upon response.

- ✔ **Eliminates the need for arguments.** You cross the limit, and the identified response follows, no questions asked.

- ✔ **Settles your mind.** You don't constantly wonder what you can put up with and how much you can take.

- ✔ **Enables unconditional love.** You can control your personal space without taking unacceptable behaviors personally. You can respond in previously agreed-upon ways that don't include withdrawing your love or attention.

- ✔ **Encourages independence.** Unclear limits lead to endless conflict — constant discussions about how to handle every situation — often repeating the same cycles ad nauseum. Given clear boundaries, individuals can make choices about their behaviors independently, with full awareness of the responses they can expect.

Effective limit-setting is a fine art that requires a detached toughness. You need to set realistic limits and devise responses that not only make your family feel comfortable, but also discourage your loved one from testing your limits and allow for him to recover his appropriate behavior patterns and get back on track. The following suggestions can help you set limits more effectively:

- ✔ **Identify one or two of the most troublesome behaviors.** Let the little stuff go. Pick one or two behaviors that you simply can't tolerate. As a caregiver, a problem behavior may be that your loved one abuses alcohol or spends money excessively. If you have bipolar disorder, a problem behavior may be that your caregiver nags you or makes insensitive comments about your condition.

- ✔ **Pick behaviors that you can easily measure.** Whether or not a person arrives home at a specific time is easy enough to determine. Whether or not a person treats you civilly is a judgment call.

- ✔ **Assign appropriate consequences.** With children, you can identify consequences and then follow through on them, such as limiting television or computer time or withholding allowance. Similar consequences are inappropriate for adults — they *infantilize* the person, taking away his adult decision-making abilities and making him feel like a child. Unless you have a true safety crisis on your hands, you want to optimize the other person's responsible decision-making. For adults, appropriate consequences are your responses to the unacceptable behavior. You can't actually change another person's behavior; you can only change your own, so responses can include disengaging briefly from the conversation until your loved one cools down or stepping out of a planned activity until appropriate behaviors return. Make sure these are consequences you can live with so you can stick to them.

✔ **Clearly communicate your limits and the associated consequences.** You can't expect your loved one to respect your limits if you don't inform him of those limits. Go over your limits and consequences at a time when emotions are stable, not during times of turmoil. You may need to write them down.

✔ **Enforce your limits consistently.** Without consistent enforcement and reinforcement, consequences become nothing more than idle threats. This may take a great deal of self-discipline on your part. The more consistent you are, the less you may need to enforce the consequences.

Setting limits doesn't mean transforming a person into the ideal human being, whatever *that* is. It means communicating your inability or unwillingness to tolerate certain words or actions in your presence or in your home. You can't control your adult loved one, but limits provide you with tools you can use to influence your loved one's behavior.

Have some family fun

Cultivating healthy relationships means more than just avoiding conflict and "getting along." It requires that you and your loved ones have meaningful discussions and share experiences that increase intimacy and strengthen bonds. When bipolar disorder enters a relationship, you can become so caught up in crisis intervention and damage control that you lose touch with each other emotionally. Encourage your loved ones to become more involved in family activities, including the following:

✔ Meal preparation

✔ Physical activities

✔ Religious or spiritual activities

✔ Family outings

✔ Family meetings to discuss plans and issues that arise

Mood medication and therapy can do wonders when it comes to controlling the symptoms of bipolar disorder, but even a successful combination of medication and therapy is rarely sufficient to return *functionality* — a person's ability to carry out duties as a family member, friend, or worker. Functionality typically improves as an individual begins to perform various activities in a supportive environment and gradually increases his level of involvement.

Take breaks from one another

Two people may make for good company for a few days, but after a couple weeks, even two begins to feel like a crowd, especially when you have to deal with a long-term health condition. You don't need to stand 24-hour watch over a loved one who has bipolar disorder. It isn't healthy for you, and it certainly isn't healthy for your loved one. When his moods are cycling, you may need to spend more time and energy as a caregiver, but when his moods stabilize, take a break to recharge your batteries and connect with other friends and acquaintances.

Encourage your loved one to do the same. After an extreme mood episode, he may withdraw from friends or acquaintances and need some encouragement to re-establish his connections. Simply mentioning that a friend or relative would like to hear from him may be enough to encourage a phone call or e-mail.

What about the kids?

If you have children living with you, they suffer from the fallout of bipolar disorder as well. As a guardian, you may need to physically protect your children from any harm during extreme mood episodes, but preventing them from learning about the disorder is usually a mistake. Perhaps even more than adults, children need to understand what's going on; otherwise, their developing brains, which are still self-centered, shift into high gear, and they may think that they're the reason why Mommy and Daddy are fighting, why Daddy can't get out of bed to play ball, or why Mommy's crying.

When explaining bipolar disorder to young children, use age-specific language. "Depression" and "mania" may mean nothing to a 5-year-old, but if you explain that "Mommy gets really excited sometimes and can't calm down" or that "Daddy can't help getting really sad, even when everything is okay," a child is more likely to understand. Explain everything — symptoms, medication, therapy, support groups, and so on — and then leave some time for questions and answers. Encourage your children to express their perceptions and emotions.

Your kids have to grow up with bipolar disorder, and they have a right to know what's going on. Consider this an educational opportunity that not only helps you bond with your children, but also provides them with a better understanding of their family and the world at large. Knowledge and understanding improve your child's ability to be resilient in the face of this challenge. (For information on raising a bipolar child, head to Chapter 18.)

Arnie's kids

Arnie came from a long line of family members with bipolar disorder and other mood disorders. His mother suffered from depression, his grandfather was an "eccentric recluse," and his father suffered from rage attacks and alcoholism. His work life had stalled in many ways after numerous big ideas collapsed, and his creative periods were followed by long periods of fatigue and fruitless labor. He was sure, however, that he was different from his parents and that he wasn't going to let himself "be labeled."

Arnie's marriage fell apart in his early 40s, primarily due to his moodiness and unpredictable behavior, but he still didn't acknowledge the possibility of a mood disorder. Over the next few years, his children became more and more aware of his difficulties and started to avoid him because his visits were so chaotic. Arnie was devastated, but he finally got in to see a doctor, who diagnosed him with bipolar disorder and began a treatment plan. Arnie's children, all in their early teens, were relieved to hear about the diagnosis and eagerly supported Arnie's treatments. Their visits became opportunities for honest conversations that brought the kids and Arnie closer together. His oldest daughter did a research project on bipolar disorder for her health class and collected articles and Web links to give to Arnie. They finally had an explanation for his difficulties, and they came up with plenty of ideas for ways to help him.

Remaining Vigilant for Warning Signs

One of the more sinister characteristics of bipolar disorder is that the person who has it may not be able to recognize the onset of symptoms until it's too late to interrupt the cycle. To keep your loved one's moods in check, she needs to have one or two friends or family members who have close, regular contact with her to remain vigilant of behaviors that may signify a major mood episode.

Not everyone has the knowledge, temperament, and sensitivity to take on this job. You don't want a Barney Fife personality who gets rattled easily and points out every blip on the mood radar, nor do you want someone who's so unaffected that major mood swings go unnoticed. The ideal candidate has the following qualifications:

- ✔ Knows and can identify the signs of an oncoming mood episode
- ✔ Has close, regular contact with the person who has bipolar disorder
- ✔ Can openly communicate observations without instigating conflict
- ✔ Has permission to contact the person's therapist or doctor

During a period of relative calm, consult your loved one to determine if she's willing to allow one or two people to help monitor her moods. Avoid getting too many people involved or being overly involved yourself. Too much vigilance and focus can make your loved one feel as though she lives in a fishbowl.

Knowing when to step in

Most people who live with bipolar disorder know the way the disorder presents itself in their lives. They may not notice it all the time, but they look back later and recognize repeating behavioral patterns. For some, increased shopping is a sign of ensuing mania; others may look to heightened sexuality, self-harm, brighter shades of makeup, or escalating irritability. Depression can begin to make itself known through withdrawal from social activities, an increased need for sleep, or an overly pessimistic view of life.

If your loved one agrees to let you monitor her moods and watch for warning signs, ask for additional details to help you determine the severity of the symptoms and the actions you should take:

- Make a list of common warning signs.
- Find out at what point you should be concerned enough to act.
- Determine the actions you should take, including relating your observations and concerns to your loved one, contacting the therapist or doctor, taking away credit cards or car keys, securing objects the person could use to harm herself, or contacting another support person for assistance.

Everyone has good and bad days. Don't assume that just because your loved one is irritable or seems a little down in the dumps, you need to contact her doctor or therapist. You should be a little more vigilant and convey your concerns, but try not to overreact.

Knowing when to step back

In the midst of a major mood episode, don't step back simply because your loved one requests that you do so. Stick with her until she takes steps to obtain the treatment necessary to stabilize her moods. Encourage your loved one to contact her doctor or therapist immediately for evaluation and consultation. A short visit with a qualified therapist is often enough to get your loved one back on the right track, and if the therapist notices any disturbing behavior, he'll have a better idea of how to proceed.

When the crisis abates, and your loved one regains control of her moods, be prepared to step back and let her manage her life once again. Let her know that you're there if she needs anything.

Let's make a deal: Drawing up a contract

During a period of relative calm and stability, sit down with your loved one and draw up a treatment contract, as shown in Figure 16-1. A useful contract should contain the following information:

- ✔ Descriptions of external signs and symptoms of depression and mania
- ✔ Descriptions of verifiable signs that your loved one can manage the disorder on her own
- ✔ Descriptions of observable signs that your loved one needs help
- ✔ Instructions on the types of help your loved one agrees to accept
- ✔ A clear statement that you may do whatever you think is best when you suspect that your loved one faces an imminent risk of harming herself or others

Taking Care of Yourself

As a caregiver, you may feel lonelier than a guy at Tupperware party. Friends and family may ask how your loved one is doing, showing little concern for how you're holding up. Even worse, your circle of friends may scatter, perhaps out of fear, ignorance, or the mistaken belief that you don't want them "meddling" in your affairs. If you let this behavior continue, you and your loved one may become isolated.

Isolation isn't healthy for you or your loved one. If you mope around, consumed by thoughts of the life you lost and the added responsibilities you bear, your loved one will recognize the pain in your expressions and gestures and feel the pangs of guilt. You need to blow off some steam, grieve for your losses, attend to your needs, get a life, and then return to the relationship refreshed and renewed.

Treatment Contract

This treatment contract specifies my limits and preferences in accepting help to manage my bipolar disorder. It is intended to help my support person, _____, determine when I need help and the type of help I prefer when specific symptoms are present.

I am able to manage my bipolar disorder when I'm doing the following:

❑ Sleeping regularly: _____ to _____ hours per night

❑ Attending work/school

❑ Seeing my doctor/therapist _____ times every _____ weeks/months

❑ Taking my medications as prescribed

❑ Getting together with friends or family ___ times a week

❑ Communicating with others without arguing

❑ Other: _____

You should be concerned when you notice any of the following symptoms of depression:

❑ I'm sleeping more than ____ hours/day

❑ I'm missing work/school

❑ I'm complaining about my health or other issues much more than usual

❑ You notice me crying almost every day

❑ My house is messy or in disarray and I don't seem concerned

❑ I'm not showering or dressing up as I usually do

❑ I'm drinking alcohol more than usual or abusing drugs

❑ I'm smoking much more than usual

❑ Other: _____

When you observe _____ or more of the symptoms lasting for more than _____ hours/days, you can help me by doing the following:

❑ Ask me how I'm doing

❑ Do not try to convince me that I'm not depressed

❑ Spend more time with me and encourage me to go out

❑ Take me to the doctor if I am unable to do so myself

❑ Stay with me until I get help

❑ Other: _____

You should be concerned when you notice any of the following symptoms of hypomania or mania:

❑ I'm not sleeping at least _____ hours per day

❑ I'm shopping much more than usual and buying impulsively

❑ I'm much more interested in sex or am engaging in risky sexual activities

❑ I'm becoming involved in gambling or risky investment schemes

❑ I'm talking faster or much more than usual

❑ I'm much more irritable or critical than usual

❑ I have lots of plans and neither the time nor resources to execute them

❑ I'm becoming paranoid or I start hearing things or thinking I know the future

❑ My physical appearance seems out of the ordinary, such as too much makeup or wild clothes

Figure 16-1:
A treatment contract sets boundaries for you and your loved one that optimize the help you can give.

Find support for yourself

Although your friend or relative may be the one who takes the direct hit from bipolar disorder, you deal with a great deal of collateral damage. Suffering in silence forces you to hold back feelings that eventually find expression through blame and criticism. Try to find a healthy outlet for your emotions:

- **Attend a support group for family members of people with mental illnesses.** A support group can provide a forum for sharing feelings and information. As we discuss in Chapter 6, the Depression and Bipolar Support Alliance (DBSA) provides free and confidential support groups for family members, friends, and patients. One DBSA parent said, "When you are a family member in the middle of a situation, it's hard to see what's happening, but when you sit in a support group across from someone who is going through the same thing, it gives you so much perspective and relief." The National Alliance for the Mentally Ill (NAMI) also offers a selection of support groups and family-education programs. Check out `www.support4hope.com/Support_Groups.html` for additional leads.

- **Discuss problems with your family and friends.** Feeling angry and bitter over what you're dealing with is normal, and you have every right to talk about it openly, but you should do it in the right setting. Loading up your loved one who has bipolar disorder with your emotional responses, no matter how reasonable they are, only stirs up more negative feelings in someone who's poorly equipped to manage them.

- **See a therapist.** A therapist can help you through the grieving process and provide you with an outlet for your emotions.

Get a life!

Bipolar disorder may be a part of your life, but it shouldn't overshadow your life. Don't fall into the martyr syndrome, in which you sacrifice your life for the life of your loved one. You have your own identity and your own life, so start living it with some of the following activities:

- Connect with old friends.
- Pursue outside interests and hobbies.
- Get involved in community activities.
- Invite friends or family members to your home.
- Do something just for the heck of it once a week.

Chapter 17

Planning Ahead for a Possible Crisis

In This Chapter

▶ Taking the time to make a plan

▶ Knowing when to take action

▶ Listing a roster of who to call for help (and who not to call)

▶ Protecting your loved one from dangerous behaviors

---

*Y*ou're too late. The intruder has already slipped past the protective barriers of medication and therapy, entered the mind of your loved one, and taken control. The erratic driving, the spending sprees, the racing thoughts, and the irritability are already in high gear, and the intruder has convinced your loved one that all is well — even better than usual. Or the intruder has cranked down the speed, wrapping your loved one in darkness and despair and forcing her to refuse your help and say, "There's no hope."

The time for asking your loved one what to do has passed. Would she want you to call the doctor? What's her doctor's name, and where's the phone number? No, not the office number, the emergency number! Do you have consent to talk with the doctor? Should you call another family member? If so, who? And if you reach someone who can help, what do you say? What medications is your loved one supposed to be taking? Has she been taking them? Should you wrestle away the car keys? The credit cards? Is there a gun in the house?

Now isn't the time to be asking these questions. You should already have the answers. If only you'd sat down with your loved one during a calmer period and developed a crisis-intervention plan, you wouldn't be so flustered now. You may still have trouble convincing your loved one to get help, but at least you have a solid plan in place and the information and resources to carry it out.

Don't let this scenario happen to you and your loved one. This chapter provides a perfect opportunity for you both to develop a customized emergency plan so that you're prepared in the event of a crisis.

Making Time to Discuss the Plan

You know you need to discuss crisis planning with your loved one, but you just don't have the time, not to mention the inclination, to deal with it. You've already invested more time and energy in controlling this condition than you thought would be necessary, and now that life seems relatively normal, you really don't want to dredge up painful memories and admit the possibility of a future crisis. You decide to take the path of least resistance — which just happens to be a recipe for disaster.

To get over the speed bump of time constraints and emotional inertia, plan ahead, and set some ground rules for getting the process going:

- **Wait for a period of relative calm.** Don't try to plan for emergencies when your loved one is actively manic or depressed. Attempting to have a rational discussion, particularly when mania is involved, is an exercise in futility. You may not have the luxury of waiting until the moods are completely settled, but look for times of relative stability.

- **Make an appointment.** Put this meeting on your calendar just as you would a meeting at work or a PTA gathering. Unless you provide advanced notice and treat this meeting as a high-priority item, you'll likely bump it lower and lower on your to-do list with each passing day.

- **Reduce distractions.** Select a quiet place — no televisions, cell phones, kids yammering for attention, or intrusive waiters. If you have kids, plan the meeting for the school day, or arrange for a babysitter and head out to a quiet place. Take a half day off work, if you have to — your efforts will save you a lot more time down the road.

- **Keep cool.** Carefully monitor your mood temperature during the meeting, and try to keep your emotions from overheating. You need to address your frustrations and disappointments, but not in this setting. You're conducting a planning meeting, not a therapy session. Introducing your issues shuts the meeting down before it gets started.

- **Involve a third party.** If this meeting seems likely to collapse into tears or yelling, or you just can't seem to get it going, consider asking a friend, loved one, or even a therapist to be part of the process. An impartial third party can act as a mediator, emotional thermostat, and taskmaster.

How Involved Should I Be?

After you carefully set aside the time and space to set up a crisis-intervention plan, the first topic needs to be what role you should eventually play in the event of a crisis. Will you play cheerleader, stepping in only when a crisis looms? Will you act as a referral service, calling others when you sense trouble? Or will you land a starting position on the mood-management team: going to the doctor, managing medications, and assisting your loved one? When you step in, how much power should you have? Consider some of the following factors when drawing up guidelines for your involvement:

✔ **Availability:** Geography and time may limit your availability. Are you close enough to your loved one to show up within moments of a problem, or do you need to hop on a plane? Can you take time from work or household responsibilities to devote to crisis prevention and management? Do you have ready access to child care? Is your boss understanding?

✔ **Past experience:** Do you perform well during crises? If you're the type who faints when someone at the office gets a paper cut, or if you wig out when the basement floods, perhaps you're not the best person for the job. You need to be able to keep a cool head, identify the signs of an impending mood episode, and act rationally in the midst of chaos.

✔ **How involved you were before the crisis:** The more involved you've been in everyday management, the more involved you can be in responding to crises. Have you been part of the everyday management of your loved one's care? Do you have a sense of the patterns that lead up to a crisis? Do you know what's been happening with your loved one's medications? Have you been talking with your loved one about the stresses in her life? Or are you more on the sidelines — ready to take action only when a crisis is brewing?

✔ **Your boundaries:** Do you want to have power of attorney so that you can intervene with things like credit cards and bank accounts? Or do you want to handle such issues informally? Does your loved one want you to know about her finances? Will you be in this person's home — pulling credit cards and car keys? These issues are the nitty-gritty of your plan that you must hammer out clearly in advance of any major problems. See Chapter 16 for more information.

✔ **How much intervention your loved one can endure from you:** If the person you're helping has patterns of becoming explosive or dangerous during a crisis, you can do so only much before involving other levels of intervention, such as a crisis team or hospital emergency room. Your role in crisis management may have an early stopping point if your attempts to help trigger outbursts or destructive reactions.

Defining the limits of your involvement depends a great deal on your and your loved one's temperaments and styles. You must identify her personal preferences and what she feels are reasonable levels of involvement. Just as important, you must communicate your comfort level for dealing with deeply personal issues such as money and health care. Your level of involvement isn't a given; it's a matter of negotiation. However, your loved one should have someone on the support team who's willing and able to step in during a crisis.

When Should I Intervene?

Determining the proper intervention point can be quite a challenge. You don't want to hit the panic button whenever your loved one looks a little glum or gets excited, but you also don't want to wait until your loved one is acting irrationally or is completely unreceptive.

Ideally, you'll be able to communicate your observations and concerns to your loved one well before a crisis occurs, assuming that you can identify the warning signs early enough and that your loved one is open to feedback. In such cases, you could mention that "you seem a little more talkative than usual" or "you seem to really be dragging lately," and your loved one knows that you're expressing the secret code for "you're getting hypomanic" or "you're getting depressed." After she accepts the situation, she can see her doctor or therapist for evaluation and any necessary treatment.

In general, the longer you wait to communicate your observations and concerns (perhaps because you don't want to become overly involved or are afraid that you'll hurt your loved one's feelings), the less receptive your loved one will be.

If you feel doubt about when to speak up, the following guidelines may help:

✔ **Act early and often.** Work on establishing open communication with your loved one about the disorder and how it affects her, as we explain in Chapter 16. Such discourse gives you greater knowledge of the warning signs and improves your ability to identify them early. It also makes your loved one more comfortable when sharing the illness with you and others and more receptive to your observations and concerns. The sooner you can identify a mood cycle and take action, the more likely you are to be successful. As a mood cycle gains momentum, your loved one's resistance to your intervention is likely to increase, and your efforts can backfire.

✔ **Keep an eye on the mood journal.** If you live with your loved one, you may not notice the subtle escalation of mood from one day to the next, but a quick glance at a one- or two-week period on a mood chart can alert you to a growing problem. Again, the more you can communicate openly with your loved one, the better your chances of gaining access to mood charts or journals. Don't peek without permission. (Chapter 12 has a mood chart you can copy for use.)

✔ **Identify "red flag" behaviors.** Is your loved one sleeping less? More? Is she beginning to lose whole evenings to shopping or planning numerous big projects? Is she eating more or less? Has your musician friend stopped listening to music or playing instruments? Behavioral changes that indicate trouble are often very unique to the individual.

✔ **Err on the side of caution.** You must balance your fear of hurting your loved one's feelings and making her angry with your desire to keep her safe. You can't manage everything in her life, but if you're worried and things don't feel right, more action rather than less is the way to go. Your loved one may be angry with you for taking action, but if it makes a difference in her safety and survival, your efforts are well worth it.

If your friend or relative is talking about suicide or behaving recklessly, you must act immediately. If she can't or won't listen to you, call for help, as we instruct later in this chapter in the section "Suicide."

Whom Should I Call for Help?

When you create your crisis-intervention plan, address the issue of who may become involved and at what point. Make a list of the people that your loved one wants you to contact and the people you consider helpful and then edit as necessary. Cross people off the list who may cause more problems than they solve; you both know who *they* are. Record your final list of names and numbers on the crisis information form we provide in the section "Putting Your Plan in Writing," later in this chapter.

If the names of doctors and therapists are on the list, they can't talk with you unless they have signed consent forms from your loved one on file, so make sure your loved one follows up on signing the necessary forms.

The following list provides an overview of the professionals, mood-management team members, and others you may need to call in an emergency:

✔ **Psychiatrist:** If your loved one gives you consent to contact her psychiatrist, that's the best place to start. When you see red-flag signs or a worrisome pattern developing, let the doctor know early enough to allow for a medication adjustment before a full-blown crisis. This step works even better if you've met the doctor and if he knows that you're a contact person on the team. Encourage your loved one to describe her escalating symptoms to the psychiatrist, but if she can't because of her emotional state, step in, assuming you have consent.

✔ **Therapist:** If your loved one consents, contact her therapist early enough so she can receive effective treatment. Even if you've already contacted the psychiatrist, giving the therapist a heads-up can provide additional support. Again, meeting the therapist before the crisis is tremendously helpful, because he knows who you are and what your role is.

✔ **Other nonprofessional support people:** Your friend or relative may have identified spouses, parents, siblings, friends, and others as people to call. Bringing them into the mix tightens the support network. Early on, you may have to call other members of the mood-management team for a second opinion on behaviors or patterns you've observed. If the mood cycle begins to escalate, you may need to call for additional assistance.

✔ **The crisis team:** Most municipalities — often at a county or district level — have crisis teams available to assess mental health patients rapidly. Sometimes these teams are based in hospitals, but in many cases, they can come to your home to do the assessment. If the crisis is quickly spinning out of control, or if you can't reach the doctor or therapist, contacting the crisis team is your next step. You can call the crisis team without consent if you feel that your loved one is in danger of hurting herself or someone else. Obtain this phone number in advance; it can be tough to track down, even during the best of times.

✔ **The hospital or emergency room:** If the situation is getting unsafe or out of hand, and your loved one will cooperate, take her to a hospital emergency room or to a predetermined psychiatric hospital for admission. The psychiatrist may refer you in this direction. Unlike an emergency room, you should call the psychiatric hospital before showing up, because it may not have a bed available. In that case, you proceed to a second hospital on the list or the emergency room. In your crisis plan, you should identify the hospitals that work with your loved one's insurance plan and doctors, and make sure you know how to call the hospitals and how to get there. See Chapter 3 for tips on preparing for a stay in the hospital.

✔ **911 or the police:** If you sense imminent danger, call for backup from professionals who can act immediately. What's "imminent danger?" Your loved one is in imminent danger if she:

- Threatens suicide

- Rages toward others

- Makes threats

- Acts so disorganized that travel becomes unsafe

- Refuses or is unable to cooperate

Calling the police isn't something that anyone wants to do to a friend or family member, but if you see a dangerous situation, and your loved one won't or can't go with you to the emergency room, call for help.

Keep in mind that you may have to call more than one person on your list. If you're trying to act early, and dangerous symptoms aren't present, you're more likely to deal with the doctor and therapist. If you're acting during a dangerous episode, you're likely to call the hospital or 911, but you need to call the psychiatrist and therapist as well.

Having your loved one admitted involuntarily

Involuntary hospitalization is the process of admitting someone to a psychiatric hospital against his will. It can only happen in three situations:

- The person poses a danger to himself.
- The person is a danger to others.
- The person can't care for himself.

This is an easier process in some states than in others, but all states require a physician to evaluate the person for danger and risk level before he can be admitted involuntarily to a hospital. You can't "sign commitment papers," like people do in the movies. The legal system considers commitment a medical process and requires that a professional — and in many states, two professionals — identify the person as being a high-risk threat to self or others. The initial hospitalization lasts only a few days; keeping a person hospitalized against his will beyond that period involves a court hearing, which can sometimes occur at the hospital.

During the 1960s, patients' rights groups and advocacy movements worked to enact laws against involuntary commitment in order to err on the side of patients' rights. For the general population, these laws are a positive step toward increased freedom, but they can be frustrating for family and friends who want to help a loved one who refuses treatment. According to these laws, you can't force treatment on someone until the person reaches a danger level that can be legally and medically established.

The issue of medicating a person against his will also falls into this area. States vary widely in their procedures, but action typically requires at least one court hearing. Some states are developing so-called *outpatient commitment* procedures that involve closely monitoring a person who has a diagnosed mental illness (including the person's medication compliance). If the person has a documented history of behavior that threatens his own safety or the safety of others, and if he requires medication to control the behavior and stops taking the medication, the law enables the state to move the person to a hospital against his will. These programs are designed for the most chronically ill patients with the highest risk of dangerous behaviors.

Bring your list of contact information to the emergency room or hospital. This saves a lot of time for the admitting team. Also keep an updated list of medications with your contact list so you can tell the healthcare professionals exactly which medications and doses your loved one is supposed to be taking.

Preventing Risky Behavior

People think nothing of buckling up for safety or wearing a bicycle helmet, but they often hesitate to take car keys away from someone who's driving recklessly or to snatch credit cards from someone whose spending is out of control. When you and your loved one discuss crisis prevention and management, confront these sorts of risky behaviors, and agree on a plan for dealing with them. Your loved one's prior approval to intervene can strengthen your resolve to act forcefully during a crisis.

In this section, we list risky behaviors that are common to bipolar disorder and provide suggestions for possible ways of dealing with them. How you choose to deal with the behaviors is up to you and your loved one and often requires some creative thinking and serious planning.

Also be aware that the clever plans you develop during your rational meeting of minds may seem completely unacceptable to your loved one during a mood episode — particularly a manic episode. Having a solid plan and taking early action can increase your chances of success, but be prepared to meet some strong resistance.

Reckless driving

Mania and depression can impair your loved one's ability to drive safely. Mania lifts inhibitions, essentially disabling the speed regulator inside the brain and pressing your friend or relative to disregard speed limits and defensive-driving techniques. Depression can impair concentration and reflexes, slowing response times and resulting in erratic driving. A driver who feels hopeless and despondent and who doesn't care whether she lives or dies may be unable to make safe driving decisions.

The obvious intervention in this case is to take away the car keys — obvious, that is, until you consider some of the ramifications. Driving is central to many of our lives and represents adulthood and independence. By grabbing the car keys, you remove your loved one's sense of independence and freedom and her ability to get to work, do her shopping, get to doctor's appointments, and perform other tasks that help her stay on track and avoid a major mood episode. Before you snatch the car keys, plan for these contingencies:

- Can someone get your loved one to work?
- How will your friend or relative get to the doctor and therapist?
- Who can pick up her kids, take them to soccer, and buy groceries?

Taking away the keys is the easy part. Keeping your loved one's life going afterward requires serious planning and attention to detail.

Runaway spending

Unrestrained spending is almost a cliché in stories about manic episodes. The logical intervention is deceptively simple — hide the cash and checkbook, snatch the credit and debit cards, and transfer the cash from the savings account to an account that your loved one can't touch. But mania has several ways to work around these minor inconveniences and get to the cash it needs:

- Your loved one may memorize the credit card numbers.
- Account information may be stored on Internet shopping sites.
- Your loved one can still shop by phone.
- Credit cards are easy to apply for over the phone or on the Internet.

In order to stay one step ahead of the mania, you need to think creatively and invent ways to counter these tactics:

- **Contact the credit card companies to place a hold on the accounts.** Procedures may vary, depending on the companies and the state in which you reside, so research the policies and credit card company phone numbers ahead of time.

- **Report the credit cards stolen.** Technically speaking, the bipolar disorder has stolen them, so you're not really lying. (Do this only in a pinch.)

- **Inspect the mail for any new credit card applications.** Most mailboxes receive a steady stream of tempting offers; shred them, or simply write "Return to Sender" on the envelope and drop it in the mail.

- **Monitor your loved one's Internet use and e-mail for any activity regarding credit card applications or transactions.** Obtain consent from your loved one prior to doing this.

Of course, potential drawbacks accompany these clever plans. If your loved one shares the accounts with a spouse or significant other, how can he or she access money to buy groceries and pay bills? It makes sense to keep at least one separate account that the person with bipolar disorder can't access — money available during a crisis. You may also want to keep the accounts in the spouse's name only to reduce the potential sources of money during a crisis.

Hypersexuality

Hypersexuality — a supercharged state of sexual confidence and desire — is a diagnostic feature of mania that often results in risky sexual behavior. It stirs up boatloads of trouble for the person with bipolar disorder and her family. Trying to reduce these behaviors presents unique challenges. Sexual behavior is private stuff. Without trailing the manic person 24/7, how can you prevent dangerous sexual behavior? For starters, try the following:

- **Take the car keys and credit cards.** No car, no money, no sex. Well, it may not be that easy, but taking driving and spending off the table blocks the main access routes to unsafe sexual connections. Of course, taking away the car keys and credit cards presents similar drawbacks, which we discuss in the previous two sections.

✔ **Restrict or monitor Internet access.** The Internet provides 24-hour access to a menu of sexual opportunities, including pornography, which may be the least of your worries. Chat rooms, online dating sites, and other virtual pickup joints are packed with people looking for sexual connections. Pornography doesn't carry the risk of sexually transmitted diseases or pregnancy, but chat rooms and dating sites can lead to physical encounters.

Restricting Internet access also has some potential drawbacks that you should discuss during your planning meeting. Can you restrict Internet access without eliminating e-mail and work communications? Will your loved one allow you to monitor her Internet activities? Tailor your plan so that both of you feel comfortable with it and confident that it will produce the desired results. Talk, talk, and more talk is the only way to cover all your bases.

Be careful not to encourage behaviors that you find enjoyable; for example, if your spouse is hypersexual with *you,* you may welcome the extra attention you're getting. Remember, however, that the fun that comes with this extra energy can easily get out of control. You need to do what's best for the person with the illness, not what feels good at the time.

Drug and alcohol abuse

Bipolar disorder doesn't mix well with drugs or alcohol. In a person whose inhibitions are already compromised, these substances melt away any vestiges of good judgment. With depression, alcohol can result in a much higher risk of completed suicide. Helping your loved one stay away from these danger zones can be lifesaving, but your options are limited:

✔ **Cut off access to money and transportation.** If your loved one can't afford drugs and alcohol and can't get to them, she can't use them. However, if she has access, she can still steal what she needs or trade stuff for it.

✔ **Restrict phone and Internet access.** If a friend or acquaintance delivers drugs or alcohol to your loved one, cutting off communications to the outside world, if possible, can help block the courier route.

✔ **Monitor your loved one's activity.** Keeping watch is incredibly intrusive and restrictive for both you and your loved one, but standing guard is the most effective option in controlling almost every risky behavior we cover in this section. Obtain assistance from others, if possible, to reduce your burnout.

Julie's college intervention

The crisis crept up slowly on Julie. She was a college student and always bright and energetic. She began to stay up very late at night doing extra work for her classes and planning multiple events for her sorority. She was thrilled that even with such little sleep, she didn't feel tired. She even had the time and energy to party with her friends all night — drinking and smoking a little pot. She felt increasingly confident and sought out companionship on the Internet and at off-campus bars. She raced through her credit card limit, buying new clothes for her liaisons and her planned activities, so she ordered a new card from the many offers she received in the mail. Her schoolwork began to drop off the radar.

Julie's friends worried about her, but she told them she had never felt better and that nothing was wrong. She became snappy with friends who voiced their concerns, and she began to think that her friends wanted to ruin her life. She even started to suspect that the college administration could have something to do with it.

When her closest friend contacted Julie's parents, she was enraged. She jumped in her car to race home and clear things up. Halfway home, an officer stopped her for speeding; she was going about 100 miles per hour. The police officer suspected that something was amiss, because she was rambling and looked "out of it." He called for an ambulance, which took her to the emergency room about an hour from home. When her parents arrived, Julie was paranoid and disoriented. They agreed to hospitalization, which she fought but gave into eventually. Over the next six months, she stabilized on medications and returned to school.

Julie and her family and friends developed an early warning system, particularly regarding her sleep. If she began sleeping less, her friends would call her parents. Julie's friends also kept her busy with activities other than drinking. Her mood cycling persisted, but her support group managed it well with early intervention, and Julie eventually found a mix of meds that kept her mood pretty even most of the time.

Agreeing beforehand about the actions you must take to curb risky behavior may make your loved one more receptive when the time comes for you to monitor behavior and enforce limits. However, any action you take to restrict behavior carries the risk of causing backlash. Your loved one may become more secretive or even decide to rebel or run away. Prepare yourself for these potential reactions, both psychologically and in your planning.

Suicide

A person with severe depression is at high risk for suicide. If you suspect that your loved one may be considering suicide, take the following steps:

1. **Keep watch, and don't leave your loved one alone.**

   If you can't stay around, call someone to come over and stay there until your replacement arrives.

2. **Listen, remain supportive by telling your loved one how much she means to you, and encourage her to talk about her feelings.**

   Don't try to argue at this point about why life is worth living, and don't dismiss her feelings.

3. **Remove any weapons or medications that could assist a suicide attempt.**

   Don't leave anything around that can make suicide an easy option.

4. **Call your loved one's doctor or therapist, or call 911.**

   If you can't connect with the doctor or therapist, don't hesitate to drive your loved one to the emergency room or dial 911.

5. **Get help from other friends or family members.**

   They can help support your loved one, as well as you, through the crisis.

Don't be afraid to ask about suicidal thoughts. Your loved one won't become suicidal just because you ask questions — the risk comes from not asking. Also, trust your perceptions and instincts. When dealing with a loved one who's becoming increasingly violent or suicidal, you may try to talk yourself out of believing that something bad can actually happen. If the situation is escalating, get help before it's too late.

Putting Your Plan in Writing

Digging through your loved one's purse or wallet for doctor names and phone numbers or rummaging through the medicine cabinet to piece together prescription information during a crisis is both bothersome and unnecessary. The one thing you should walk away with from your crisis-planning meeting is a single sheet of paper listing every piece of critical information you need in the event of a crisis.

With the help of your loved one, fill out the Crisis Information Sheet shown in Figure 17-1, distribute it to all the people on your mood-management team, and keep it handy at all times.

Keep several copies of the Crisis Information Sheet on hand: one at home, one at work, one in your purse or briefcase, and one on your computer or PDA (Personal Digital Assistant). Update the information whenever your loved one changes doctors or therapists or has a medication adjustment so you have the most recent information at all times.

Contact Information		
To Call	**Name**	**Phone Number**
Psychiatrist		Office: Emergency:
Therapist/ Social Worker		Office: Emergency:
Primary Care Physician		Office: Emergency:
Hospital		
Local Mental Health Crisis Team		
Local Support Group Crisis Responder		
Local Police		
State Police		
Friend/Relative		
Friend/Relative		
Friend/Relative		
Friend/Relative		

Medication		
Medication	**Dose**	**Times Per Day**

Figure 17-1:
Filling out
a Crisis
Information
Sheet
makes it
easier to
make
decisions
during a
crisis.

Insurance Information	
Insurance Company	
Member Services Phone Number	
Mental Health Services Phone Number	
Member ID	
Group ID	

Work Information	
Employer Name	
Employer Phone Number	
Supervisor Name	
Human Resources Contact	

Responding in a Crisis

Depression and mania can both lead to situations that build up to a crisis or an emergency situation. As a support person, your job is to quickly and accurately assess the potential danger; keep cool; and take the necessary actions to protect yourself, your loved one, and any others in close proximity. When a crisis begins to brew, take the following steps to defuse it and obtain the necessary treatment for your loved one:

1. **Protect yourself and others.**

   If you feel that the situation endangers your safety or the safety of others in the household, exit as soon as safely possible. If your loved one is violent or threatening, call 911; inform the dispatcher of any previous hospitalizations, and request that the police not brandish any weapons.

2. **Defuse the situation, if possible.**

   Confronting an individual in the throes of mania or arguing with someone during a bout of depression is perhaps the worst thing you can do. Remain calm and rational, talk in a soft tone, and encourage your loved one to seek help voluntarily. Don't threaten or try to restrain your loved one.

3. **Call your loved one's doctor or therapist.**

   If you can't reach the doctor or therapist, contact the local crisis team or hospital. If your loved one is able, let him talk to the doctor or therapist; otherwise, you do the talking. If your loved one has been taken somewhere, provide the doctor or therapist with the necessary information to follow up.

Being arrested and incarcerated are extremely traumatic events, especially for people who suffer from a mental illness. Your goal is to get your loved one to a hospital or other treatment center where he can obtain medication and therapy. If your loved one commits a crime that someone witnesses, you can petition for involuntary commitment rather than jail time. Jail isn't where your loved one needs to be.

Chapter 18

Backing Your Bipolar Child

Something's not quite right with your child. She's moodier than the other kids — yelling at you one minute, crying uncontrollably the next. When things don't go the way she wants, she flies into a rage, sometimes breaking her favorite toys or tearing up her artwork. She doesn't have any close friends, and just when you think she's about to strike up a friendship, she does something to drive her friend away. The entire household is on edge, afraid that any wrong word or gesture will upset the delicate balance.

Need some advice? You'll find plenty. When it comes to raising children, everyone's an expert. Comments about your child's behavioral problems come freely and loudly, and from all directions. Your family, your neighbors, and even the lady behind you at the supermarket offer their expert advice and observations: "She just needs a good spanking" or "She's a spoiled brat!" In your mind, you're wrestling with guilt and fear, wondering what you did to cause the problem and if you can do anything to make it better.

Trying to tough out the situation with advice from daytime television and the neighborhood peanut gallery won't work. This complicated medical problem needs the same care and attention you'd give a child with diabetes or severe asthma.

In this chapter, you discover how bipolar disorder typically affects children and teenagers, and why the diagnosis is so tricky. You find out what an evaluation should involve and how to obtain an evaluation for your child. We also review the treatment options for a child with bipolar disorder and offer a brief introduction to the world of special education services for children with bipolar disorder.

Recognizing the Diagnostic Difficulties

Many adults with bipolar disorder will tell you that they had their first symptoms when they were kids, even though they didn't recognize the symptoms as symptoms back then. For a long time, psychiatrists thought that bipolar disorder was only an adult problem and that children couldn't get depressed or manic. Until the late 1980s, most experts believed that children couldn't suffer from depression, but research from the past few decades has shown that they clearly can. The question of mania has come up even more recently, and professionals are still debating and discussing the issue.

Kids' brains really are different from adult brains. Their neurons are still connecting and configuring to create a grown-up person. Just as babies must babble before they talk, kids must have immature emotional reactions before they can have mature ones. Human moods and behaviors become more defined and modulated as people develop through childhood and adolescence. When problems arise with moods and behaviors in kids, they can appear more vague. In kids, bipolar disorder may exhibit some of the following differences:

- ✔ **Duration:** Depression and manic episodes may not compare to the full duration of adult episodes. The two weeks of depression and the week of mania or hypomania required by DSM-IV (see Chapter 2) for a diagnosis of bipolar disorder aren't always part of childhood bipolar disorder.

- ✔ **Definition:** The periods of depression and mania may not be as clear-cut — mixed types of episodes may be more prominent in many children with bipolar disorder.

- ✔ **Details:** Children typically don't go on a worldwide tour or a shopping spree when manic; however, they may start spending all night counting their baseball cards and begin "collecting" frantically, even stealing cards from other kids.

Older adolescents often exhibit traditional bipolar symptoms. A common onset age is late adolescence and early adulthood. In younger teens and especially in children under 12, the diagnosis is much trickier. During the earlier years, children may simply appear overly angry, hyperactive, depressed, or oppositional.

The angry kid

Plenty of kids throw fits — that's their job. After all, they're living, breathing human beings with brains, and nobody likes to be told what to do. In junior high, kids specialize in moodiness as they rebel against rules and authority and test the boundaries of free expression. But sustained patterns of daily mood and behavioral explosions, and a persistent inability to meet the demands of daily life without falling apart, are red flags for mood disorders in kids.

Tantrums, a "short fuse," and "mood swings" aren't enough to officially diagnose bipolar disorder. The following general symptoms can arise from a host of other causes and conditions:

- ✔ **Unipolar depression:** Frequent anger and tantrums can be symptoms of childhood depression without mania. Adults with depression are often irritable and short-fused. Depressed kids, with even less ability to express their feelings clearly and fewer skills for managing unbearable sadness, may seem really angry.

- ✔ **Anxiety:** Fears and worries can paralyze kids and make them unable to carry out requests. They may be terrified of someone getting hurt at home, for example, so they're terrified of leaving the house to go school. A battle rages over school every morning, complete with tears, flying toys, kicking and biting, and gnashing of teeth. The child hasn't clearly identified the fear, so he just looks defiant.

- ✔ **Obsessive-compulsive disorder:** OCD is a subtype of anxiety disorder in which kids have repeated irrational thoughts and fears, along with behaviors that they must repeat over and over again to try to reduce the fears. A child who must walk through doorways five times forward and five times backward has a lot of trouble moving along with his class through the hallways. He may not be able tell you what's going on in his head, or he tries to hide the behaviors because he's embarrassed. The result is a kid who looks as though he's "oppositional," with fits of anger and "meltdowns."

- ✔ **Language and learning problems:** Undiagnosed or undertreated language and learning problems are wildly frustrating for kids. They can't do what teachers or parents ask of them, so they're labeled "difficult," and no matter what they do, they can't seem to succeed or change their behaviors. They cycle into a pattern of failure, which leads to negative/ avoidance behaviors and explosions whenever they encounter demands.

- ✔ **Sleep problems:** Kids with irregular sleep patterns and difficulty staying asleep can look terribly irritable and reactive when their bodies and minds are simply tired.

- ✔ **Medical problems:** Migraine headaches, stomach problems, and asthma are some of the most common ailments in children that can cause irritability.

- ✔ **Stress reactions:** Chronic family conflict at home can cause kids to be irritable and reactive. Illness or loss in the family, financial problems, moving, new siblings, and substance abuse in the family can all wreak havoc on a child's ability to tolerate daily life without big, emotional reactions. School situations can be just as overwhelming — being bullied or having a fight with a teacher can cause severe emotional distress.

Not every angry kid has bipolar disorder. A brief interview isn't adequate for a diagnosis. Get a careful evaluation, preferably with a board-certified child-and-adolescent psychiatrist, before you accept a bipolar diagnosis in your child.

The hyperactive kid

In children, ADHD (Attention Deficit Hyperactivity Disorder) and bipolar disorder, particularly the mania, can look like identical twins. Some studies show that large numbers of kids in psychiatric hospitals and kids diagnosed with ADHD actually have bipolar disorder, although some experts suggest that this claim may be an exaggeration. Distinguishing between mania and ADHD is critical because their treatments are so very different. The stimulants used to treat ADHD, such as Adderall and Ritalin, can wreak havoc with a manic child, and mood stabilizers don't help ADHD.

Shared symptoms between bipolar disorder and ADHD

To grasp just how challenging a child's diagnosis can be, check out the following symptoms that bipolar disorder and ADHD share:

- **Increased motor activity:** In both conditions, kids "bounce off the walls." They can't sit still, and they seem restless and easily bored.

- **Increased talking:** Both conditions often create "motor mouth," where kids talk constantly and can never seem to catch a breath. They often interrupt conversations or pipe up with comments irrelevant to the discussion around them. They talk about what interests them without paying attention to how other people respond. They blurt out feelings or opinions that may hurt someone's feelings or cause major problems.

- **Poor impulse control:** Increased motor activity and talkativeness are examples of limited impulse control. In mania and ADHD, poor impulse control is a core problem. Performing dangerous stunts without thinking is the most problematic part of either diagnosis. A hyperactive or manic kid may jump off bookshelves or dash across the street without realizing the danger involved. Kids with ADHD are more likely to try drugs and alcohol, just like kids with mania. Stealing and lying are common problems in both conditions. In manic and hyperactive teens, impulsive decisions about sexual partners can present serious problems.

- **Impatience/low frustration tolerance:** More subtypes of impulse-control problems. Kids who can't wait their turn, who grab things from other kids, or who melt down over minor frustrations can have ADHD or mania.

How can I tell the difference?

What are the differences between the two conditions? How do you sort them out? In adults, the distinction is fairly straightforward. In kids, for several reasons, the distinction can be more difficult. The following areas are important to consider:

- **Cycling:** In bipolar disorder, the manic and hypomanic symptoms typically come in episodes. In ADHD, the impulse-control issues are chronic and don't shift markedly in severity or degree. Impulsivity certainly shifts, but not to the degree of a cycling mood disorder.

✔ **Change from baseline:** To identify mania, you must notice a variation from the norm — a person doesn't feel like himself. With kids, they may have always behaved like this, leaving you with no point of comparison. Because a kid hasn't lived as long, the manic behavior could be his baseline — he may not have a "usual" state — but the doctor still looks for evidence of shifts from a baseline as part of the diagnosis of a mood disorder in your child.

✔ **Grandiosity:** Mania causes you to be full of yourself and quite certain that you can do anything and everything that comes into your head. Although kids with ADHD may act impulsively, overconfidence and the tendency to misjudge their abilities aren't parts of the ADHD diagnosis. In fact, these kids typically struggle with low self-confidence and a sense that that they're doomed to failure. Grandiosity is a red flag for mania.

✔ **Sleep disturbance:** Kids with ADHD often have trouble quieting their minds to sleep, making bedtime quite difficult. In mania, the entire sleep/wake cycle is disturbed. These kids seem to need little sleep — they stay up late, get up early, and keep on going. Kids experiencing mania eventually crash and appear exhausted, but they typically have periods of high energy with less need for sleep.

✔ **Presence of "euphoric mood" episodes:** Mania can be diagnosed in someone with only angry, irritable moods, a symptom that's also associated with ADHD. But the presence of euphoria — an expansive, overly happy mood with a persistent sense that everything is "beyond wonderful," even when life throws its usual curve balls — is much more likely in bipolar disorder than in ADHD.

Could my child have both?

How common is it for kids with bipolar disorder to also have ADHD? Can you have both? Evidence suggests that the combination is fairly common and that overlapping areas of the brain are involved in both disorders, but the exact relationship between the two disorders still isn't clear in the scientific research.

Not all individuals with bipolar disorder have problems paying attention. Some people can focus quite well when hording baseball cards, memorizing trivia, and convincing you that they're right and you're wrong. But many people with bipolar disorder do seem to have trouble with *executive function* — the ability to organize, sort, and manage incoming information and make decisions. ADHD often includes executive-function problems as well. The brain's CEO may be compromised in both disorders, and that may explain why the conditions seem to overlap so frequently.

The depressed child or adolescent

Child-and-adolescent depression is a condition that tragically results in one of the leading causes of death in teenagers: suicide. But depression can be tricky to spot, particularly in teens who already seem moody and impulsive. Depression in kids and teens doesn't always look like it does in adults; depressed kids can appear angry, bored, or withdrawn rather than sad and dejected. Parents often think that a kid doesn't have depression if he can still smile or have fun: "He can have fun with his friends, so how can he be depressed?" Kids, like adults, try to keep functioning in public for as long as they can to avoid being noticed and to keep from being embarrassed in front of their peers. And like adults, when a teen feels depressed, he tries to do something to make himself feel better, and being with friends may be the only activity in his life that feels remotely positive. School and home, with the demands and judgments, are painful. Friends are comforting.

How can you decide whether your child or teenager is being "dramatic" or is sinking into a serious depression? Look for the following signs:

- **Persistent changes in function:** Everybody has good and bad days or weeks. Inconsistency is a hallmark of humanity, but when your child or adolescent begins to experience extended periods of time when he's "not himself," you need to pay attention. Changes in grades, friends, activities, energy, and enthusiasm that go on for more than a couple of weeks are worth looking into.

- **Any self-harm or talk of suicide:** These are big red flags that you must respond to immediately. Even if you think your child just wants attention or wants to manipulate you, the fact that he's using suicide or self-injury as his tool is already a problem. A child with adequately developing mood and behavioral coping mechanisms doesn't typically use this method to communicate a need for attention or to manipulate his environment.

   Always take threats of suicide seriously. Don't try to determine yourself if your child really means it. Get a professional opinion immediately.

- **Withdrawal:** Kids like their personal space, and adolescents particularly spend plenty of time in their rooms. But kids who hardly leave their rooms, stop spending time with friends, or start dropping their after-school and weekend activities are showing signs of depression. This behavior can happen gradually and may be hard to notice.

- **Sleep/energy changes:** Kids change sleep patterns throughout their development. As teenagers, we seem to develop a need to stay up late and sleep later into the day. The trend is fairly universal; however, a kid who changes his patterns and starts sleeping a lot more or a lot less than usual may be depressed. If your child's energy levels seem to be dropping and not rebounding after a couple of weeks, schedule a medical exam. If the doctor finds no medical cause, depression may be a possibility.

- **Substance use:** Drinking and marijuana use seem to be ubiquitous in high schools nowadays. Keeping kids from these experiences is a difficult challenge, but a kid who uses substances regularly or significantly increases his use may be self-medicating. Don't convince yourself that "all kids do it." If your kid gets high or drunk every weekend, you need to look into it. Depression is closely related to substance abuse.

If depression is part of the diagnostic picture in a child or adolescent, you automatically raise a red flag for bipolar disorder. People who develop depression early in life are more likely to develop bipolar disorder than someone who develops depression at a later age. Not every kid who suffers from depression eventually receives a diagnosis of bipolar disorder, but your child's doctor may look a little closer for any warning signs, including some of the following:

- ✓ **Repeated depressions:** A child or teen who experiences numerous episodes of depression is a more likely candidate for a bipolar diagnosis eventually. If the episodes are brief (three months or less), the risk increases.

- ✓ **Family history of mania/bipolar disorder:** The risk of developing bipolar disorder is higher if you have a first-degree relative with the illness (a parent or sibling). If you have identical twins, and one twin develops bipolar disorder, the other one has an 80 percent chance of developing the disorder, too.

- ✓ **Manic or hypomanic response to antidepressants:** A manic response is a suggestive symptom, but it isn't diagnostic of bipolar disorder. People can become manic or agitated on antidepressants without having bipolar disorder.

- ✓ **Lack of response to antidepressants:** Difficult, severe depressions that don't respond to antidepressants are associated with a bipolar pattern.

- ✓ **Drop-off in response to antidepressants:** People who respond to antidepressants temporarily (even after dose increases and medication changes) are more apt to receive a bipolar diagnosis.

- ✓ **A "larger than life" temperament:** People with baseline hyperthymic personalities are considered a high bipolar risk. *Hyperthymic* is a medical term for "high energy" — very outgoing and active, often highly confident, sometimes seen as arrogant or narcissistic.

These factors aren't diagnostic for bipolar disorder; just count them as big red flags. This realization is important, because treating bipolar disorder with antidepressants alone can be risky — it can trigger mania or agitation. If your child's doctor identifies a number of these warning signs, she may choose different medications than she would for a kid without these characteristics. Bipolar disorder often requires at least two medications: one to treat mania and the other for depression (see Chapter 7 for more information). If bipolar disorder is unlikely, the medication choices are often, but not always, clearer and less dangerous, which is why a full history and extended interview are such important parts of treating a child or adolescent with depression.

The oppositional kid

The term "oppositional kid" may seem redundant to most parents and teachers. Every child is oppositional at times. The attitude is part of growing up.

By the time a child reaches the terrible twos, he's mastered the word "no" and uses it quite appropriately to mark his parents' limits. Adolescence is another time of life characterized by oppositional behaviors — teenagers want to do things their way, not their parents' way.

For most kids, these behaviors respond fairly well to the usual carrot-and-stick parenting techniques, but oppositional kids exhibit a much more tenacious defiance. Their entire lives seem to revolve around the word "no." Either the kid constantly says "no" or hears "no." Parents describe the child as "stubborn," "strong willed," or simply "a pain in the neck." When this pattern creates significant problems in function — at school, at home, with friends, or during activities — a doctor or therapist may suggest a diagnosis of ODD (Oppositional Defiant Disorder). The problem with this diagnosis is that oppositional behavior, like anger, is a symptom shared among a host of diagnoses and conditions, resulting in what professionals technically refer to as a "real muddle." So even if the ODD diagnosis fits, you want to know what else is going on. Here are some possible explanations:

- **Mood disorders (depression or bipolar):** Mood conditions can create a pattern of defiance. A kid whose mood, rather than logical thinking, drives his brain has less mental muscle to do what he has to do in life. Depression saps energy and interest, and mania clouds judgment and inhibition.

- **Temperament:** Kids start out in the world loaded with certain basic tendencies. The ability to "go with the flow," as opposed to sticking with an agenda, is called *cognitive flexibility.* Some people (kids included) are more naturally inflexible and have a harder time negotiating the demands of life. Beyond a child's natural tendencies, mismatches of temperament between a child and the adults in his life (parents and teachers) can exacerbate or even trigger significant oppositional behavioral patterns.

- **Anxiety:** Anxiety, like a mood problem, takes over the brain and gets in the way of good decision-making. The only thing an anxious person can concentrate on is reducing his anxiety, so telling him that he has to do his homework may not register if he can't stop worrying that a robber is in the house and wants to kill him.

- **ADHD:** Kids with less impulse control can't follow directions as well or limit negative behaviors as effectively as other kids. Kids who can't pay attention often don't hear the directions the first few times.

- **PDDs (Pervasive Developmental Disorders):** These include diagnoses such as Asperger's disorder and high-functioning autism. Kids in this category are, by definition, cognitively rigid and tend to *perseverate,* or get stuck on certain activities that interest them. They have a particularly hard time moving through commands and instructions on a day-to-day basis. Although more severe forms are obvious in their diagnoses, doctors sometimes miss the subtle forms.

✔ **Learning and language disabilities:** Anything that gets in the way of a kid's ability to correctly take in, process, and produce responses to information from the world can create oppositional and defiant behavior patterns.

An oppositional kid can easily get labeled as a "problem child," resulting in more frequent negative interactions with adults in his world. The potential for a chronically angry and explosive kid with problems at school and home is enormous, and a diagnosis of bipolar disorder often gets thrown into the mix. Before making any diagnostic decision, you and your child's doctor should consider all the possible causes for your child's pattern of behavior.

When dealing with an oppositional child, open your mind to other possible reasons why he may be acting defiant. Don't just look at what you or others may have done to spoil the child or make him manipulative or "bratty." Although your assessment may be that you need to work on your skills as a disciplinarian, try looking at your child's temperament and other possible contributions to this pattern that make it hard for him to choose more cooperative behaviors. He may not want to drive you crazy; he may just be stuck in a pattern. A more positive, flexible approach on your part can neutralize some of the power struggles and reduce some of the defiance and conflict, thereby reducing the likelihood of escalating explosions and mood reactions. In other words, sometimes you may need to back off on the less important issues. *The Explosive Child,* 2nd Edition, by Ross Greene (HarperCollins), is an excellent reference that provides plenty of detailed suggestions.

The law-breaking kid

If your child or teenager has run-ins with the law, you should strongly consider screening for psychiatric disorders. Mood disorders, particularly mania, are much more common in kids who commit crimes. In many cases, substance abuse buddies up with a psychiatric illness, creating a dangerous duo that lead your child to trouble's door. Alternative schools and detention centers are populated with an inordinate percentage of adolescents who suffer from bipolar disorder, anxiety disorders, or ADHD.

Legal problems are usually the result of multiple factors, but evaluating for a psychiatric disorder and treating the disorder effectively can make a big difference for some kids. The courts are overburdened and unlikely to recommend evaluations for many cases. Parents and mental health professionals need to advocate for these psychiatric workups and treatments when their children are heading down this path. Don't assume that the system will do what's best for your child.

Requesting a Professional Evaluation

Maybe after reading the previous ten pages, the only conclusion you can draw is that your child has *some* characteristics that *may* be caused by one of a *dozen different things,* including your parenting skills and your relationship with your spouse. Now what? Now you get your child to a professional who can help you sort out the possible causes and pinpoint one or two that can steer you toward obtaining proper treatment.

How can I find the right doctor?

A good starting point is your family doctor or pediatrician. Pediatricians are becoming increasingly familiar with psychiatric diagnoses in kids and can guide you and your child to the appropriate psychiatric help. Also, the pediatrician can conduct a full medical examination to rule out the presence of any health issues that could be contributing to your child's problems. Conditions such as thyroid disease and some anemias can generate mood symptoms. The doctor can also address general health issues such as sleep and growth, which may be important factors in a mood disorder.

After a physician rules other illnesses out, if you still have serious concerns about mood disorders, the next step is to consult a board-certified child-and-adolescent psychiatrist. Some adult psychiatrists work with adolescents and may be comfortable diagnosing and treating kids over 16. Younger teens and children, however, should see a psychiatrist trained and experienced in working with kids' brains.

Beware of doctors who proceed with a "diagnosis by prescription." The doctor spends 15 minutes with you and your child; hands you a prescription for Ritalin or an antidepressant; and then, when your kid ends up in the hospital, he tries a different medication to see if it will work. A thorough evaluation takes time, input from various sources, and detective work. Is there a child-and-adolescent psychiatrist in the house?

Finding a child-and-adolescent psychiatrist may take some work, depending on where you live. This field has a shortage of qualified professionals, particularly in some areas of the country. Even if you can locate a number of child doctors in your area, finding one who fits into your insurance plan can be a nightmare. Look to the following sources for leads:

- ✔ Your child's pediatrician
- ✔ The school system's special education department
- ✔ Friends or relatives
- ✔ A counselor or therapist who works with your child

✔ The American Academy of Child and Adolescent Psychiatry Web site at `www.aacap.org`

✔ Your local medical society

✔ The Depression and Bipolar Support Alliance (DBSA) Web site, `www.dbsalliance.org/resources/referral.html`, which has a peer-to-peer doctor recommendation section and online discussion forums for parents and families where you can discuss caring for your child with people who've been there

✔ The National Alliance for the Mentally Ill (NAMI) Web site at `www.nami.org` (use the site to find contact information for a local chapter of NAMI)

✔ The Child and Adolescent Bipolar Foundation Web site at `www.bpkids.org`, which offers a professional directory that includes names of doctors who have some expertise in working with kids with bipolar disorder

✔ A local children's hospital or a medical school or university hospital (places that may have a department of psychiatry)

Chapters 5 and 6 describe the process of finding and choosing a psychiatrist and assembling a mood-management team and support network. This information is valuable for putting together a team for your child's care as well.

If your child expresses suicidal thoughts or behaviors, *run,* don't walk, to your nearest mental health professional or emergency room. Don't wait to find someone through referrals or plans. You can do that later. Get help right away, and sort through your long-term options later.

What else can I do at this stage?

As a parent and/or guardian, your role at this stage is to find a doctor you think is best qualified to evaluate and treat your son or daughter and to provide that person with the most accurate and complete history you can possibly present. Your child may be unable or unwilling to describe symptoms or to relate the details of various incidents that can help the doctor accurately assess the situation, so you need to supply that information without running your child's self-esteem through the grinder. The following suggestions come from others who have been in the trenches:

✔ **Be open and honest.** If you and your spouse are having marital problems, or if one of you has a drinking or substance-abuse problem, don't keep it a secret. Family problems can have a significant impact on your child's moods and on the diagnosis. Don't let your child be misdiagnosed because you want to protect a family secret. Family therapy may be a necessary first step in treating your child.

✔ **Mention any history of mental illness in the family.** Genetics plays a strong role in bipolar disorder. If your family has a history of bipolar disorder, schizophrenia, depression, or other mental illness, be sure to mention it.

✔ **Recollect the history.** When did you and others first become concerned? Record descriptions and details of any incidents that your child has been involved in that raised concern. Concentrate on home, school, your child's friends, and activities outside the home. Include dates. Also be sure to record periods of relative calm, when you have observed few problems. Keeping a mood chart and sleep log for one or two weeks before your appointment can help (see Chapter 12 for copies of these logs).

✔ **Gather input from others.** Ask caregivers, teachers, youth ministers, coaches, and others who deal with your child for their observations and input. Some therapists and psychiatrists have standard forms for collecting this data as part of their evaluation processes. Parents can have a skewed vision of their child's behavior, so additional input may help form a more balanced report.

✔ **Meet with the doctor personally.** Everyone closely involved should get a chance to meet with the doctor privately. Parents need to honestly report their concerns without shaming the child, and the child needs to be able to speak openly about his symptoms. Exactly how this plays out depends on the patient's age and temperament, but the doctor needs to obtain information from both sources. Confidentiality weighs heavily in this situation, especially with teenagers. The usual arrangement is that a doctor won't tell parents what the patient says unless a safety risk is involved. Clarify the boundaries of confidentiality with your child's doctor from the start.

✔ **Obtain a copy of the evaluation.** In this day and age, people change doctors more often than they change clothes. Having the evaluation and any diagnoses in writing can smooth the transition to another doctor or therapist.

If you don't feel sure about the diagnosis or treatment plan or comfortable with the answers to your questions, obtain a second opinion. Given the complexity of the situation, a second viewpoint can be valuable in helping you make the best decisions and treatment choices.

Breaking Out the Treatment Toolbox

With a diagnosis in hand and the assistance of your child's doctor and support network, your family can prepare to embark on a course of treatment. Your journey will meander along a path strewn with starts and stops, successes and failures, fatigue, and financial drain, but it eventually leads to the land of stabilization for your child and family. The journey may be rough, but you have several tools at your disposal to help you reach your destination:

✔ **Medications:** Balancing and calming the overcooked nervous system usually requires at least some period of medication. Although you and your doctor may have concerns about using medications in children and teenagers, the right medication combination can ultimately be a lifesaver.

✔ **Therapy:** Individual therapy, family and parenting therapy, and group and social-skills therapy are the building blocks of treating children with bipolar disorder. Cognitive behavioral types of therapy are probably most commonly used, but other techniques are certainly employed as well.

✔ **School support and intervention:** Kids spend much of their daily lives in school, and mood disorders disrupt school life in many ways. Building the right educational setting and support system, which we discuss in the section "Tending to school matters," later in this chapter, is as critical as any other intervention on the menu.

✔ **Lifestyle/expectations management:** Throughout this book, we discuss the beneficial effects that lifestyle changes can have on the treatment outcome. This discussion applies to children, too, but in the case of children, the parents must accept, implement, and encourage these lifestyle changes so the child doesn't feel pressured to fulfill unrealistic expectations.

✔ **Hospitalization:** Hospitalization is a last resort, but it may be the only option if your child may harm himself or others, such as siblings. Managing the disorder without hospitalization is possible, but children with bipolar disorder are commonly hospitalized at least once for the illness.

Cautiously treating the developing brain

The idea of treating a child with psychiatric medications may send shivers down your spine. People often find it hard to imagine that children can hurt so much emotionally that they need medication. "Kids should just be happy and do what they're told." "If parents would give their kids a good spanking when they needed it, the kids wouldn't be such spoiled brats." The idea that bipolar disorder is a physical illness is hard enough to grasp when you see it in adults; in kids, for some reason, people are even more unlikely to accept this scientifically clear premise.

When a child's mood problems are destroying her chances of safely making the transition to adulthood, or the symptoms are disrupting her development, medications are often the only viable solution. Despite all the diagnostic challenges, when a child's depression, mania, or rage hijacks her life, chemical adjustments become necessary. Much like bipolar disorder itself, the process of medicating a child is complicated.

Complicating factors for medication

The study of psychiatric medication in children is still in its infancy. Other disorders, such as ADHD and anxiety disorder, have been studied in kids, but scientists are just beginning to look closely at biological treatments for bipolar disorder in kids — including depression, mania, and cycling. Chapter 7 describes in detail many of the medications used in treating bipolar disorder in adults. Doctors also prescribe most of these medications for children, using the adult research and what little information is out there about kids with the disorder. For many reasons, doctors must be especially careful with children and teenagers. Here are some of the difficulties:

- **Different brains, different reactions:** Child and adolescent brains differ from adult brains. Medications affect the wiring and structures in the brain, and in kids, these elements are immature, so the medications may work differently on bipolar symptoms in kids. The potential benefits and side effects of medications aren't as predictable in children as they are in adults, based on current science, because the science comes from studying adult brains.

- **Changing brains, changing reactions:** Not only do young brains differ from those of adults, but they also change constantly. Treating a child's brain is like trying to hit a moving target. You may get things stabilized just right and then puberty strikes or some physiological event occurs. Now the brain sits in a new chemical environment, and the medication combinations need adjusting.

- **Murkier symptoms:** Bipolar symptoms in children aren't as clear-cut as they are in adults. When a child tantrums and rages, you must ask: Is she depressed, anxious, manic, or sleep deprived? The answers determine the choice of treatment, and they can be very difficult to tease out.

- **Lack of understanding/noncompliance:** A child's understanding of her illness varies with her age and developmental stage. Including her in conversations as much as possible in age-appropriate ways is important. Over the course of kids' lives, they'll need to manage their moods and behavioral symptoms, and now is the time to start. But given that many of the symptoms of bipolar disorder include being oppositional and explosive, convincing a kid to cooperate with treatment often makes or breaks treatment plans. And just like adults, kids can feel flattened by the medicine or dislike side effects such as weight gain or sedation.

- **Parental conflict:** Parents often disagree about the diagnosis of bipolar disorder and the necessity of medication in kids. Media images of psychiatric medication and the stigma associated with mental illness can weigh heavily on parents' minds as they make difficult choices. If a parent has bipolar disorder, her personal experiences may color the decisions about treating her child. And if parents don't see eye to eye, the child often gets caught in the middle.

What do you do then, sitting in the psychiatrist's office, trying to make the best decision for your child? How can you decide which way to go? Your best bet is to gather as much information as you can before making a decision.

Questions to ask and consider with the doc

Here are some things to consider or review with your child's doctor before you make medication decisions:

- ✔ **How did you make this diagnosis?** You want to know your doctor's thought process, not just a pronouncement. Given the complexity of a bipolar diagnosis in kids, don't just accept it without a careful review of how the doctor arrived at her conclusion. You can think more critically and carefully about your child's condition with this information.

- ✔ **How did you choose this particular medication?** Just like making a diagnosis, choosing a medication is a layered process with many pieces to it. You want to know your doctor's thought process so that you can understand it and then evaluate her recommendations. If the doctor hands you a prescription with no explanation, find another doctor.

- ✔ **Have there been studies in children with this medication?** Find out if the medication has been studied in kids and how often it has been used for children. Ask if the medication has an *FDA indication,* which means that the Food and Drug Administration approves the medication for this particular use in kids. Many psychiatric medications don't have FDA indications in children — they're used *off label*. This practice is completely legal, very common, and often the right choice, but you want to know what information is out there.

- ✔ **What are the target symptoms?** What are the goals of this particular medication, and how can you measure if it's working or not? Keeping mood charts, rage counts, and sleep journals are some ways that you and your doctor can follow your child's progress (see Chapter 12). Otherwise, sorting out the response can be quite difficult, because all the tantrums melt together in your head after a while.

- ✔ **What are the side effects?** What side effects should you look for, and how can you measure them? Do you need to watch for any dangerous side effects? If you're concerned about a side effect, how can you get in touch with the doctor? Will she return your calls?

- ✔ **How often will you see my child?** How closely does the doctor need to monitor your child on this medication? How long are the meetings? How often will the doctor talk to you, the caregiver? Do you need to follow up with laboratory tests or medical exams?

- ✔ **How long will my child be on this medication?** If your child does well on a medication, how long will she need to stay on it? If she doesn't do well, how long should your child stay on this medicine before moving on to another? What are the criteria for stopping or changing a medicine? How will the doctor make that decision?

Getting the right medication combination can take a while. Avoid the temptation to throw in the towel and give it all up when nothing seems to work. Persistence pays off.

✔ **Will you talk to other caregivers?** Will the doctor communicate with your child's therapist? Pediatrician? Neurologist? Teacher? Can you expect the doctor to give you a written report? Does this cost more?

Bring a written list of questions with you and a pad of paper to write down the answers. During these meetings, you and your doctor exchange a lot of information in a short period of time — you won't remember it all.

Parenting a child with bipolar disorder

Parenting is quite a challenge even when kids have the standard amount of control over their thoughts and emotions, but parenting children with bipolar disorder poses greater challenges. Sure, the medication can help stabilize the neurons and chemistry in your child's brain, but the chaos of everyday life outside the brain — bedtime, the morning rush, sibling rivalries, family discord, and other commotion — requires intensive care as well. Many of the therapeutic approaches we discuss in Chapter 8 work effectively for both adults and children, but with children, the approach usually requires a slightly higher dose of family therapy.

Some standard parenting approaches aren't only ineffective, but also aggravate your child's condition; negatively affect her self-esteem; and make you feel powerless, guilty, and resentful toward your child. To survive as a parent and avoid the everybody-loses confrontations, keep the following suggestions in mind:

✔ **Don't take your child's behavior personally.** You're not a bad parent just because you can't control your child's behavior.

✔ **Don't blame your child for negative behaviors.** Remember that bipolar disorder significantly impairs a person's self-control. Most negative behaviors grow out of your child's distress, not a desire to break the rules or anger you. This doesn't mean that you should abandon limits and consequences, but staying calm and picking your battles buys you some peace of mind.

✔ **Avoid shaming your child or using highly punitive discipline.** These tactics only make matters worse. If your child can't meet the demands you place on her because of her mood instability, anxiety, or low energy, for example, consequences won't change her inability to meet your expectations, so you and your child end up feeling more hopeless and angry.

✔ **Do what you can to help your child accept herself as she is and to integrate the disorder into her life.** Acceptance and integration are the primary goals of therapy, and as a parent, you can help tremendously. Like adults, children must work toward understanding that they aren't bipolar, but *have* bipolar disorder. It doesn't define them, although it's a big part of their lives. Their frustrations will be numerous.

✔ **Allow your child and yourself to grieve.** Your child grieves over the differences between herself and her peers. As a parent, you grieve the loss of the child you expected and some of the dreams you may have had for her. Everyone must move forward. A skilled therapist can guide you and your child through this long and arduous process.

Parenting a child with such unique emotional and behavioral needs requires specialized skills. The therapist and your psychiatrist can provide you with strategies and techniques for managing everything from the biggest crisis to mundane matters such as getting your child out of bed in the morning.

BIPOLAR BIO

Sam's journey

Sam was adopted at birth. He was full of life, affectionate, loving . . . and challenging. Early on in his childhood, he struggled with severe separation anxiety and would rage whenever his parents left the house. Going to school led to a daily meltdown, even into fifth grade. At that point, the rages increased in frequency, taking over the family life. Sam began to exhibit depression, expressing hopelessness and despair when he wasn't raging and breaking things. At the age of 12, he threatened to kill himself.

After several evaluations, he was diagnosed with bipolar disorder and comorbid anxiety. Medication trials took months and continued for years. Antidepressants and antianxiety medicines were essential, but they often agitated him. Lithium was effective, but he couldn't tolerate the weight gain. Periods of stability occurred for months at a time, but then a life change or developmental problem (girlfriends, school failure, and medication side effects, including his inability to concentrate) would demand medication adjustments. When he hit

his junior year in high school, he stopped taking some of his medications because of the side effects, and he relapsed into severe mood cycles, requiring repeated hospitalizations. It wasn't clear if he would even receive credit for the school year.

Sam's family felt exhausted and full of despair. His younger sister became depressed and anxious. Despite enormous financial pressures, his mother put in for family leave from work to manage the many medical visits and school issues that were essential to Sam's recovery and to give the whole family some downtime. Sam continues to recover from the junior-year episode and has re-entered school. His school is doing all it can to help him regain lost time and credits. The doctor is still adjusting Sam's medications, but Sam is able to function. Sam and his doctor are now communicating more effectively regarding Sam's concerns about side effects so he doesn't take matters into his own hands again. The process of recovery and management continues, and everyone involved becomes more hopeful with each passing day.

Judgment, criticism, and demands may seem to have a place in parenting, but finding other, more positive ways to communicate with your child is far more successful, particularly in a child with bipolar disorder.

Tending to school matters

Kids with bipolar disorder are sensitive and reactive. They have less buffer than most kids and can be extremely reactive to teacher temperament, schedules, peer conflict, and unanticipated change. Oppositional behavior, meltdowns, and social drama dot the landscape of school for a child with bipolar disorder. Teachers and administrators can develop negative attitudes and expectations for your child, which only makes success more difficult.

How can you minimize the damaging impact of bipolar disorder on school? Is it possible that school can be part of the process of recovery and prevention?

Taking advantage of available services

Just like all kids, a child with mental health issues needs and is entitled to an appropriate education. Other kids with special needs, such as physical challenges and language differences, are entitled to appropriate modifications in the educational setting. Children with bipolar disorder are just as deserving of appropriate services that enable them to participate in the educational process — services mandated by law. Your options include the following:

✔ **Special Education Services:** The Individuals with Disabilities in Education Act, or IDEA, which Congress updated in 1997, requires that schools provide these services under certain conditions:

• **To obtain services, you must request, in writing, that your child be evaluated for special education services.** Usually, this request goes to the director of special education in your school district.

• **The school district has a designated time frame to respond to your request.** Schools typically have 30 days to respond — 30 school days, not 30 calendar days.

• **The evaluation includes a minimum of three types of assessments: psychological, educational, and social.** School or district psychologists and social workers usually conduct these evaluations.

• **An IEP team considers your child's case.** After the evaluations are completed, an IEP (Individualized Educational Plan) team holds a meeting to determine if your child meets the criteria for services.

• **The team must include you, your child's teacher, a district special education representative, and a special education teacher.** States often require that a *parent advocate* (often another parent from the district) be on the team.

- **The team develops an IEP.** If your child is eligible to receive services, the team develops an IEP to outline where and how the school will educate your child, based on her needs.

- **You must agree with and sign off on the IEP for it to proceed.** This ensures that you have the final say in the IEP.

✔ **Section 504 Services:** Section 504 of the Rehabilitation Act of 1973 and the Americans with Disabilities Act proscribe laws to provide for modifications to the educational program that allow your child to participate without being discriminated against for a disability:

- **Section 504 plans typically address less-severe needs than special education services.** You may have more success convincing your child's school to provide special services under Section 504 than under the IDEA.

- **Section 504 services are defined locally.** Procedures for obtaining these services vary from district to district.

- **The evaluation process varies.** In some cases, the school may need to evaluate your child; in other cases, you simply need to produce a letter or report from your child's doctor.

- **Modifications are based on your child's unique needs.** Modifications can include providing extended time on testing, separate testing locations, oral rather than written tests, and computer use in class, to name a few.

Now you've taken the necessary steps to get your child the proper education. However, your child isn't the only one who needs a lesson.

Educating the educators about bipolar disorder

The process of obtaining an appropriate education for your child is often daunting. Schools are inundated with demands for services, and budgets are stretched thin. The educational community has a track record of inconsistent understanding and awareness of mental health needs in kids. Stigma and a lack of understanding about bipolar disorder are rampant everywhere, including in schools. During the process, you can expect to educate the educators. Advocacy is your mission. Keep the following in mind as you proceed:

✔ **Communication is key:** Begin by talking and staying in touch with your child's teachers to get their takes on your child's needs. Get to know the guidance counselor or social worker who's involved. Ongoing communication provides you with information and demonstrates your concern and involvement — important tools in your ongoing negotiations with the school and the district.

✔ **Gather supporting data:** Get reports from your psychiatrist and therapist. Bring them to meetings. Encourage phone or e-mail communication between the school and your medical team.

✔ **Know your rights:** Federal education law mandates that every state maintain parent resource and training centers that provide guidance and information for parents as they navigate the special education system. The centers are sometimes referred to as *advocacy centers.* Your state department of education or your special education department should be able to give you a list of these places.

✔ **Network with other parents:** Special education PTAs or more informal gatherings of parents who are in your child's school system can provide a wealth of information, as well as camaraderie and support.

Practicing lifestyle management

Lifestyle changes can enhance the management of bipolar disorder and often alleviate symptoms. Many of the suggestions we offer here and throughout this book apply to children with bipolar disorder as well:

✔ Ensure proper health and nutrition — see Chapter 14.

✔ Adjust expectations and develop more structured schedules and routines — see Chapter 13.

✔ Pace your family life and your child's activities — see Chapter 11.

✔ Map and track moods — see Chapter 12.

All these strategies and techniques can contribute to your child's treatment success. Battling with your kids over things like food and exercise may not always be advisable — if you create rages or meltdowns, for example — but over time, working to establish some healthy lifestyle habits eventually pays dividends.

Keep track of your expectations and demands for your child. Letting go of your expectations and embracing the child you have, not the child you expected, empowers and liberates you and your child. Grieving the loss of that "expected child" is important work, but a healthy grieving process eventually helps you let go. Until that work is done, you can't move forward.

Turning to hospitalization for suicide prevention

Bipolar disorder is a potentially lethal disease. People with this disorder often kill themselves. Suicide is a leading cause of death in adolescents, and bipolar disorder increases this risk significantly. To prevent suicide, keep the following guidelines in mind:

✔ **Never ignore threats of suicide or self-harm.** Don't try to determine if your child "really means it." Let an expert evaluate your child to assess the risk.

✔ **Pay attention to substance abuse.** Alcohol intoxication dramatically increases the risk of completed suicide.

✔ **Watch for covert signs.** Maybe you notice your child organizing and giving away belongings (preparing for "when I'm gone"), experiencing sudden and extreme changes in activity levels or socialization, or talking of despair and hopelessness or death, even if you don't hear her speak of suicide in particular.

✔ **If you have concerns, don't be afraid to talk about them.** Bringing up suicide won't give your child the idea; you don't create suicidal thoughts by talking about it. Not talking about your worries is much more dangerous.

If your child appears suicidal or out of control, your doctor may recommend hospitalization. Psychiatric hospitalization is only for brief periods of time (often fewer than ten days) and is only for safety and crisis management. Hospitals don't do extended evaluations anymore, because insurance doesn't cover it. When considering hospitalization:

✔ Talk to your doctor about where he admits people or if he uses a hospital where another doctor does the inpatient treatment (this varies regionally).

✔ Review hospital choices with your insurance company, because it may contract only with certain hospitals.

✔ Expect a long day during admission, and expect to spend as much time at the hospital as you can during your child's stay. Being a presence, even when your child says she doesn't want to see you, is critical for getting good care and for your child's well-being.

✔ Ask the hospital staff about the hospital's policies regarding seclusion and restraint and *prn* meds — meds given if a child is out of control. Make sure the staff informs you if either of these measures is necessary. Make sure they know you're watching.

In some cases, children can't stabilize at home and may require long-term care at a residential facility. This process is beyond the scope of this chapter, but you can obtain additional information from your doctor, your child's school system, or the Child and Adolescent Bipolar Foundation Web site (www.bpkids.org). This site offers an array of information and support for families dealing with a child who has bipolar disorder.

Part VI
The Part of Tens

The 5th Wave   By Rich Tennant

"I've tried Ayurveda, meditation, and aromatherapy but nothing seems to work. I'm still feeling nauseous and disoriented all day."

In this part . . .

We couldn't call this a *For Dummies* book without a Part of Tens, so here it is. We provide 10 probing questions you should ask a psychiatrist or therapist during your initial interview. We provide 10 cost-cutting tips to make psychiatric visits, therapy sessions, and medications more affordable. And, because advocating is so important in helping to eliminate the stigma of mental illnesses and to ensure fair and equitable treatment for you, your loved one, and for all people who've been diagnosed with various psychiatric disorders, we describe 10 ways that you can become more active in the bipolar community.

Chapter 19

Ten Questions to Ask a Psychiatrist or Therapist

In This Chapter

▶ Evaluating the professionals who evaluate you

▶ Contacting your caregivers in an emergency

▶ Identifying the signs that you're getting better

▶ Knowing what to do if you start feeling worse

*W*hen your doctor or therapist starts asking you questions, you may begin to wonder who's serving whom. As a savvy consumer, you should be prepared to ask questions in order to assess the caregiver's credentials and qualifications, make informed treatment choices, determine how you can tell if the treatment is working, and know what to do if you begin feeling worse.

This chapter provides a list of ten questions you should ask a psychiatrist or therapist in order to obtain the information you need. Of course, you may have additional questions, so be sure to write them down so you remember to ask.

How Much Experience Do You Have in Treating Bipolar Disorder?

Some psychiatrists and therapists are like general practitioners, and others specialize in particular areas, such as bipolar disorder, depression, anxiety disorders, or schizophrenia. Professionals who have more experience in treating bipolar disorder are typically more apt to spot symptoms and warning signs and are more aware of what you may be experiencing and the types of treatments that have worked for other clients. More specific questions include the following:

- ✔ Are you licensed/certified?

  Your psychiatrist should be *board certified* in psychiatry. Therapists typically are licensed, using a title such as LCSW (Licensed Clinical Social Worker), or they have a degree, such as CSW (Clinical Social Worker) or MSW (Masters in Social Work). Counselors may be licensed in some states.

- ✔ What are your specialties?

- ✔ Approximately how many people with bipolar disorder have you treated?

For links to state licensing boards for counselors and psychologists, visit `www.m-a-h.net/hip/stateboards.htm`. To check on psychiatrists, go to the American Medical Association Web site at `www.ama-assn.org`. This site enables you to check the credentials of almost every licensed physician in the United States.

Is It Tough to Get an Appointment?

If you can't get in to see your doctor or therapist when your moods begin to cycle, he can't help you much, so before you choose a psychiatrist or therapist, make sure you won't have to wait three months before your next appointment.

When you begin treatment, you quickly discover the tricks and techniques for getting appointments:

- ✔ Schedule at least three appointments in advance at regular intervals. After each appointment, schedule another appointment so you always have three scheduled.

- ✔ If you anticipate having difficulties scheduling appointments during a particular season, set up appointments in advance. Most mental health-care providers get very busy around Thanksgiving and Christmas.

- ✔ If you set up several appointments in advance and realize that you don't need a particular appointment, cancel it 24 to 48 hours in advance. (Find out how far in advance you need to cancel or reschedule an appointment before the clinic charges you for it.)

- ✔ If you need to see your doctor or therapist, and the schedule is booked solid, ask to be notified if another client cancels an appointment. Provide all your contact numbers: home, cell phone, and work.

Can I Contact You During a Crisis?

Nights, weekends, and holidays. The three times you most need your doctor or therapist, she's at home, spending time with her friends and family. The nerve of these medical people! Everybody, even doctors and therapists, needs some time off, but as a person with bipolar disorder, you need some numbers to call in a crisis:

- ✔ Office number
- ✔ Cell phone or home number
- ✔ Name and number of the person who covers for your doctor or therapist when she's out of town
- ✔ Emergency number of the hospital or mental health center where you should go in a crisis

Ask how long it typically takes your doctor or therapist to return calls if you need to leave a message. (See Chapter 17 for more information on how to plan ahead for a crisis.)

What's the Diagnosis, and How Did You Arrive at It?

Most people who have bipolar disorder first report symptoms when they're depressed, so unless your doctor sees you during a hypomanic or manic episode, he's likely to make a diagnosis of depression and prescribe antide-pressants, which could induce mania. Your evaluation, therefore, should screen for a family history or any past symptoms of elevated mood. Make sure your doctor considers the following:

- ✔ Family history of mood disorders, particularly bipolar disorder, suicide, or eccentric behaviors, that may not have been diagnosed
- ✔ Family history of schizophrenia, which was often mistakenly diagnosed in cases of bipolar disorder in the past
- ✔ Prior history of elevated moods. (Your doctor may have you fill out a mania scale or ask questions about previous periods in which you felt much more alert, productive, and inspired)
- ✔ Medical conditions that could possibly cause symptoms similar to bipo-lar disorder. (Your psychiatrist may ask you if you've seen your family physician)

Chapter 4 covers the many ways to arrive at an accurate diagnosis.

What's the Treatment Plan?

Your doctor may hand you one or more prescriptions for antidepressants, mood stabilizers, antipsychotics, or sedatives, but your medication doesn't make up your complete treatment plan. A treatment plan should include a combination of medication, therapy, lifestyle changes, and peer support. In most cases, you should have a doctor and a therapist; ideally, they work together to develop a treatment plan specifically for you. In practice, the doctor typically handles the medications, and the therapist deals with everything else. Your treatment plan should include the following:

✔ Medications

✔ Individual therapy

✔ Family education and, possibly, family therapy

✔ Instructions on what to do if your moods begin to cycle

Want more info about treatment plans? Flip to Chapter 5.

When Can 1 Expect to See Improvement?

Your doctor and therapist often tell you to remain patient, and we do too, but you should know up front what "patient" means. A week? A month? Two months? In most cases, you can expect to see some improvement in one to two weeks, but ask your doctor and therapist to be sure.

Typically, your doctor follows up with you in two to four weeks to assess the effectiveness of the treatment and monitor for side effects. If the doctor tells you to come back in more than one month after you start a new medicine, find out why he doesn't want to follow your situation more closely.

How Will 1 Know When My Condition 1s 1mproving?

With bipolar disorder, feeling better may convince you that you are better, particularly if you're cycling into mania. Ask you doctor for more objective signs that your mental health is improving.

When recovering from an episode of depression, signs of recovery may include the following:

✔ Sleeping less (or sleeping more, if depression interfered with your sleep)

✔ Doing more with less effort

✔ Socializing more

✔ Crying less

✔ Diminished thoughts of death or suicide

When recovering from an episode of mania, signs of recovery may include the following:

✔ Sleeping more, with less restless sleep

✔ Fewer and less-intense confrontations with others

✔ Improved ability to control impulses

✔ Less irritability

What Should I Do If I Feel Worse?

Although your doctor may be able to predict with some degree of certainty the way you'll respond to a medication based on her experience with other patients, she can't know for sure. Some medications may not work for you or may have an adverse effect on you. If your condition fails to improve or worsens, or if you have a bad reaction to the medication (such as a rash or shortness of breath), you should contact your doctor, who may suggest one or more of the following steps:

✔ Stop taking the medication.

✔ Keep taking the medication to see if the side effect settles down or the desired effects kick in, and call or come in to the office in a few days.

✔ Take a lower dose of the medication.

✔ Take a higher dose of the medication.

✔ Add something else to the medication.

What Side Effects Should I Watch For?

Most doctors hand you a prescription for the medication(s) that she thinks is going to be most effective and have the least chance of causing serious side effects. If you want to be involved in the decision, pipe up before your doctor reaches for the prescription pad. For every medication prescribed, you should obtain answers to two questions:

- ✔ How effective is the medication at treating the symptoms I have? Are there more effective medications?

- ✔ What are the potential risks and side effects of this medication, and what are the chances that I'll experience them? Are there any medications that have fewer, less-serious side effects?

You should always know the side effects of a medication before you begin taking it so you know what to watch out for. After you have a list of the most common and most serious potential side effects, ask what you should do if you notice any signs of one of these side effects. For a complete tour of the bipolar pharmacy, head to Chapter 7.

Will You Work Along with My Other Treatment Providers?

Coordinated treatment, especially between your doctor and therapist, is an essential component of success. Ask your doctor and therapist if they're willing to exchange notes, and make sure they have each other's contact information and signed consent forms that enable them to exchange information.

If you want family members, friends, and other nonprofessionals to enter the treatment discussion, ask the doctors if they're willing to talk with people in your support network. Your doctor and therapist can't legally discuss your condition or treatment with anyone unless they have signed consent forms from you. (To build your mood-management team, check out Chapter 6.)

Chapter 20

Ten Ways to Fight the High Cost of Treatment

In This Chapter

▶ Devising clever ways to get treatment without paying for it

▶ Helping yourself for free

▶ Finding cheap or free insurance for your child

▶ Pitching a payment plan to your psychiatrist or therapist

Mental healthcare isn't cheap. Even if you have health insurance, few plans offer *parity* of coverage for mental illnesses; that is, the plans provide less coverage for mental illness than they do for other medical illnesses. Mental health advocacy organizations are actively lobbying to have this changed. In the meantime, you may be footing the major portion of your bills for psychiatric care, leaving you to ask the question, "Can I afford to be sick?"

In this chapter, we help you answer that question by introducing various ways you can avoid paying for mental healthcare and by tracking down sources of financial assistance. Through self-help, community assistance programs, mental health agencies, and the flexibility of your psychiatrist and other mental healthcare professionals, you may be able to create a custom financial package that meets your needs.

Find a Community Mental Health Clinic

Many communities realize that not treating people with mental illnesses is more costly than offering affordable treatment, and they invest in community-based mental healthcare clinics. These clinics typically offer a wide range of treatment options and assistance to people who qualify, and if you can't afford private treatment, you should qualify. Services typically include

✔ Psychiatric visits

✔ Therapy

✔ Payment plans

✔ Housing or assisted-living arrangements

✔ Job training and placement for people who can work

✔ Transportation

✔ Assistance securing Social Security and disability benefits

Consider contacting your local Mental Health Association for assistance. You should be able to find the number for your state or county Mental Health Association in your telephone directory or by contacting the National Mental Health Association at 800-969-6642. If you have Internet access, you can search a directory of Mental Health Associations online at www.nmha.org. The directory enables you to pull up a list of NMHA affiliates in any state. The NMHA has over 340 affiliates.

Track Down a University Program

Because universities are often on the cutting edge of research, they can provide the latest treatment options and may even offer free treatment, especially if you're willing to take part in a study. If you do go through a university, try to talk directly to a bipolar expert who's in charge of the program. Some university psychiatrists have several trainees studying under them, and if you get shuttled from one trainee to another, you may find yourself constantly changing from one medication or treatment to another to your detriment. By recognizing this risk, you can take steps to ensure continuity of treatment:

✔ **Keep in touch with the supervising physician or psychiatrist.** Make sure she's notified of any medication adjustments or other changes to your treatment plan. Get a phone number — both her office number and a number to call in emergencies.

✔ **Request explanations for any changes to your medications or treatment.** Why is the trainee or doctor requesting the change? What are the desired results? How long should it take before you see a positive change in your condition? What are the possible side effects? And what should you do if your condition worsens? See Chapter 19 for more questions to ask.

✔ **Coordinate communication with all members of your treatment team.** If you have a therapist or doctor working with you outside of the university, make sure the healthcare providers at the university keep him in the loop.

Although becoming involved in a controlled study is an excellent way to obtain access to the newest medications and to help the cause, ask additional questions of yourself and your care providers before you sign up. Discover the possible risks of the new medication and how likely it is that you'll receive a *placebo* (a "sugar pill" with no medication in it). Make sure your moods are stable enough to handle a change in medications, if that's what the study calls for. If you're doing well on your current medication and adjunctive treatments, we recommend that you stick with what's working.

Find Peer Support

Everyone has something valuable and unique to teach you — whether it involves a golf swing or a new therapy technique — and no one knows bipolar disorder better than someone who's living with it.

Naturally, you may feel reluctant to sit in a room full of strangers and talk about your life, but don't write off peer support until you've tried it. It can be a relief to be with people from whom you don't have to hide the fact that sometimes your brain short-circuits with unpredictable results. For details on tracking down peer support groups in your area, turn to Chapter 6.

Contact Religious Organizations

Churches and other religious organizations often have qualified counselors on staff who can provide therapy and other assistance for free. Many of these services are offered free or at a reduced cost to church members, but even if you're not a member, you may find that the organization has an open door. Religious organizations are always looking for new, dedicated members, and offering help to the people who need it most is one of the best evangelistic tools they have.

Be at least as careful when shopping for "free" counseling as you are when shopping for private therapy. The quality of training varies widely, and many religious organizations have their own agendas, which may not quite follow proven treatment protocols. Avoid any organization that's against the use of psychiatric medications or requires you to make drastic changes to your life that you aren't completely comfortable making.

Obtain State Medical Assistance

Most states have a medical assistance office that can provide information about available state and federally funded health insurance programs. Starting your search at the local or state level is usually more efficient than starting at the federal level, even though the latter may be where you eventually find the assistance you need. If you need help navigating the system, contact your local Mental Health Association or community mental health clinic.

File for Disability and Medicaid

If you (or a loved one) are disabled by bipolar disorder or any of the other medical illnesses associated with it, you may qualify for disability payments and Medicare coverage. (Disability includes not being able to work for a period of time until you find effective treatment.) You can find out more at www.ssa.gov or by calling 800-772-1213. For more specific information, contact your local Social Security office; details differ from state to state.

In Chapter 13, we provide a list of tips and tricks for winding your way through the Social Security Administration to obtain disability benefits and Medicaid. You need a good dose of patience and persistence to succeed. And if at first you don't succeed, call a good lawyer who specializes in Social Security disability claims.

In some states, the only way to get Medicaid coverage for children with mental illnesses is to surrender your parental rights to the state. These states won't cover such care unless the child has become a ward of the state's child protection agency. Advocacy groups are working with Congress to change this, but it's still the only option for parents in some parts of the country. Find out everything you can about the laws in your state from mental health advocacy organizations, and get help from an attorney or legal-aid organization before signing any papers that take away your parental rights.

Check Out the "Insure Kids Now!" Program

If you can't afford to insure a dependent child, the U.S. Department of Health and Human Services sponsors a program called "Insure Kids Now!" that helps states provide low-cost or no-cost insurance to qualifying families. Call 800-543-7669 or visit www.insurekidsnow.gov for more information.

Trying to obtain affordable healthcare for yourself or family members can be incredibly frustrating, even for someone with a clear mind. If you're ill, now is the time to enlist the aid of a friend or family member to help with what is often a very challenging process. For more information on building a good support network, refer to Chapter 6. For emergency contact help, flip to Chapter 17.

Locate a Prescription Assistance Program

Individuals with mental illnesses often face the very real choice of paying for food or medication. When you rely on medication to stabilize your moods and give you a fighting chance at earning a living, that's no choice at all. Fortunately, several pharmaceutical companies, healthcare groups, and local organizations offer prescription assistance programs that provide prescription medications at no cost or at discount prices. In most cases, you need to provide the following information to qualify:

- Your doctor's written consent

- Proof that you have no health insurance or that your health insurance doesn't offer a prescription benefit or doesn't cover the specific medication you need

- Proof that you qualify financially

To find out more about available prescription assistance programs, check out the following sources:

- HelpingPatients.org at www.helpingpatients.org is a nonprofit organization that's dedicated to helping low-income, uninsured patients find free or affordable pharmaceuticals. At this site, you answer a few questions to gain access to programs for which you qualify and obtain the paperwork you need to apply.

- Mental health advocacy organizations can help you track down programs for which you qualify. See the section "Find a Community Mental Health Clinic" earlier in this chapter.

- If you qualify for Medicare, go to www.medicare.gov/AssistancePrograms to find out more about Medicare's prescription drug card and to see if you qualify for it.

- Pharmaceutical companies may offer their own prescription assistance programs for people whose total family incomes are low. Your doctor or pharmacist or sometimes your prescription label can tell you the manufacturer of your medication, and you can find contact information online or in the phone book. In some cases, your doctor must contact the company on your behalf.

- Search the Web for "prescription assistance program" to find links to several other companies that provide information on prescription drug cards, generic medications, and other cost-savings plans.

Your doctor may be able to provide an informal prescription assistance program simply by supplying you with free samples. Many pharmaceutical companies provide doctors with a good supply of samples.

Make a Deal with Your Psychiatrist or Therapist

Some psychiatrists and therapists offer payment plans that allow their patients to pay off their bills gradually. If you don't have insurance, your psychiatrist or therapist may offer you a discount. Many clinics and university settings and some private practitioners offer a *sliding scale,* where the fee is based on your ability to pay. You usually have to fill out some type of financial worksheet to determine if you qualify for reduced fees. Most large insurance companies negotiate with providers in this way to save on costs, so doctors and therapists commonly offer similar discounts to patients who don't have insurance. Always ask to be sure.

Help Yourself

If you go to a doctor for heart problems and want to have the best chance of getting better, you'll probably change your diet, exercise, and learn more about heart health. You can do the same with bipolar disorder. Although you can't treat yourself, even if you're a professional, you can discover ways to cope with situations and symptoms that would've upended your life before you got treatment. Your healthcare providers can help you learn real-world coping skills and ways to avert crises.

The more that you and your family and friends can do to stabilize your moods, the less that you need to rely on professionals to help. Completely replacing professional care with self-help isn't prudent, but investing time and effort in becoming more knowledgeable about your illness and learning ways to reduce stress can help you reduce your need for professional intervention or hospitalization. By reading this book and following our suggestions, you're already well on your way to helping yourself.

Chapter 21

Ten Ways to Help the Bipolar Community

In This Chapter

▶ Spreading the word about bipolar disorder

▶ Joining a mental health advocacy group

▶ Contacting your government representatives

▶ Advocating for fair treatment and equal rights

*W*hen you're chin deep in a battle to reclaim your life, nobody expects you to become an outspoken advocate for the bipolar community, but when life settles down a bit and becomes more manageable, you may consider contributing some time and effort (or funds) to the cause. After all, if people who have a psychiatric illness and their loved ones don't advocate for fair treatment and equal rights, who will?

In this chapter, we offer several ways that you can become more involved in spreading the word about mental health issues and working toward ensuring fair treatment and equal rights for people who suffer from mental illnesses.

Begin Advocacy at Home

The battle against stigma is a grassroots war that begins in your immediate and extended family. You can start winning the battle against ignorance by educating family members. Those close to you may be a little gentler in their criticism than the outside world, but criticism cuts deep, no matter what form it takes.

If you notice that your family has little understanding of bipolar disorder or other mental illnesses, you can educate them by describing the struggles you've experienced and the lessons you've learned. You don't need to become confrontational — simply bringing up the issue and then offering to answer any questions can get the conversation rolling.

Take the Battle to Your Insurance Company

When it comes to mental health issues, many insurance companies are stuck in the 1920s, when mental health issues were considered purely psychological. They can't admit that bipolar disorder and other mental illnesses are physical in nature and that people who suffer from mental illnesses deserve equitable care to establish and maintain their health. Advocates commonly refer to equitable treatment as *parity* of benefits.

Although insurance companies insist that parity would be too expensive and they would have to raise premiums, many public health studies show that parity actually saves on medical costs in the long run. It just makes sense. By successfully treating a person's depression, you reduce the amount of time the person must take off from work, which increases productivity and decreases the incidents of related illnesses and risky behavior.

You can advocate for parity by becoming a more vigilant and active consumer:

- **Compare co-payments for physicians and mental healthcare providers.** Does the insurance company require a higher co-pay for psychiatric and therapy visits than for "doctor" visits? If so, that's certainly unfair. Call and complain. Write a letter to the company.

- **Compare treatment benefits.** Does the insurance company allow for unlimited visits to other physicians but only a limited number for psychiatric and therapy visits? Call your insurance company and ask why. Write a letter.

- **Compare lifetime benefits.** Insurance companies commonly provide lifetime benefits for psychiatric disorders that amount to less than half the benefits offered for treatments of other illnesses.

- **Compare hospitalization benefits.** Does the insurance company shell out considerably less for psychiatric hospitalizations than it does for standard hospitalizations? Many do. Check to make sure.

- **If you have any say in selecting insurance providers, pick a company that offers the highest parity of coverage.** This enables you to vote with your wallet.

- **If your insurance company denies a claim for a visit to a psychiatrist or therapist, contest the denial.** Most insurance companies allow consumers to contest denials. Find out when and how to submit your protest. Go all the way to the top, and make plenty of noise.

Join an Advocacy Group

When you join an advocacy organization, you join millions of people working for change. Most offer you a chance to meet people with similar life experiences so you can empower one another through education, support, and a common cause.

Get to know the advocacy organizations near you. Chances are you'll find one that fits your needs and connects you to people with whom you can relate. If you aren't ready to shout from the rooftops yet, a small donation goes a long way to help a mental health advocacy organization spread the word. If you don't know whom to contact, start with the biggies:

- **NAMI (National Alliance for the Mentally Ill):** If you're itching to help in some way, but you're not sure how, NAMI can offer dozens of ideas and find a role for you in its organization. You can teach NAMI classes, head a local support group, write letters to local and national politicians, donate money, or contribute in many other ways. With NAMI, you can become just as involved as you want to be. For more information, visit NAMI's Web site at www.nami.org, call 800-950-NAMI (6264), or call your local NAMI chapter.

- **DBSA (Depression and Bipolar Support Alliance):** DBSA is best known for its peer support groups, but it's also heavily involved in advocacy. In fact, the DBSA Web site at www.dbsalliance.org features an Advocacy link you can click to access an entire electronic booklet on advocacy that covers everything from defining it and explaining why it's important to how the legislative process works and how to contact your legislators. The booklet is an excellent how-to manual if you want to become involved on the political level.

Get Involved in Local Support Groups

To become an effective advocate, you need to educate yourself, and one of the best ways to learn is to get connected with other similarly interested people locally. Local support groups are grassroots information kiosks where people freely exchange information and advice about doctors, therapists, medications, insurance companies, IEPs (Individualized Education Plans), work-related issues, and legal issues.

In addition to providing you with valuable information, support groups put you in touch with the people-power you need to promote any initiatives you seek to enact at the community level. Your presence at support meetings gives others the confidence and power to speak out as well.

Teach Classes on Mental Health Issues

Local support groups and other organizations frequently offer classes on various mental health issues. As a person with bipolar disorder or a person who has a loved one with bipolar disorder, you have valuable first-hand experiences and insights to offer others, particularly in a classroom setting — teaching a class, acting as a guest speaker, or simply joining in as a participating group member.

Many organizations offer training programs and services for consumers, family members, providers, and the general public, including NAMI's Family to Family and C.A.R.E. programs and numerous others (see `www.peersupport.org/PeerTrng.htm` for a list).

Write to Your Government Reps

You may think that politicians look out for their constituents' best interests, but politicians often sacrifice what's morally right for what appeals to the masses. In order to tip the scales in favor of what's morally right, you and like-minded individuals need to raise your collective voice above the collective voice of the majority. You do that by writing letters and discussing issues with your representatives.

Find out who represents you on the state and local levels and on the national level. Get to know your representatives by name, and find out how to contact them via e-mail or snail mail. Also, get involved in letter-writing campaigns, such as those that your advocacy organization sponsors. Learn to use the Web to track down the information you need:

- ✔ You can get on an e-mailing list at `capwiz.com/ndmda/home` or `www.nami.org` to be notified of any legislation that's up for a vote and how action is proceeding on issues you care about.

- ✔ Go to `www.senate.gov` to find contact information for U.S. senators in every state.

- ✔ You can find your state representative in the U.S. House of Representatives, using your ZIP code, by going to `www.house.gov`. This site also features a link you can click to write your representative via the Web. The U.S. Capitol switchboard at 202-224-3121 can also help you find your representatives and senators. Still on the goose chase? Try to track them down at `www.congress.org` or `Thomas.loc.gov`.

- ✔ Don't be afraid to go right to the top — write to the president himself at `president@whitehouse.gov`.

Fight Stigma in the Workplace

Most people need jobs to eat and pay their bills. If you have a mental illness, however, a job can mean much more. It can help structure your days, make your life more meaningful, expand your social circles, and provide you with a sense of independence. At your workplace, you may have several opportunities to fight stigma and improve conditions for yourself and anyone else who's struggling with a mental illness:

- ✔ If a coworker is diagnosed with a mental illness, help educate supervisors, managers, and workers so they can become more accepting.

- ✔ Stick up for a coworker who has a mental illness.

- ✔ Try to influence hiring practices to encourage the employment of people with mental illnesses. Your local chamber of commerce or department of labor may be able to assist you.

- ✔ Speak out for parity of benefits when selecting health insurance plans.

- ✔ Encourage proper job placements or reasonable accommodations for those who have a mental illness.

Protest Stigma in the Media

People like to joke about the most painful issues and poke fun at differences. Mental illness makes people uncomfortable, so they commonly joke about it as well, but sometimes the joking goes too far, and when the person poking fun isn't suffering from a particular disorder himself, the joke goes from a coping mechanism to an insensitive attempt to demean others. In addition, it sends people a hidden message that making fun of those "crazy people" is okay.

When you or loved ones have a mental illness, however, such jokes are jabs, and you don't need to just laugh it off. If you witness insensitivity in the media, call the station or paper and complain, or write a letter. Many advocacy organizations have their own corps of volunteers who keep an eye out for stigma in the media. Consider joining.

Become Involved in Your Schools

Schools tend to herd students like cattle. If a kid doesn't fit in, the stampede tramples him. All kids have something very valuable to offer their schools and communities, and each child should have the opportunity to achieve his potential and contribute in his unique way. Get involved in your school to ensure that your child and other kids have the tools and resources they need to succeed.

Consider joining your school's PTA and seeing what you can do to have a guest speaker do a presentation on mental illnesses, or try to schedule an open-discussion forum on the topic. Find out what your school does to support children with bipolar disorder, ADHD, and other mental illnesses, and find out what you and others in the community can do to help.

For more about supporting a child with bipolar disorder, refer to Chapter 18.

Work through Your Church

If you belong to a church or other religious organization, you may be able to redirect a portion of its resources and people-power to improve mental health services in your community. Almost all places of worship have meeting rooms that are ideal for hosting support groups or mental health classes. If your community has no support group, consider starting one yourself.

Another great way to help out through your place of worship is to create a directory of members who are willing to have another member stay at their homes in times of need.

Appendix

A Glossary of Bipolar-Related Terms

- -

acute: The stage of a manic or depressive episode that comes on rapidly, lasts a relatively short time, and is severe.

adjunctive: Complementary to the main treatment.

affective disorder: A category of psychiatric disorders that includes depression, bipolar disorder, and seasonal affective disorder (SAD). Affect is a medical term for "mood."

anticonvulsant: A class of medications developed primarily to prevent epileptic seizures. Many anticonvulsants, including valproate and carbamazepine, are also useful in treating mania.

antidepressant: A class of medications that have proved effective in treating the symptoms of depression.

antipsychotic: A class of medications developed to reduce the frequency and severity of psychotic episodes, which sometimes occur during mania or depression. Antipsychotics have also proved useful in treating mania and the psychoses that sometimes accompany depression and mania.

bipolar disorder: A psychiatric condition characterized by extreme mood states of mania and depression. A person may have bipolar disorder even if he has experienced only one of the extreme mood states, making diagnosis very challenging.

Bipolar I: A type of bipolar disorder characterized by at least one full-blown manic episode that doctors can't attribute to another cause, such as a medication or substance abuse. A Bipolar I diagnosis doesn't require an episode of major depression.

Bipolar II: A type of bipolar disorder characterized by at least one major depressive episode that doctors can't attribute to another cause, along with experiencing one or more hypomanic episodes. People with Bipolar II are often misdiagnosed with chronic depression and prescribed antidepressants, which may induce mania.

Bipolar NOS: A type of bipolar disorder characterized by hypomanic, manic, or depressive episodes that don't fit in any of the other bipolar categories and can't be ascribed to unipolar depression.

bipolar spectrum: A continuous range of mood disorders that extends from highly reactive moods and mood regulation problems to more classical bipolar disorder. The term is used as an umbrella concept to cover all types of bipolar disorders.

board certified: The status of a physician that indicates she has passed a standardized exam that qualifies her to specialize in a particular field of medicine.

circadian rhythm: An individual's biological pattern of sleep, wakefulness, and energy that plays out through the course of a day. Some studies show that irregularities in a person's circadian rhythm can destabilize moods.

cognitive behavioral therapy (CBT): A therapy that attempts to identify negative thoughts and thought processes and their resulting behaviors and retrain individuals to think and act more positively. Several studies show that CBT is highly effective for treating some forms of depression.

comorbid: Any medical condition that presents along with and often independent from another condition. People who have bipolar disorder can have other comorbid conditions — such as ADHD, alcoholism, or anxiety disorder — that complicate the diagnosis and treatment of the bipolar disorder.

cyclothymia: Sometimes referred to as "bipolar lite," cyclothymia is a muted form of bipolar disorder that nevertheless interferes with your life. It involves multiple episodes of hypomania and depressive symptoms, which don't meet the criteria for mania or major depression. Symptoms must last for at least two years, during which you have no more than two months without symptoms.

differential diagnosis: The process of distinguishing between two or more diseases or conditions that feature identical or similar symptoms. A doctor commonly performs a differential diagnosis to rule out other possibilities.

dopamine: Generally considered the feel-good neurotransmitter, dopamine is linked to feelings of pleasure. It modulates attention and focus as well as muscle movements and is also related to psychosis.

DSM-IV: Short for Diagnostic and Statistical Manual of Mental Disorders, version 4, this is the bible of psychiatry that describes various syndromes and conditions and the symptoms that must be present to establish a particular diagnosis.

dysphoria: An unpleasant, irritable mood. The opposite of euphoria.

dysthymia: Chronic, low-level depression, commonly characterized by irritability and an inability to feel pleasure or joy.

electroconvulsive therapy (ECT): A medical procedure in which a low-level electrical current is applied to the brain to induce a mild seizure in order to treat depression. ECT is often successful in treating depression that doesn't respond to medicine or therapy or in cases in which patients prefer it to any of the other treatment choices. ECT can also be an effective treatment for mania.

essential fatty acid (EFA): A healthy fat, which your body uses for tissue development and other purposes, that you must obtain through diet. Omega-3 is a source of several EFAs that may be valuable in treating many health problems, including mood disorders.

euphoria: A feeling of elation, which is great unless it becomes exaggerated, as it sometimes does with the onset of hypomania or mania.

euthymic: Moods considered to be in the normal range — not manic or depressive.

executive function: The ability to organize, sort, and manage incoming information and make decisions. Many psychiatric disorders weaken executive functioning, often leading to impaired judgment and uninhibited behavior.

expressed emotion: Highly charged attitudes that people express in words or gestures, that are part of a family pattern, and that affect the person who has the mood disorder. All expressed emotion can be dangerous for a person with bipolar disorder, but the most damaging consists of criticism, hostility, and emotional overinvolvement.

gamma-aminobutyric acid (GABA): An amino acid neurotransmitter that can either cool down or excite brain cells, depending on other chemicals surrounding it.

glutamate: A neurotransmitter that's involved in revving up the central nervous system. Glutamate may play a significant role in causing mania.

G-protein: Short for *guanine nucleotide binding protein,* a protein found in neurons that's part of the "second-messenger" system that regulates signal transmissions in the brain. The study of genetic variations in this protein may eventually play a role in diagnosing bipolar disorder.

hypersexual: Having an excessive interest or involvement in sexual activity.

hyperthymic: A medical term for "high energy" — very outgoing and active, often highly confident, temperamental, and sometimes arrogant or narcissistic.

hyperthyroidism: A malfunction of the thyroid gland that results in the over-production of hormones; the symptoms can mimic those of mania.

hypomania: An elevated mood that doesn't qualify as full-blown mania but that typically involves increased energy, less need for sleep, clarity of vision, and a strong creative drive. These changes are noticeable to others but don't significantly impair daily function.

hypothyroidism: A malfunction of the thyroid gland that results in the under-production of hormones; the symptoms can mimic depression.

Individual Education Plan (IEP): A personalized program for teaching a child or adolescent with developmental, medical, or psychiatric conditions that affect school and learning.

insight: A clear acceptance and understanding of a psychological disorder and the ability to objectively observe one's own behaviors and attitudes that are characteristic of the disorder.

interpersonal and social rhythm therapy (IPSRT): A therapy developed specifically to maintain mood stability through strict scheduling, learning about personal roles, coping with transitions, developing healthy routines, increasing social contact, and resolving and preventing interpersonal problems.

kindling: The gradual increase in susceptibility to mood episodes with each successive occurrence of a mood episode. The kindling model is based on a process that occurs in the brains of people with seizures; some experts believe that the same model applies to bipolar disorder.

maintenance dose: An amount of a prescription medication that's intended to prevent the onset of symptoms rather than treat existing symptoms.

major depressive episode: An extreme low mood lasting at least two weeks and characterized by symptoms such as despair, fatigue, loss or increase in appetite, loss of interest in pleasurable activities, sleeping too much or the inability to sleep, and thoughts of death or suicide.

mania: An extremely elevated mood typically characterized by euphoria, excessive energy, impulsivity, nervousness, impaired judgment, irritability, and a decreased need for sleep.

manic depression: Another name for bipolar disorder.

manic episode: A period of elevated mood, either euphoric or irritable, typically characterized by impulsivity, nervousness, impaired judgment, irritability, and a decreased need for sleep. The period must last at least one week.

MAO inhibitor: A class of antidepressant medications that slow the action of monoamine oxidase, an enzyme responsible for breaking down dopamine, serotonin, and norepinephrine in the brain. Doctors often prescribe MAO inhibitors only if a person reacts poorly to other antidepressants because of the strict diet changes needed when taking MAO inhibitors.

mechanism of action: The way a medication acts on the biology or physiology of the brain to produce the desired effect.

mixed state: A mood episode in which depression and mania are both present, typically resulting in excited irritability.

mood chart: A graph that shows the rise and fall of mood levels over time. Mood charts are very useful in predicting the onset of mood episodes and documenting the response to medications.

mood disorder: A psychiatric condition that results in persistently disrupted moods and/or mood regulation.

mood stabilizer: Strictly speaking, a medication that prevents depression and mania. The term typically describes any medications that have antimanic effects, even if they don't treat depression.

neuroleptic: Another name for antipsychotics, neuroleptics led the charge in pharmacological treatment of mental illness in the 1950s and 1960s.

Neuroleptic Malignant Syndrome: A potentially fatal but very rare side effect of antipsychotic medications that results in high temperature, muscle rigidity, and altered consciousness.

neurotransmitter: A chemical in the brain that carries messages between brain cells.

norepinephrine: Best known for its role in your fight-or-flight response, norepinephrine is a neurotransmitter that functions to regulate mood, anxiety, and memory.

off label: A legal use of a prescription medication to treat symptoms that the FDA (Food and Drug Administration) didn't officially approve it to treat.

omega-3: A source of several essential fatty acids that some experts believe are essential in the healthy development and functioning of the brain. Omega-3 is present in high concentration in cold-water ocean fish, including sardines, herring, and salmon; in walnuts; in flaxseed; and in supplements.

p-doc: Nickname for psychiatrist.

phase delayed: The condition of having your daily rhythm out of sync with the rising and setting of the sun. Night owls are considered phase delayed.

phototherapy: The use of light to stimulate mood changes.

presenting symptoms: The signs of discomfort that prompt you to visit your doctor.

prodromal symptoms: The early signs that indicate an impending mood episode.

prophylaxis: A fancy word for prevention. Doctors commonly prescribe a maintenance dose of a medication to prevent the onset of symptoms.

protein kinases: A group of second messengers that trigger changes to proteins inside the neuron.

psychiatrist: A physician who specializes in the biology and physiology of the brain. A psychiatrist's primary role in treating bipolar disorder is to diagnose and prescribe medication, but psychiatrists also provide patient education and psychotherapy.

psychoeducation: A type of therapy that consists primarily of educating the afflicted person about the condition, its causes, and its treatment so he can more effectively manage the condition.

psychologist: A professional who specializes in thought processes and behaviors. A psychologist can play a critical role in stabilizing moods by helping the sufferer adjust negative thoughts and thought processes and control self-destructive behaviors.

psychopharmacology: The study of the effects of medications on the functioning of the brain.

psychosis: A brain malfunction that blurs the line between the real and the imagined world, often causing auditory hallucinations, irrational fears, and delusions.

psychotropic substances: Any chemical substance (usually a medicine) that affects mental functioning, emotions, or behavior.

rapid cycling: A state in which mood alternates between depression and mania more than four times in a year.

repetitive transcranial magnetic stimulation (rTMS): The application of strong, quick-changing magnetic fields to the brain to produce electrical fields indirectly. Some consider this less stressful than electroconvulsive therapy.

schizoaffective disorder: A psychiatric disorder in which symptoms of bipolar disorder and schizophrenia are both present.

schizophrenia: A psychiatric disorder in which thought becomes dissociated from sensory input and emotions and is accompanied by hallucinations and delusional thinking. Bipolar disorder may be misdiagnosed as schizophrenia, especially in men.

seasonal affective disorder (SAD): A mood disorder that's strongly linked to the change of seasons. People who have SAD commonly experience major depressive episodes in the winter months.

second messenger: A chemical that carries signals within a brain cell rather than between brain cells.

seizure: A sudden, involuntary muscle contraction caused by a brain malfunction.

Selective Serotonin and Norepinephrine Reuptake Inhibitor (SSNRI): A class of antidepressant medications that prevent the brain from absorbing and breaking down the neurotransmitters norepinephrine and serotonin after their use, thus increasing the concentration of both chemicals in the brain.

Selective Serotonin Reuptake Inhibitor (SSRI): A class of antidepressant medications that prevent the brain from absorbing and breaking down the neurotransmitter serotonin after its use, thus increasing the concentration of serotonin.

self-medicate: The attempt to stabilize your moods by taking nonprescription chemical substances, including alcohol and marijuana, or by regulating your doses of prescription medication without a doctor's assistance.

serotonin: A neurotransmitter that helps regulate mood, anxiety, fear, sleep, body temperature, the rate at which your body releases certain hormones, and many other body and brain processes.

stigmatize: To brand someone as disgraceful or shameful.

stressor: Anything that revs up your brain and body. Stressors are usually negative, but even exciting and positive events can be stressful.

support group: A group of patients and/or family members who meet to discuss and empower one another in the face of a common illness.

tardive dyskinesia: A condition — sometimes caused by the long-term use of neuroleptics — that results in abnormal, uncontrollable muscle movements, often in the mouth and face.

therapeutic level: The concentration of medicine in the bloodstream required for the medication to be effective.

thyroid: A gland situated below the Adam's apple that produces hormones that control growth and influence moods.

total sleep deprivation (TSD): A controversial therapy for depression that consists of subjecting a patient to 36 hours without sleep followed by a 12-hour recovery sleep. Some studies show that TSD alleviates depression, but it poses a risk of inducing mania.

tricyclic antidepressant: A class of medications developed to treat depression by limiting the reuptake of the neurotransmitters serotonin and norepinephrine.

unipolar depression: A mood disorder characterized by episodes of major depression without symptoms of mania or hypomania.

zeitgeber: A German word that literally means "time giver," a zeitgeber is an external sign that indicates the approximate time of day and thereby sets the body's internal clock, such as the rising of the sun or a late-night talk show.

Index

• T •

BUSINESS, CAREERS & PERSONAL FINANCE

Grant Writing For Dummies
0-7645-5307-0

Home Buying For Dummies
0-7645-5331-3 *†

Also available:
- Accounting For Dummies †
  0-7645-5314-3
- Business Plans Kit For Dummies †
  0-7645-5365-8
- Cover Letters For Dummies
  0-7645-5224-4
- Frugal Living For Dummies
  0-7645-5403-4
- Leadership For Dummies
  0-7645-5176-0
- Managing For Dummies
  0-7645-1771-6

- Marketing For Dummies
  0-7645-5600-2
- Personal Finance For Dummies *
  0-7645-2590-5
- Project Management For Dummies
  0-7645-5283-X
- Resumes For Dummies †
  0-7645-5471-9
- Selling For Dummies
  0-7645-5363-1
- Small Business Kit For Dummies *†
  0-7645-5093-4

HOME & BUSINESS COMPUTER BASICS

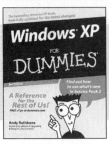

Windows XP For Dummies
0-7645-4074-2

Excel 2003 All-in-One Desk Reference For Dummies
0-7645-3758-X

Also available:
- ACT! 6 For Dummies
  0-7645-2645-6
- iLife '04 All-in-One Desk Reference
  For Dummies
  0-7645-7347-0
- iPAQ For Dummies
  0-7645-6769-1
- Mac OS X Panther Timesaving
  Techniques For Dummies
  0-7645-5812-9
- Macs For Dummies
  0-7645-5656-8

- Microsoft Money 2004 For Dummies
  0-7645-4195-1
- Office 2003 All-in-One Desk Reference
  For Dummies
  0-7645-3883-7
- Outlook 2003 For Dummies
  0-7645-3759-8
- PCs For Dummies
  0-7645-4074-2
- TiVo For Dummies
  0-7645-6923-6
- Upgrading and Fixing PCs For Dummies
  0-7645-1665-5
- Windows XP Timesaving Techniques
  For Dummies
  0-7645-3748-2

FOOD, HOME, GARDEN, HOBBIES, MUSIC & PETS

Feng Shui For Dummies
0-7645-5295-3

Poker For Dummies
0-7645-5232-5

Also available:
- Bass Guitar For Dummies
  0-7645-2487-9
- Diabetes Cookbook For Dummies
  0-7645-5230-9
- Gardening For Dummies *
  0-7645-5130-2
- Guitar For Dummies
  0-7645-5106-X
- Holiday Decorating For Dummies
  0-7645-2570-0
- Home Improvement All-in-One
  For Dummies
  0-7645-5680-0

- Knitting For Dummies
  0-7645-5395-X
- Piano For Dummies
  0-7645-5105-1
- Puppies For Dummies
  0-7645-5255-4
- Scrapbooking For Dummies
  0-7645-7208-3
- Senior Dogs For Dummies
  0-7645-5818-8
- Singing For Dummies
  0-7645-2475-5
- 30-Minute Meals For Dummies
  0-7645-2589-1

INTERNET & DIGITAL MEDIA

Digital Photography For Dummies
0-7645-1664-7

Starting an eBay Business For Dummies
0-7645-6924-4

Also available:
- 2005 Online Shopping Directory
  For Dummies
  0-7645-7495-7
- CD & DVD Recording For Dummies
  0-7645-5956-7
- eBay For Dummies
  0-7645-5654-1
- Fighting Spam For Dummies
  0-7645-5965-6
- Genealogy Online For Dummies
  0-7645-5964-8
- Google For Dummies
  0-7645-4420-9

- Home Recording For Musicians
  For Dummies
  0-7645-1634-5
- The Internet For Dummies
  0-7645-4173-0
- iPod & iTunes For Dummies
  0-7645-7772-7
- Preventing Identity Theft For Dummies
  0-7645-7336-5
- Pro Tools All-in-One Desk Reference
  For Dummies
  0-7645-5714-9
- Roxio Easy Media Creator For Dummies
  0-7645-7131-1

* Separate Canadian edition also available
† Separate U.K. edition also available

WILEY

SPORTS, FITNESS, PARENTING, RELIGION & SPIRITUALITY

0-7645-5146-9

0-7645-5418-2

Also available:
- ✔Adoption For Dummies
  0-7645-5488-3
- ✔Basketball For Dummies
  0-7645-5248-1
- ✔The Bible For Dummies
  0-7645-5296-1
- ✔Buddhism For Dummies
  0-7645-5359-3
- ✔Catholicism For Dummies
  0-7645-5391-7
- ✔Hockey For Dummies
  0-7645-5228-7

- ✔Judaism For Dummies
  0-7645-5299-6
- ✔Martial Arts For Dummies
  0-7645-5358-5
- ✔Pilates For Dummies
  0-7645-5397-6
- ✔Religion For Dummies
  0-7645-5264-3
- ✔Teaching Kids to Read For Dummies
  0-7645-4043-2
- ✔Weight Training For Dummies
  0-7645-5168-X
- ✔Yoga For Dummies
  0-7645-5117-5

TRAVEL

0-7645-5438-7

0-7645-5453-0

Also available:
- ✔Alaska For Dummies
  0-7645-1761-9
- ✔Arizona For Dummies
  0-7645-6938-4
- ✔Cancún and the Yucatán For Dummies
  0-7645-2437-2
- ✔Cruise Vacations For Dummies
  0-7645-6941-4
- ✔Europe For Dummies
  0-7645-5456-5
- ✔Ireland For Dummies
  0-7645-5455-7

- ✔Las Vegas For Dummies
  0-7645-5448-4
- ✔London For Dummies
  0-7645-4277-X
- ✔New York City For Dummies
  0-7645-6945-7
- ✔Paris For Dummies
  0-7645-5494-8
- ✔RV Vacations For Dummies
  0-7645-5443-3
- ✔Walt Disney World & Orlando For Dummies
  0-7645-6943-0

GRAPHICS, DESIGN & WEB DEVELOPMENT

0-7645-4345-8

0-7645-5589-8

Also available:
- ✔Adobe Acrobat 6 PDF For Dummies
  0-7645-3760-1
- ✔Building a Web Site For Dummies
  0-7645-7144-3
- ✔Dreamweaver MX 2004 For Dummies
  0-7645-4342-3
- ✔FrontPage 2003 For Dummies
  0-7645-3882-9
- ✔HTML 4 For Dummies
  0-7645-1995-6
- ✔Illustrator CS For Dummies
  0-7645-4084-X

- ✔Macromedia Flash MX 2004 For Dummies
  0-7645-4358-X
- ✔Photoshop 7 All-in-One Desk Reference For Dummies
  0-7645-1667-1
- ✔Photoshop CS Timesaving Techniques For Dummies
  0-7645-6782-9
- ✔PHP 5 For Dummies
  0-7645-4166-8
- ✔PowerPoint 2003 For Dummies
  0-7645-3908-6
- ✔QuarkXPress 6 For Dummies
  0-7645-2593-X

NETWORKING, SECURITY, PROGRAMMING & DATABASES

0-7645-6852-3

0-7645-5784-X

Also available:
- ✔A+ Certification For Dummies
  0-7645-4187-0
- ✔Access 2003 All-in-One Desk Reference For Dummies
  0-7645-3988-4
- ✔Beginning Programming For Dummies
  0-7645-4997-9
- ✔C For Dummies
  0-7645-7068-4
- ✔Firewalls For Dummies
  0-7645-4048-3
- ✔Home Networking For Dummies
  0-7645-42796

- ✔Network Security For Dummies
  0-7645-1679-5
- ✔Networking For Dummies
  0-7645-1677-9
- ✔TCP/IP For Dummies
  0-7645-1760-0
- ✔VBA For Dummies
  0-7645-3989-2
- ✔Wireless All In-One Desk Reference For Dummies
  0-7645-7496-5
- ✔Wireless Home Networking For Dummies
  0-7645-3910-8